Fieldnotes in the Critical Study of Religion

Critiquing Religion: Discourse, Culture, Power
Series editor: Craig Martin

Critiquing Religion: Discourse, Culture, Power publishes works that historicize both religions and modern discourses on "religion" that treat it as a unique object of study. Using diverse methodologies and social theories, volumes in this series view religions and discourses on religion as commonplace rhetorics, authenticity narratives, or legitimating myths which function in the creation, maintenance, and contestation of social formations. Works in the series are on the cutting edge of critical scholarship, regarding "religion" as just another cultural tool used to gerrymander social space and distribute power relations in the modern world. *Critiquing Religion: Discourse, Culture, Power* provides a unique home for reflexive, critical work in the field of religious studies.

Christian Tourist Attractions, Mythmaking and Identity Formation
Edited by Erin Roberts and Jennifer Eyl

French Populism and Discourses on Secularism
Per-Erik Nilsson

Reframing the Masters of Suspicion: Marx, Nietzsche, and Freud
Andrew Dole

Religion, Nationalism and Foreign Policy
Filiz Coban Oran

Representing Religion in Film
Edited by Tenzan Eaghll and Rebekka King

Rethinking Christian Martyrdom: The Blood Is the Seed?
Matt Recla

Spirituality, Corporate Culture, and American Business: The Neoliberal Ethic and the Spirit of Global Capital
James Dennis LoRusso

Stereotyping Religion: Critiquing Clichés
Edited by Brad Stoddard and Craig Martin

Stereotyping Religion II: Critiquing Clichés
Edited by Brad Stoddard and Craig Martin

Fieldnotes in the Critical Study of Religion

Revisiting Classical Theorists

Edited by
**RICHARD NEWTON AND
VAIA TOUNA**

BLOOMSBURY ACADEMIC
LONDON · NEW YORK · OXFORD · NEW DELHI · SYDNEY

BLOOMSBURY ACADEMIC
Bloomsbury Publishing Plc
50 Bedford Square, London, WC1B 3DP, UK
1385 Broadway, New York, NY 10018, USA
29 Earlsfort Terrace, Dublin 2, Ireland

BLOOMSBURY, BLOOMSBURY ACADEMIC and the Diana logo are trademarks of
Bloomsbury Publishing Plc

First published in Great Britain 2023

Copyright © Richard Newton, Vaia Touna, and contributors, 2023

Richard Newton and Vaia Touna have asserted their right under the Copyright,
Designs and Patents Act, 1988, to be identified as Editors of this work.

For legal purposes the Acknowledgements on p. xix
constitute an extension of this copyright page.

Cover image © Yi Lu / EyeEm. Getty Images

All rights reserved. No part of this publication may be reproduced or transmitted in
any form or by any means, electronic or mechanical, including photocopying,
recording, or any information storage or retrieval system, without prior permission
in writing from the publishers.

Bloomsbury Publishing Plc does not have any control over, or responsibility for,
any third-party websites referred to or in this book. All internet addresses given in this
book were correct at the time of going to press. The author and publisher regret any
inconvenience caused if addresses have changed or sites have ceased to exist,
but can accept no responsibility for any such changes.

A catalogue record for this book is available from the British Library.

A catalog record for this book is available from the Library of Congress.

ISBN: HB: 978-1-3502-5164-9
PB: 978-1-3502-5165-6
ePDF: 978-1-3502-5166-3
eBook: 978-1-3502-5167-0

Series: Critiquing Religion: Discourse, Culture, Power

Typeset by Newgen KnowledgeWorks Pvt. Ltd., Chennai, India

To find out more about our authors and books visit www.bloomsbury.com
and sign up for our newsletters.

Contents

List of Contributors vii

Preface: Taking *Notes* in the *Field* of Religious Studies: Critical Methods xi
   Vaia Touna

Acknowledgements xix

List of *field notes* xxi

Introduction: Revisiting the Past ..., Again 1
   Aaron W. Hughes and Russell T. McCutcheon

1 Friedrich Max Müller 11
   Brent Nongbri

2 William James 19
   Emily Suzanne Clark

3 Edward B. Tylor 29
   Mitsutoshi Horii

4 Joseph Kitagawa 39
   Christopher M. Jones

5 James G. Frazer 49
   Krista N. Dalton

6 Wilfred Cantwell Smith 59
   Edith Szanto

7 Sigmund Freud 69
   Robyn Faith Walsh

8 Gerardus van der Leeuw 77
   Tenzan Eaghll

9 Rudolf Otto 87
   Martha Smith Roberts

CONTENTS

10 Carl Jung 97
Lauren Horn Griffin

11 Bronislaw Malinowski 111
Brett J. Esaki

12 Mircea Eliade 123
Joseph Winters

13 Max Weber 133
Andrew Tobolowsky

Afterword: *Revisiting Classics* and Plotting Futures for the *Field* of Religious Studies 141
Richard Newton

Notes 153
Bibliography 177
Index 193

Contributors

Emily Suzanne Clark is Associate Professor of Religious Studies at Gonzaga University. She is the author of the award-winning book, *A Luminous Brotherhood: Afro-Creole Spiritualism in Nineteenth-Century New Orleans* (2016) and co-editor of *Race and New Religious Movements in the USA: A Documentary Reader* (2019). She is currently working on a project on American Spiritualism and material culture.

Krista Dalton is Assistant Professor of Religious and Jewish Studies at Kenyon College. She is a cultural historian of religion, working primarily with the texts and traditions of ancient Judaism within the Mediterranean context. Her research analyzes the performance of rabbinic expertise and the cultivation of donor networks in late antiquity. Dalton is coeditor-in-chief of the digital journal, *Ancient Jew Review*.

Tenzan Eaghll is Senior Researcher and Lecturer for the Department of Global Buddhism at the Institute of Science, Innovation, and Culture at Rajamangala University of Technology Krungthep, Bangkok. He has been published in *Method and Theory for the Study of Religion, Religion Compass, Implicit Religion*, and the Bloomsbury series *Critiquing Religion*. He is the coeditor of *Representing Religion in Film* (2022).

Brett J. Esaki (PhD, North American Religions, University of California, Santa Barbara, 2012) is Assistant Professor of Practice in the East Asian Studies Department at the University of Arizona. He researches Asian Americans, especially their connections with African Americans, on subjects of spirituality, popular culture, and comprehensive sustainability. His book *Enfolding Silence: The Transformation of Japanese American Religion and Art under Oppression* (2016) explores artistic strategies of silence that Japanese Americans used to preserve religion, communal history, and the memory of social silencing.

Lauren Horn Griffin, is Assistant Professor in the Department of Philosophy and Religious Studies at Louisiana State University. Her research and teaching focus on religion, media, and technology. Her current project investigates discourses on tradition and modernity in Catholic communities in the U.S. and around the globe.

Mitsutoshi Horii is Professor of Sociology at Shumei University, Japan, and based in the UK, as Principal of Chaucer College, which is Shumei's overseas campus. His recent research focuses on the function of modern Euro-American categories, such as "religion," and examines the ways in which these categories authorize and normalize specific norms and imperatives in a variety of colonial and postcolonial contexts, including Japan, as well as social theories and sociology. He is the author of *The Category of "Religion" in Contemporary Japan: Shūkyō and Temple Buddhism* (2018). His monograph is titled *"Religion" and "Secular" Categories in Sociology: Decolonizing the Modern Myth* (2021).

Aaron W. Hughes is the Dean's Professor of the Humanities and the Philip S. Bernstein Professor of Religious Studies at the University of Rochester. He has held visiting positions at the Hebrew University of Jerusalem, McMaster University, the University of Oxford, and the Aga Khan University. His research has been supported by the Social Sciences Research Council of Canada (SSHRC), the Lady Davis Fellowship Trust (Jerusalem), the Killam Foundation, the National Endowment of the Humanities (NEH), and Fulbright Canada.

Christopher M. Jones is Assistant Professor of Religious Studies at Washburn University. He has held academic positions at Augustana College and Beloit College. He graduated with a PhD in Hebrew and Semitic Studies from the University of Wisconsin–Madison in 2014. His scholarly publications cover Second Temple Judaism and pedagogical issues in the academic study of religion.

Russell T. McCutcheon is University Research Professor and Chair of the Department of Religious Studies at the University of Alabama. His work concerns the practical implications of classification systems and often draws on case studies form the history of the academic study of religion.

Richard Newton is Associate Professor of Religious Studies at the University of Alabama. He is the author of *Identifying Roots: Alex Haley and the Anthropology of Scriptures* (2020), and editor of the *Bulletin for the Study of Religion*. Newton's research focuses on the anthropology of scriptures and the study of religion as occasion for social theorizing. He is also the founding curator of Sowing the Seed: Fruitful Conversations in Religion, Culture, and Teaching (sowingtheseed.org).

Brent Nongbri is Professor of History of Religions at MF Norwegian School of Theology, Religion, and Society in Oslo. He leads "The Early History of the Codex: A New Methodology and Ethics for Manuscript Studies (EthiCodex)," a project sponsored by the Research Council of Norway (2021–6). His most recent book, *God's Library: The Archaeology of the Earliest Christian*

CONTRIBUTORS

Manuscripts (2018), was the winner of the 2019 DeLong Book History Prize awarded by the Society for the History of Authorship, Reading and Publishing.

Martha Smith Roberts is Assistant Professor of Religious Studies at Fullerton College. Her current research and teaching interests include religious diversity, pluralism, race and ethnicity studies, and minority and new religious movements. Her courses focus on the diversity of the global and American religious landscapes, especially the ways in which race, gender, and ethnicity are connected to religious identities and the significance of material culture and lived religious experience in everyday life.

Edith Szanto is Assistant Professor of Religious Studies at the University of Alabama. She previously taught for eight years at the American University of Iraq, Sulaimani. Szanto received her PhD in religious studies from the University of Toronto in 2012. She has extensively published on Islam, particularly Twelver Shi'ism, in Syria, Iraq and Iraqi Kurdistan, as well as issues relating to women and other minorities such as the Zoroastrians in the region.

Andrew Tobolowsky is Associate Professor at the College of William and Mary, focusing mainly on the study of the Hebrew Bible, Ancient Israel, Greek Mythology, and how traditions are inherited and redescribed. He is the author of *The Myth of the Twelve Tribes of Israel* (2022), which explores how the identity of Israel was used and reused by groups all over the world.

Vaia Touna is Associate Professor in the Department of Religious Studies at the University of Alabama, Tuscaloosa. She is author of *Fabrications of the Greek Past: Religion, Tradition, and the Making of Modern Identities* (2017) and editor of *Strategic Acts in the Study of Identity: Towards a Dynamic Theory of People and Place* (2019). Her research focuses on the sociology of religion, acts of identification and social formation as they relate to discourses of the past, and methodological issues concerning the use of the category "religion" in the study of the ancient Graeco-Roman world.

Robyn Faith Walsh is Associate Professor of the New Testament and Early Christianity at the University of Miami, Coral Gables. Her most recent monograph, *The Origins of Early Christian Literature: Contextualizing the New Testament within Greco-Roman Literary Culture*, was released with Cambridge University Press in 2021. Her articles have appeared in *Classical Quarterly* and *Jewish Studies Quarterly*, among other publications. She is also an editor at the Database of Religious History and editor of the *New Directions in Gospel Literature* series at Fortress/Lexington.

Joseph Winters is Associate Professor at Duke University in Religious Studies and African and African American Studies. His interests lie at the intersection of African American religious thought, black studies, and critical theory. His research examines the ways Black literature and aesthetics develop alternative configurations of the sacred, piety, (Black) spirit, and secularity in response to the religious dimensions of anti-Black violence and coloniality. Winters is the author of *Hope Draped in Black: Race, Melancholy, and the Agony of Progress* (2016). He is currently working on a second manuscript, tentatively titled *Disturbing Profanity: Hip Hop, Black Aesthetics, and the Volatile Sacred.*

Preface

Taking *Notes* in the *Field* of Religious Studies: Critical Methods

Vaia Touna

> As students of myth, we can turn our attention to the mythmaking of our scholarly, as well as that of other, ancestors, secure in the knowledge that our descendants will one day return us the favor.[1]

The opening quote by Bruce Lincoln is a nice reminder, at least in my reading of it, that on the one hand the scholarly work of our predecessors can be seen as a type of mythmaking, and on the other, and perhaps most importantly, that we are as much implicated in the mythmaking process as them, and that our work will be put by future scholars under the same scrutiny that we put the work of our predecessors. To me, then, the "favor," that Lincoln speaks of, is *how* we choose to return to the work of our ancestors, how we choose to approach it, knowing that it may one day apply to our own. Should we dismiss the work of an earlier generation of scholars as *passé* and outdated, should we elevate it to a status of authority that will dictate our work or is there an alternative approach. This volume explores exactly that, alternative methods by which we can critically approach what are now understood by many as classic scholars in the field of religious studies.

Over the past fifty years, with a turn toward offering courses on method and theory as part of the curriculum of many religious studies departments, there have been many publications that, whether intentionally or not, produce canons for the field, that is, lists of classic scholars that are thought to constitute an authorized, collective past for religious studies. Like all origin's stories, though, things are a lot messier when we look a little more closely at these canons. Undoubtedly, the field of religious studies was born, over one hundred years ago, out of a broad spectrum of scholars writing on and about religion and its many derivatives (from its adjective religious to concepts that are associated with religion, such as sacred, holy, faith, ritual, myth, etc.). Scholars from a variety of what are now distinct fields and disciplines from within the humanities—from theology, religious studies alter ego, as well as sociology and economic/political science, from history and psychology to classic studies and anthropology—all for their reasons became interested in exploring what is religion or the role that it plays in societies and psyches, and so their work inevitably, whether implicitly or explicitly, touched on issues of what we today refer to as theory and method. But which one of those now long past scholars will be chosen to become part of a given canon of the field (i.e., added to the list of so-called classics) depends to a large extent, of course, on who is making the canon and the research area and agenda that it is meant to serve. For example, in my field of research, that is, studies in the ancient Graeco-Roman world, there are certain names that are widely considered classics, such as Jane Ellen Harrison (1850–1928), James Frazer (1854–1941), Martin Nilsson (1874–1968), and, more recently, Walter Burkert (1931–2015), to name just a few, who may not be familiar or may not be considered at all relevant to someone working, say, on biblical studies or Buddhism. In other words, given the larger field's variety of areas of expertise and the diversity of research interests, the work of some classic scholars is only known within a specific area or subfield and so, all depending on who is telling the origins story of the field and what one wants to accomplish in offering such a tale, different scholars will be chosen from the archive of the past to form an authorized list, that is, canon. Though, of course, there are some names that seem to be more knowable across the various subfields than others. Nevertheless, and perhaps not surprisingly, when one is diving into the archive there are some theoretical and methodological issues that are common across areas of expertise, making them potentially of interest to a wide variety of people working in the field of religious studies or is interested in the history and development of the study of religion in general.

A once well-known attempt to include in a single publication a large number of foundational scholars from across fields and disciplines was Jacques Waardenburg's 1973 edited volume *Classical Approaches to the Study of Religion*. According to his preface to the 1999 paperback edition of the volume, his effort was "to make clear that for the study of religions to be recognized as a distinct field of research—and not just a matter of personal taste or gifts—questions of theory and method had to be discussed."[2] The book, therefore, includes long excerpts from what Waardenburg considered to be classical scholars' works that explicitly addressed—at least according to what he thought to be—questions of theory and method. In 2017 the second edition of the volume was published with a foreword by Russell McCutcheon

PREFACE

xiii

in which he argues that there is great value in looking at the work of previous scholars; as he writes,

> The ongoing and still-current nature of what are in fact very old methodological debates on the role of similarity and difference, for example, or controversies concerning theories intent on explaining causes rather than interpreting meanings suggests that something may be gained by studying past chess moves and their players, inasmuch as we all still seem to be playing on much the same board and debating the same rules.[3]

Looking through that volume and its excerpts from those classic scholarly works there are several things that may attract our attention today. Obviously, there's a once prominent scholarly language that one can now easily, and rightly so, judge as racist; moreover, it's a bygone language that is filled with ethnic and gender stereotypes and misconceptions of the "other"; in fact, it is a language that, in many respects, predictably mirrors the time in which those scholars were writing (Waardenburg's volume covers the late nineteenth to the early twentieth century). At the same time, though, and especially in the earlier works, one can also see in their debates, and their struggles, the *naissance* of the field of religious studies as it tries to find its own distinct voice, to differentiate itself from its alter ego, that is theology, and thereby gain a place of its own, first within the European and then North American academy. It is also fascinating to observe the way that they were debating ideas, some of which, in one way or another, we are still debating today.

Although a work such as Waardenburg's is no doubt of value in its own right, the reason that I mention it is because it became a point of discussion with my colleagues at the University of Alabama, Russell McCutcheon and Richard Newton, not only about the extent to which so-called classic scholars are of relevance to us now (i.e., whether there is, and if so what kind of, value still to be found in their work) but also how we should approach them today, both in our research and in our classrooms. Out of those discussions the idea for the current volume was born. For we concluded that the field needed a work that will demonstrate for students and newcomers in the field a critical method to be applied in specific examples from past scholarship, a method in how to read our predecessors—whether we today agree with them or not. For when engaging in discussions with the work of such classic scholars, we may see that some themes that we thought were long gone may still, in one way or another, be around, something that would help us rethink them and potentially advance the academic study of religion by addressing those recurring themes in novel ways that break through their circle and, maybe, move beyond them.

xiv PREFACE

As I mentioned previously, and as I and Richard have both observed in our teaching as well as in our research, earlier scholarly work is either dismissed by our contemporaries as outdated, or it is approached as an authority that possesses timeless meanings or even timeless descriptions of the people once studied. For example, we often rely on classic scholarship to fill in the blanks of our own descriptive efforts, assuming that these are merely "settled facts" that are obviously timeless, and so we end up picking and choosing those "facts" often uncritically as if they are not part of the whole which they represent and which, as Hayden White once noted, is discursive in its entirety.[4] Moving beyond this kind of binary thinking then, beyond dismissing or endorsing classic scholars, we instead invited our contributors to look at their work anew, as a piece of data which we may be able to put in the service of some theoretical questions of our own; in short, we asked them how could we engage with such works in a critical manner.

Fieldnotes in the Critical Study of Religion comes out from these questions and observations; it is primarily a demonstration of methods on *notes* taken by revisiting or continuing with an ethnographic language, and *by observing* the work of classical scholars in the field. Those notes then are put in front of thirteen scholars of religion from various areas of expertise, to engage and discuss them. More specifically, this multi-authored collection invites contemporary scholars of religion to contextualize and engage with a quote of *our choosing*, as editors, from nineteenth- and twentieth-century scholars of religion who were once widely recognized as authoritative/influential in the field. The quotes we have chosen are like broad strokes from an earlier time in the field, like notes taken by ethnographers in their fieldwork research and which, like fieldnotes, do not tell the whole story but are nonetheless critical in serving the research interests of the ethnographers, in this case the methodological and theoretical interests of mine and Richard's. Hence, in putting together this volume we had to make choices regarding which scholars to include, and we are fully aware that "the archive of the past contains far too much, and so we have no choice but to make selections whenever we refer to it—and, inevitably, there are consequences to the choices we make."[5] *Fieldnotes* though does not attempt, explicitly at least, to create or recreate another list that aspires to become its own origins tale of the field or some kind of canon; instead, our selection of the scholars was primarily driven by what *we* found curious enough in their work to make us want to read on, a little more. To be sure, there were far too many scholars that we would have liked to include in this volume but, given practical limitations, inevitable choices had to be made. In looking at the work of those earlier scholars some of the criteria by which we chose those quotes was the element of surprise occasioned by reading them, of something that we, at least, wouldn't have expected to read in a scholar from a hundred or so years ago, but also quotes

PREFACE

that we thought could serve as a fresh opportunity to be put in the service of some theoretical question to be engaged with and critically analyzed in light of current debates in the field which, not surprising, are actually "new versions of old problems that we thought we had long ago moved beyond."[6] It will be fair to say, then, that we were not so much concerned with the *who* but rather about the *what* to include, not that who is included is any less significant or should not equally attract our attention, but we hope readers will be paying attention to the tensions of those quotes and the issues that they bring to light as well as the methods by which our contributors are dealing with the quotes that they have been assigned—assignments that sometimes involved surprises too. For the way that we paired the quotes to the contributors was not necessarily based on the familiarity we thought the latter might have of the classic scholar in question; in fact, we steered away from doing that to the extent possible. Our logic was that a perspective from a different area of expertise applied to a quote of an author not particularly familiar within that area would be more beneficial and productive. This might offer, we thought, a novel way into writing both a history and ethnography of the field as well as helping readers to see how it has changed while inviting them to consider what—if anything—endures and thereby unites these diverse authors both in time and space, that is, both the classical scholars as well as the contributors, into a common field.

The volume starts with an introduction by Aaron Hughes and Russell McCutcheon who outline the reasons for the constant development of new scholarly approaches against the backdrop of higher education's changes while providing a case study from the late nineteenth century inviting scholars as well as readers in general, to see it in light of current interests and curiosities. The following thirteen chapters open with a quote of a classical scholar selected by Newton and myself and each contributor is then invited to identify the assumptions it presupposes while testing and challenging them in light of the field's current conditions and aims. Brent Nongbri investigates, through Friedrich Max Müller's quote and his ideas on the "science" of religion and comparison, the extent to which they are both still prominent in the field. Emily Suzanne Clark tackles William James's ideas on religious experience to discuss the current interest in affect theory and materiality. Mitsutoshi Horii, in looking at the critiques of Edward Tylor's once-repeated use of the term "savage," questions whether modern scholarship achieved a better understanding of non-modern forms of life. Christopher M. Jones takes the often-neglected work of Joseph Kitagawa on a trip to contemporary debates about sui generis "religion" and the role of the scholar in interpreting and explaining religious data. Krista N. Dalton traces "lived religion" from James Frazer to recent scholarship and discusses the consequences it has for the study of religion. Edith Szanto looks at the still influential idea of interfaith dialogue as was developed by Wilfred Cantwell Smith and the issues it may pose to the field today. Robyn Walsh examines Sigmund Freud's contemporary "popular" legacy and the implicit reification of his ideas that come through this praise. Tenzan Eaghll pairs Gerardus van der Leeuw with Friedrich Nietzsche and he argues for their shared theoretical origin. Martha Smith Roberts connects Rudolf Otto's idea of the uniqueness of religious experience with contemporary debates regarding the study of religious experience and affect theory. Lauren Horn Griffin uses a quote from the work of Carl Jung as a jumping-off point to discuss issues of definition as well as the implicit and explicit consequences of using his concepts. Brett J. Esaki makes an analogical comparison of theoretical blind spots between the work of Bronislaw Malinowski and contemporary theories of religion. Joseph Winters traces the implications of Mircea Eliade's thought for Black religion, Black studies and decolonial thought. Finally, according to Andrew Tobolowsky, Max Weber's quote summarizes a problem still prominent in the study of religion which Tobolowsky uses as a way into discussing meaning and sacrifice. The volume ends with a substantial essay by Richard Newton on the future of religious studies.

What has been particularly nice to see as these chapters were submitted to us, one by one, and which I think is in fact one among the strengths of this volume, is the amount of overlap that we saw in the responses of our contributors, of which we invite our readers, like *field* ethnographers themselves, to take *note*. For, as already mentioned, the book asks readers to consider whether past scholarly work continues to be relevant or is best read as an historical artifact from an earlier and long past time. Instead of representing scholars and their works as virtually timeless, each contributor provides sufficient background on the classic work in question so that students and newcomers to the field not only understand its novelty and place in its own time but are also able to arrive at a critical understanding of whether its approach to studying religion continues to be useful or not to them today.

It should be obvious by now that *Fieldnotes in the Critical Study of Religion* is neither a dismissal, nor even an endorsement of any of these classic scholars, but rather the contributors of this volume demonstrate a variety of methods on how we can critically engage the work of our "ancestors" for the benefit and the advancement of the academic study of religion. From historicizing and contextualizing, to discourse analysis, and comparison, the authors of this volume demonstrate the breadth of the field as well as the tensions and debates of the present as seen through the quotes we have put before them. And what is revealed is that the past is never really about the past but rather about contemporary interests. A careful reader, perhaps, and unbeknownst to the contributors themselves, may therefore notice that the discussion on issues relating to the field is happening on two levels, one obviously within the individual chapters and in response to the quote but also another between the contributors themselves, inasmuch as certain themes and issues are routinely brought up and addressed in varying degrees among our authors. Yet, it should not go without mentioning that, on more than one occasion, the reason that *we* picked a quote and the way it was engaged by the contributor we assigned it to did not necessarily overlap, which speaks to the fact that the reading of those past quotes is informed to a large extent by our contemporary and shared scholarly interests and our common theoretical questions; and so we invite our readers to take part in the conversation too, to think equally critically on the quote of *our* choosing. In that regard we hope that this book is ideal for a class setting, as it can be used to introduce students to issues, concerns and debates in the field, of course, but also to demonstrate for them, through a variety of methods, how they too can critically engage with classical scholars, and perhaps invite them to apply those methods to a quote from a classical or even contemporary scholar of their choosing. What follows is a list of the "field notes" that were chosen by Richard and I, that is, the scholarly quotes that open each of the volume's chapters.

Acknowledgements

This volume comes out of discussions we have had over the years with colleagues as well as our experience in classes, especially graduate courses, that we have taught. The common denominator in all of these was our observation that there was a lack of method/methods to approach a previous generation of scholars who, whether we like it or not, have been important in establishing what we now refer to as the field of Religious Studies. One day we found ourselves in the office of Russell McCutcheon, our chair at the time and good colleague of ours, in the Department of Religious Studies at the University of Alabama, talking about this very topic. It is actually quite common to see his door open and as you pass by to be invited to participate in a discussion already underway with another colleague. And so there we were talking about our frustrations on this, making the point that it's not about dismissing those scholars as passé or irrelevant, but about an ability that we thought was lacking in the field, that is the ability to critically engage with these scholars. And by "critically" we certainly had in mind something other than simply a "negation" or "refutation" of a scholarly position. At the end of the discussion Russell wondered if that could be an edited book and as is usually the case, he planted that day the idea which eventually turned into this volume; and so, we are immensely grateful to him for all his mentorship over the years as our department chair, colleague and friend.

We also want to thank our good friend and colleague Craig Martin, the editor of this series, for when we approached him with the idea of this volume, he was very positive and supportive. We also want to thank the publishing team at Bloomsbury, especially Lalle Pursglove (publisher) and Lily McMahon (assistant editor), for all their help and support during the process of this publication. Special thanks also to Andie Alexander, who did such a great job making the index to this volume. Last but not least, we would like to thank each and every one of our contributors for accepting our invitation to be part of this volume and to demonstrate for our readers methods on how to engage critically with classical scholars in a manner that can be both productive and educational: Aaron W. Hughes, Russell T. McCutcheon, Brent Nongbri, Emily Suzanne Clark, Mitsutoshi Horii, Christopher M. Jones, Krista N. Dalton, Edith

ACKNOWLEDGEMENTS

Szanto, Robyn Faith Walsh, Tenzan Eaghll, Martha Smith Roberts, Lauren Horn Griffin, Brett J. Esaki, Joseph Winters, Andrew Tobolowsky.

Richard Newton and Vaia Touna
Tuscaloosa, Alabama
December 10, 2022.

List of *field notes*

Each of the following quotes opens a chapter in this volume and represents a *note* from the *field*'s classical theorists. They have been selected by the editors of this volume and function as invitations to the authors to engage with in a critical manner.

Friedrich Max Muller (1823–1900)

"The Science of Religion will for the first time assign to Christianity its right place among the religions of the world; it will show for the first time fully what was meant by the fulness of time; it will restore to the whole history of the world, in its unconscious progress towards Christianity, its true and sacred character." (1867)

William James (1842–1910)

"The individual's religion may be egotistic, and those private realities which it keeps in touch with may be narrow enough; but at any rate it always remains infinitely less hollow and abstract, as far as it goes, than a science which prides itself on taking no account of anything private at all." (1902)

Edward B. Tylor (1832–1917)

"While anthropology, as regards the collection of materials for study of the religions of the world has gained of late vastly, the time has come for a more thorough criticism of these materials, so as to separate in the religions of the lower races the genuinely early and native part from the accretions and transformations due to contact with civilized foreigners." (1892)

Joseph Kitagawa (1915–1992)

"[The history of religions'] aim is to study the nature and structure of the religious experience of the human race and its diverse manifestations in history, such as the manner in which humankind has perceived and developed various models of the universe. In other words, the task of the history of religions is to delineate the religious meaning of humankind's religious experience and its expressions through the integration and "significant organization" of diverse forms of religious data." (1857)

James G. Frazer (1854–1941)

"Hence every inquiry into the primitive religion of the Aryans should either start from the superstitious beliefs and observances of the peasantry, or should at least be constantly checked and controlled by reference to them. Compared with the evidence afforded by living tradition, the testimony of ancient books on the subject of early religion is worth very little." (1890)

Wilfred Cantwell Smith (1916–2000)

"We should be able to arrive at a point where we can understand, not with complete assurance but with reasonable confidence, and not fully but in significant part, what the faith of other persons, other groups, even other ages, is and has been. This becomes the new and challenging business of "Comparative Religion" studies—a task that is just beginning at this level and is assuredly difficult but assuredly rewarding." (1962)

Sigmund Freud (1856–1939)

"First of all, it must be said that it is useless to question savages as to the real motivation of their prohibitions (es habe keinen Sinn, die Wilden nach der wirklichen Motivierung ihrer Verbote) or as to the genesis of taboo (Genese des Tabu). According to our assumption (Voraussetzung) they must be incapable (unfähig) of telling us anything about it since this motivation is "unconscious" to them (denn diese Motivierung sei ihnen "unbewußt")." (1913)

Gerardus van der Leeuw (1890–1950)

"For the "primal experience," upon which our experiences are grounded, has always passed irrevocably away by the time our attention is directed to it. My own life, for example, which I experienced while writing the few lines of the preceding sentence, is just as remote from me as is the "life" associated with the lines I wrote thirty years ago in a school essay, I cannot call it back again: it is completely past. In fact, the experience of the lines of a moment ago is no nearer to me than is the experience of the Egyptian scribe who wrote his note on papyrus four thousand years ago. ... The immediate, therefore, is never and nowhere "given"; it must always be reconstructed." (1933)

Rudolf Otto (1869–1937)

"Nature can only be explained by an investigation into the ultimate fundamental forces of nature and their laws: it is meaningless to propose to go farther and explain these laws themselves, for in terms of what are they to be explained? But in the domain of spirit the corresponding principle from which an explanation is derived is just the spirit itself, the reasonable spirit of man, with its predispositions, capacities, and its own inherent laws." (1958)

Carl Jung (1875–1961)

"The psychologist has to contend with the same difficulties as the mythologist when an exact definition or clear and concise information is demanded of him. The picture is concrete, clear, and subject to no misunderstandings only when it is seen in its habitual context. In this form it tells us everything it contains. But as soon as one tries to abstract the "real essence" of the picture, the whole thing becomes cloudy and indistinct. In order to understand its living function, we must let it remain an organic thing in all its complexity and not try to examine the anatomy of its corpse in the manner of the scientist, or the archaeology of its ruins in the manner of the historian." (1954)

Bronislaw Malinowski (1884–1942)

"But since the moral rules are only one part of the traditional heritage of man, since morality is not identical with the Power or Being from which it is believed to spring, since finally the metaphysical concept of "Collective Soul" is barren in anthropology, we have to reject the sociological theory of religion." (1925)

Mircea Eliade (1907–1986)

"The world (that is, our world) is a universe within which the sacred has already manifested itself, in which, consequently, the breakthrough from plane to plane has become possible and repeatable. It is not difficult to see why the religious moment implies the cosmogonic moment. The sacred reveals absolute reality and at the same time makes orientation possible; hence it founds the world in the sense that it fixes the limits and establishes the order of the world." (1957)

Max Weber (1864–1920)

"The external courses of religious behavior are so diverse that an understanding of this behavior can only be achieved from the viewpoint of the subjective experiences, ideas, and purposes of the individuals concerned—in short, from the viewpoint of the religious behavior's 'meaning.'" (1922)

Introduction: Revisiting the Past ..., Again

Aaron W. Hughes and
Russell T. McCutcheon

The story of the study of religion's beginnings in late-nineteenth-century Europe, and its subsequent development (both there and elsewhere) that we were told when earning our graduate degrees in the United States and Canada, respectively, was largely an intellectual history in which a fairly stable canon of scholars debated big ideas concerning such things as the declining role of religiosity during that period known as early modernity and the eventual emergence of nation-states along with the sociopolitical arrangement commonly known today as secularism. It was a story about what is usually characterized as the Enlightenment's application of coolheaded rationality to study *all* aspects of human beings, seeing them as but elements of the natural world—culminating early on in the Scottish philosopher, David Hume, and his still classic *A Natural History of Religion* (1757), as well as his posthumously published *Dialogues Concerning Natural Religion* (1779). This was followed, as that story went on, by the Romantic era's visceral reaction to what many have characterized as the Enlightenment's disenchantment of the world, a response perhaps represented early on by the work of the Prussian Protestant theologian, Friedrich Schleiermacher, such as his *Uber die Religion: Reden an die Gebildeten unter ihren Verächtern* (1799; English: *On Religion: Speeches to Its Cultured Despisers*) and, later, his once influential two-volume work in systematic theology, *Der Christliche Glaube* (1830–1; English: *The Christian Faith*). He defended religion by seeing it as being akin

2   FIELDNOTES IN THE CRITICAL STUDY OF RELIGION

to an aesthetic experience or feeling that therefore defied or evaded a critical, rational gaze. Or so the story went.

But the story continued right up to the present day. For the continuing conflict between these two intellectual stances—that, on the one hand, religion is a special case which is rightly exempt from the scholarly methods normally used to study human beings, while, on the other, religion is seen as a mere secondary or what some would term an accidental feature, a derivative effect of an assortment of prior and even more basic human and historical conditions (from psychology to economics)—went on to animate our field's once prominent debate between (largely Christian) theology and an academic field taking shape across the twentieth century that, at least in North American, came to be known as Religious Studies (though it goes by many names throughout the world, from Comparative Religion and the History of Religions to the Science of Religion). As noted, and regardless the side of this disagreement that one adopted and defended, this was the narrative told from the early years of the field (e.g., Morris Jastrow's essay, "The Study of Religion—Its History and Character," the opening chapter in his 1902 collection, *The Study of Religion*) right up to the contemporary period (e.g., the detailed opening essay in Jacques Waardenburg's anthology, *Classical Approaches to the Study of Religion* (1973)), and, of course, Eric J. Sharpe's once widely read book, *Comparative Religion: A History* (1975)). It was an account that was pretty much repeated whenever so-called progress in the field was being assessed (we have in mind here all of those "retrospect and prospect" volumes that once assessed the state of the field), such as twenty years later in Walter Capps's *Religious Studies: The Making of a Discipline* (1995), a book that presents the field's development in the classic history of ideas format, centering around a cast of the usual suspects having intellectual debates over what Capps saw as the field's four enduring topics: the definition, origin, description, and function of religion.

Of course, the specific intellectual issues driving this narrative can vary, sometimes dramatically, all depending on who was chronicling this adventure of ideas (to borrow a phrase from the once well-known British philosopher, Alfred North Whitehead); for example, compare the Canadian Harold Coward's sense of the fields history being propelled by an increasing desire for an understanding of religious diversity (see his book, *Fifty Years of Religious Studies in Canada: A Personal Retrospective* (2014)) to J. Samuel Preus's account of the gradual rise of naturalistic explanations (such as in his still important book, *Explaining Religion: Criticism and Theory from Bodin to Freud* (1987)). Although these two narratives are most definitely at odds with each other—or, at least provide contesting origins tales and trajectories that each serve as the grounds for a very different sort of study of religion (for while the former interprets meanings the latter explains prior causes)—they both differ

INTRODUCTION

from a more recent turn toward the material in the study of religion. Now, by this we don't mean what is currently considered by some to be a subfield of the study of religion called material religion (an approach that builds on previous developments in such fields as anthropology and social history) and which focuses on items of so-called material culture, seeing a wide variety of seemingly ordinary artifacts as the sites where religion is said to be either expressed or manifested. (It is an approach, we should add, that to us bears some striking similarities to what for many is the already discredited descriptive and interpretive approach known as the phenomenology of religion.) Instead, by the term "material" we simply aim to convey something rather more in line with a classic Marxist approach; for, although the turn in scholarship that we're describing (one which came into its own about an academic generation ago) is hardly limited to those who adopt an explicitly Marxist analysis of religion it does share a focus on what scholars will often call the material conditions or practical situations (e.g., who owns what and who has access to it) in which those supposedly intellectual debates were taking place.

A longstanding distinction employed by European philosophers—between idealist and materialist approaches—is handy here, with the former (in which ideas and thus scholarly debates and methods are represented as somehow aloof or removed from their historical circumstances) dominating this and many other academic fields for quite some time. It's no accident, in other words, that the study of religion for so long focused on studying things characterized as faiths, experiences, or beliefs, as if they were each the pristine, animating force for people's later actions and social organizations. Accordingly, the imperial setting in which the study of religion first arose, in late-nineteenth-century European universities, is therefore hardly ever mentioned in many of the histories of the field. For the dominant approach's focus on mere ideas and scholarly debates concerning other people's ideas, sentiments, and worldviews—whether emphasizing religion to be either a special source of meaning or instead a mundane element of the natural world—was largely silent on the fact that, from the earliest years of the field to its formative period in the mid-twentieth century (when fieldwork and thus first-hand experience on the part of researchers was the field's gold standard), European and then North American scholars' backdrop was the violent institution known as colonialism (which, if we're being thorough and honest, was intimately connected to the past centuries international slave trade), by which industrialized European nations, over the course of a few centuries, raced each other to claim and then exercise control over distant lands and, more specifically, their natural resources and, indeed, their populations as well. Simply put, the new information about what were once seen as the curious practices of exotic people did not spontaneously make its way to universities in London, Berlin, or Amsterdam all throughout the nineteenth century. And the distant lands to

FIELDNOTES IN THE CRITICAL STUDY OF RELIGION

which the first generation of anthropological ethnographers later traveled, such as in the first third of the twentieth century, were, as you might now predict, often still under colonial control or were newly independent after long and bloody wars of independence from European governance. A classic example of this would be the early advocate of doing long-term fieldwork among the people being studied, the Polish anthropologist, Bronislaw Malinowski, whose once important book, *Argonauts of the Western Pacific* (1922), was based on his time on what many of us know as the Trobriand Islands, off the southeast coast of New Guinea. But for some it would be surprising to learn that these islands not only were named after one of the crew of the French ship that landed there in the late-eighteenth century (a fellow named Jean François Sylvestre Denis de Trobriand) but that they eventually became the home to Australian colonial administrators, themselves an arm of what was by then a worldwide British imperial effort. Without this already established (and enforced) colonial infrastructure, let alone a convenient means for traveling on an imperial nation's ships across the globe, it is fair to assume that what was initially the European field of anthropology, let alone the study of religion and a variety of other adjacent academic fields, might never have arisen; for what Jonathan Z. Smith once called "an explosion of data," sparked by the reports of "missionaries, colonial officials, and travelers,"[1] would then have never happened let alone the resulting intellectual but, yes, also the political, industrial, and military need for Europeans to "make sense" of newly discovered similarities and differences with people deemed unfamiliar to those who were back in Europe. For although it wasn't ever analyzed at the time, even as late as the mid-twentieth century the explicit linkage between governance, coercive force, and knowledge was profoundly apparent to any critical reader of Huston Smith's once famous but still in-print world religions textbook. There its early readers learned that the study of religion might come in handy for the military, when "dealing with the peoples they were studying as allies, antagonists, or subjects of military occupation. Under such circumstances it would be crucial for them to predict their behavior, conquer them if worse came to worst, and control them during the aftermath of reconstruction."[2]

And so we arrive at the present, when those material and thus practical institutional conditions are, at least for some, no longer overlooked when telling the story of our field's past and its subsequent developments—a time when it is difficult to read Smith's 1958 textbook without finding the above passage, linking comparative religion to geopolitics and war, as rather curious and in need of further consideration. The danger, of course, is that when all of this overlooked, as if the field is only about big ideas, deep meanings, and uniquely aesthetic experiences, such prior conditions became authorized and naturalized, as if a European scholar in the early twentieth century should, of

INTRODUCTION

course, have just naturally been able to travel to, and spend time in, those distant south Pacific islands named after a French sailor (who is said to have died in Haiti's independence war, once known as Saint-Domingue, a colonial possession of France that it had gained from Spain in the mid-seventeenth century). And so, unlike the many previous iterations of the now ever-present handbook or companion in the study of religion, Richard King's recent edited resource, *Religion, Theory, Critique: Classic and Contemporary Approaches and Methodologies* (2017), aims not to overlook all this, by featuring a chapter by Nelson Maldonado-Torres entitled "Religion, Modernity, and Coloniality"; and that essay's opening sentence reads as follows: "The concept of religion most used in the West by scholars and laypeople alike is a specifically modern concept forged in the context of imperialism and colonial expansion."[3] Thus, the material turn, as we've chosen to define it here, brings us all the way back to examine the once overlooked practical situations that led to the very idea of certain parts of society or even the self as being set aside and designated *as* religious, as special, as somehow different from the rest of daily life.

Perhaps some readers will already understand why we opted to begin our introduction to this book in the way that we have, for we hope that it illustrates that there is something significant to be gained by revisiting earlier periods in a group's past—not to mention the stories that we tell ourselves about that past—even if that group is an academic field that's part of the modern university. For even the realists among us, who think that the past is tangible, real, and thus out there somewhere, behind us in time, just waiting to be discovered and then described by the careful archivist, will surely have to admit that there is more to the past than any contemporary observer can ever hope to grasp; after all, much of the past is quite literally lost, what with such things as fires and floods destroying homes and libraries, and thereby erasing any material reference to a variety of past actors and their situations. If we complicate this view of history by recognizing that different things will become apparent and thus noteworthy in the always expansive archive of the past (to borrow a phrase from the Haitian anthropologist Michel-Rolph Trouillot (1995)), all based on the particular curiosities and thus the questions posed by the one who is writing the historical narrative (ensuring that the past is always a creation of a particular present—a point that the historian Hayden White made so well), then there's an even better reason to periodically revisit the seemingly settled facts of our collective past: to see what *we* make of them today, that is, to see if they even still stand out as worth talking about and, if so, then how.

And so the editors of this volume have wagered that there may be something to be gained (and we won't know for sure if it's worth it until we do it and see what we think of our results) from having contemporary scholars of religion spend some time in that dusty archive, to see what they now make of

6   FIELDNOTES IN THE CRITICAL STUDY OF RELIGION

a past that we can't argue our field out of having had. The question, though, is whether, once we do this, that past ends up being more familiar to us today than we might have at first imagined or whether, referencing the title of a 1985 book by the historian David Lowenthal, the past remains a foreign country.

Often, we find that it is the latter stance that scholars adopt, especially those today who carry out their work in a rather different register from the approaches that were once commonly used by those who helped to establish the field well over one hundred years ago. After all, for many scholars today the past of our field is a series of problems from which we feel that we are luckily distanced or even insulated today—as if the pre-professionalized field, once populated by amateurs and armchair anthropologists, as they were called (studying distant people from the comfort of a library by reading other people's travelogues and diaries), suffered from problems from which we today are free. For example, thinking back to the work carried out by scholars in the late-nineteenth century, it was not uncommon to find the comparative method used to survey the variety of things that were designated as, for example, Buddhist or Muslim, as part of a search for the essential or defining trait that did or did not make them all examples of some particular family (i.e., the Oriental mind, as some once called it). Difference, in such an approach, was the problem to be overcome and comparison was the method used to discover what was said to be an underlying sameness—an identity presumed to indicate a deep and timeless quality shared by items despite their apparent or merely surface (and thus non-essential) differences. Thus, for a scholar on our side of the material turn, as mentioned above (such as one who is now very interested in issues of power and identity), there may seem to be little in common with those long past scholars carrying out their work in an explicitly colonial context, where the differences among peoples was almost naturally assumed to indicate a hierarchical ranking among populations, arranged on an evolutionary scale from so-called savages and primitives at the bottom to the heights of the civilized world (with scholars themselves always numbering themselves among the latter, of course). That the later nineteenth century's application of the still novel biological theory of evolution to understand how social groups (i.e., nations or races of people) changed over time (so-called Social Darwinism) was deeply problematic must be acknowledged, to be sure; for many today, it is often a challenge to read scholarship from that era—even if reading it as data and thus a relic from a bygone time—what with its frequent references to "the barbarous primitives" or "the noble savages" and its often harsh and undisguised value judgments about other people's inferior and underdeveloped status. But we think that scholars today would be wise to look for more in the work of their disciplinary predecessors, relying not just on our initial reaction to work from what is most certainly a day, and sets of interests as well as assumptions, far removed from our own today; for

INTRODUCTION

the contemporary sensibilities that many scholars now share and which they bring to their work is itself an historical fact, that is, it did not arise on its own, fully formed. Rather, the positions to which many of us have come today are the result of scholars both inheriting from, but also debating and critiquing, their seniors; for each generation builds the basis of its own work on what they learn from, but also see to be the failures of, their elders (and yes, we ourselves are not only the teachers but we will inevitably also be among those failures for those who come after us and who are intent on building something of their own). This means that, whether we like it or not, there is an intimacy between us and them, between the contemporary world of scholarship and what we now see as those terribly flawed scholarly forerunners who came well before us, with assumptions and interests that in many regards are quite alien to our own today. While we do not have to agree with them—and in many cases we certainly will not, *not whatsoever*—it may be that, here or there in their works, we will come across an unexpected passage that reads as being far more familiar or suggestive than we would have imagined; or perhaps we'll find something that, though undoubtedly strange in so many ways, nonetheless hints at what we might now see as a scholarly trajectory that somehow led to a position that we today now take for granted. What is therefore gained in revisiting the past, again and again, and always with fresh eyes, is the possibility of an appreciation for a present that invariably has roots in worlds that may strike us today as not just distant but also problematic.

So, we might ask ourselves, what happens when the editors of a book such as this select a number of authors long removed from the current field yet all part of its complex and ambiguous history, and invite a collection of contemporary writers to see what they make of something from their work? The following chapters provide us with the answer to that question—an answer that, we predict, will complicate both our present and the view of its past that we carry with us.

As but one initial example, consider a brief quotation from Edward Burnett Tylor's once very influential two-volume work, *Primitive Culture: Researches into the Development of Mythology, Philosophy, Religion, Art, and Custom* (1871). Tylor (usually known by his initials, as E. B. Tylor), an English scholar, was among the generation who established what became known as the field of anthropology; in fact, in 1896 he was the first person named a Professor of Anthropology at Oxford University. Amidst a variety of claims throughout his work that would today be read as, well, understandably offensive by many, we come across the following brief passage:

> It follows that the general similarity of interjectional utterance among all the varieties of the human race is an important manifestation of their close physical and intellectual unity.[4]

8   **FIELDNOTES IN THE CRITICAL STUDY OF RELIGION**

In this part of the book, a chapter entitled "Emotional and Imitative Language," Tylor is arguing for inferring something about "mental structures" (perhaps we could today refer either to theory of mind, cognition, or intentionality?) from utterances (the way that sounds are made), such as our ability to infer something about the emotions of an animal from the way that they make noises, whether it's a dog barking or a cat purring. Reasoning from this (i.e., "it follows ..."), Tylor draws the above conclusion, by assuming that the rest of the natural world provides an analogy for the study of human beings (seeing humans as but one more elements of the natural world was a position increasingly common, though still controversial, throughout the nineteenth century). While this may not be an earth-shattering position to hold today— inasmuch as most now take for granted that all contemporary human beings belong to the common species, known as *Homo sapiens*—when seen in its own historical context (a time when it was not unusual at all to find European scholars arguing that non-Europeans were inferior inasmuch as they lacked abstract thought or were incapable of remembering the past, thereby living in an eternal present), Tylor's presumption of what others termed the "psychic unity of mankind" explicitly countered what we would today undoubtedly (and rightly, to our minds) term the widespread biological racism of the era: the view that different contemporary groups of people actually represent different human species (with some being seen as virtually locked in amber, thereby making them a modern-day survival of an otherwise long extinct form from which we had somehow evolved). By the mid-nineteenth century such writers as the physician James Cowles Prichard—in his two-volume work, *Researches into the Physical History of Man* (1813)—and then also the German psychologist, Theodor Waitz—notably in his six-volume work, *Die Anthropologie der Naturvölker* (1859–72; English: *The Anthropology of Peoples That Live Close to Nature*; the last two of which appeared after Waitz's death in 1864), which examined what was known at the time about so-called primitive peoples—argued against a variety of scholars who, at that time, supported the view that there were such significant and basic observable differences between groups of people that they each should be considered to constitute their own kind; instead, using such things as early reports from a variety of sources (hardly what an anthropologist today would call ethnographies but they worked with what was at hand at the time), Prichard and Waitz argued— almost always in ways that date their work to that era, to be sure, such as Prichard's comments on the writing of Moses as being among the resources for such work let alone taking into account that the biblical flood might be considered an historical event—that, despite some observable differences, there were sufficient fundamental similarities across all human communities to conclude that *there was but one human species*. As Prichard phrased it, "I think we may deduce ... a presumptive argument, that all mankind are of

INTRODUCTION

one species".[5] Despite the predictable persistence of the now problematic concept of race in such early works, and the ease with which such scholars could rank various instances of humankind along a hierarchy, this conclusion of fundamental similarity and thus identity, elaborated and further supported by subsequent scholars, played no small role in how we today arrived at our contemporary understanding of the human; and, despite current readers surely having good reason to disagree with large parts of his obviously early work, it is firmly in this camp that we should place a scholar such as Tylor. For this presupposition on the common human family provides the basis for his entire comparative enterprise, allowing him to conclude that studies of "them" illuminated "us" (or at least what scholars at that time assumed to be the supposed evolutionary pre-history of the species).

Our point? A serious treatment of past scholarship should read it in its historical context and then address both the agreements and disagreements that we may have with it today, while being open to finding some surprising points of overlap despite identifying the often dramatic gaps between current work and past scholarship. Moreover, such an approach means seeing one's own work as depending on a long line of others who were themselves working in different settings, likely pursuing very different goals, but nonetheless producing a view of the world that happened to be useful to others who came after, who may have been advancing very different interests and reaching rather different conclusions. For, as already indicated, our scholarly work today is not sui generis (to call upon a term well-known in our field), that is, it is not unique and it is not self-caused or self-sufficient; rather, it came from somewhere which, in turn, came from somewhere else. And so on, and so on. That means that we should expect to sometimes see surprising overlaps despite the gaps when reading work from the past, at least if we're taking seriously its historical nature and not merely judging it by contemporary standards.

This all means that contemporary readers may come to realize that they are in much the same position as their scholarly predecessors once were; for both are challenged with looking for similarities and differences between themselves and the social worlds they took for granted, on the one hand, and, on the other, the reports of people who are geographically or culturally distant from them. That the distance in the case of this book is now chronological doesn't change much, we think, for the challenge of similarity and difference remains, now taking place within an academic field long removed from the situation of its founders. So, what remains in common—if anything—and how might revisiting the past tell us something new about the present at which it happens to have arrived? These are not just the questions that must be answered by the following authors but by their readers as well.

1

Friedrich Max Müller

Brent Nongbri

The Science of Religion will for the first time assign to Christianity its right place among the religions of the world; it will show for the first time fully what was meant by the fulness of time; it will restore to the whole history of the world, in its unconscious progress towards Christianity, its true and sacred character.[1]

Friedrich Max Müller (1823–1900) is widely considered to be a—or perhaps even *the*—founding figure of the academic field that would eventually become known in North America as religious studies.[2] As a student in Leipzig, Müller studied philosophy and at age nineteen completed a doctoral dissertation on Spinoza's *Ethics*. At the same time, he mastered several languages and became especially adept at Sanskrit. Following further study in Paris and Berlin, Müller settled at Oxford in 1850 and deepened his linguistic knowledge by working on unedited Sanskrit manuscripts that had been gathered by the British East India Company. After being passed over for a chaired professorship in Sanskrit at Oxford in 1860, Müller turned his attention to comparative linguistics and religion. By 1868, Oxford had established a chaired professorship in comparative philology, to which Müller was the first person appointed. During his time at Oxford, Müller wrote prolifically in both academic and popular outlets and became a well-known public intellectual in the UK and beyond. At the heart of his work were the convictions that (1) the comparative study of languages could offer deep insight into human thought, mythology, and religion, and (2) that just as scholars had been able to develop a systematic and comparative "Science of Language" in the mold of the emerging fields of geology, chemistry, and biology, they could and should also be able to develop an analogous "Science of Religion."[3]

The quotation that opens this chapter is extracted from the preface to the first volume of *Chips from a German Workshop*, a collection of lectures and articles that Müller produced in the 1850s and 1860s while he was working on an English translation of the *Rigveda*, a large collection of ancient Sanskrit hymns. Most of the essays in *Chips from a German Workshop* take an explicitly comparative approach (for instance, "Genesis and the Zend-Avesta"), and such comparisons were a regular feature of Müller's work. Our quotation's placement of Christianity "among the religions of the world" fits comfortably within Müller's relentlessly *comparative* approach to the study of religion. As he phrased it elsewhere, "He who knows one, knows none."[4] For Müller, a truly scientific approach to religion had to be comparative. This emphasis on comparison has left a strong imprint on the academic study of religion up to the present day. For a considerable period in the twentieth century, almost any study of religion in university contexts was carried out under the banner of "Comparative Religion."[5] Even now most university curricula emphatically stress the importance of comparison in the study of religion, although what exactly is meant by "comparison" varies from scholar to scholar, as I will discuss later.

While Müller's focus on the importance of comparison may thus feel familiar to twenty-first-century students of religious studies, the overt Christian bias in the opening quotation will certainly strike some as odd and inappropriate. That the "Science of Religion" should (scientifically!) establish the superiority of Christianity over other religions is a position that no critical scholar would embrace today. Yet, this was a very common view in the nineteenth century when the academic study of religion was beginning to take shape. Comparison involved value judgments, and the "scientific" study of religion could have quite practical outcomes. As Müller noted in a passage that follows shortly after our opening quotation, "To the missionary more particularly a comparative study of the religions of mankind will be, I believe, of the greatest assistance."[6] That is to say, knowledge of "other" religions could be helpful for Christians seeking to win converts. For Müller, there was no contradiction between an objective "Science of Religion" and the obvious preeminence of Christianity. He was not alone. The Dutch scholar and theologian Cornelis Petrus Tiele (1830–1902) shared Müller's concern that the study of religion should be comparative. And like Müller, Tiele sought "to treat Christianity simply as a subject of comparative study, from a scientific, not for a religious point of view." Nevertheless, Tiele's "scientific" examination led to a classification and hierarchical ranking of religions. The "highest" religions were those he categorized as "universal": Islam, Buddhism, and

Christianity. And for Tiele, "Christianity ranks incommensurably high above both its rivals."[7] A generation after Müller and Tiele, Louis Henry Jordan (1855–1923) would frame the general principle of agonistic comparison in clear terms: "Comparative Religion is that Science which compares the origin, structure, and characteristics of the various Religions of the world, with the view of determining their genuine agreements and differences, the measure of relation in which they stand one to another, *and their relative superiority or inferiority when regarded as types*."[8] Given the European and North American setting of much of this early scholarship, it should come as little surprise that "scientific" analyses of religions in the nineteenth and twentieth centuries strike these tones of Christian triumphalism.

If these founding figures of the "Science of Religion" were operating within what now seems to be such a problematic framework, what light can Müller's quotation cast on the *current* state of the academic study of religion? I would like to draw out three strands of thought from Müller's statement— the practice of religious studies as a legacy of Christian identity formation, the framing of the study of religion as a "science," and the ongoing emphasis on comparison in academic approaches to religion.

It is not controversial to point out that Müller, Tiele, and others of their generation operated with ideas about religion that were decisively shaped by the Christian contexts in which they lived and worked, just as we all are products of our social locations. Indeed, a common way of narrating the history of the academic discipline of religious studies is to plot it as a story of a progressive liberation from Christian theological presuppositions: While the early practitioners of the discipline may have been impaired in some respects by their Christian assumptions, subsequent generations of scholars studying non-Christian cultures have become increasingly aware of Christian theological "biases" and "distortions" and eliminated them with greater and greater success as the years have passed. Yet, one of the insights of the last several decades of reflection on the concept of religion is the recognition that religion is not a native category for most cultures. The concept of religion is itself a relic of specifically Christian disputes over identity that took place during the era of the Protestant Reformation and the age of European colonial expansion.[9] Europeans' efforts to understand newly discovered peoples around the world drew upon comparisons with warring factions of Christians back in Europe. The idea of a world populated by people belonging to different religious groups is a result of what the historian Peter Harrison has aptly described as "the projection of Christian disunity onto the world."[10] It is this projection that helped to generate the "world religions" studied by Müller and his contemporaries. It is not the case, as Müller and many others have imagined, that religions are simply part of the natural world and form a natural category common to all cultures.[11] Thus, while the narrative of a progressive

14   FIELDNOTES IN THE CRITICAL STUDY OF RELIGION

"de-Christianizing" of the study of religion may in some regards ring true, the overall enterprise of the study of religion, even in its twenty-first-century manifestation, has an inescapably Christian orientation.

This state of affairs leads to a second point that should catch our attention, Müller's characterization of the academic study of religion as a "science." At first glance, this term may seem insignificant, simply the result of a clumsy translation of the German word *Wissenschaft*, which both had and still has a broader meaning than the English word "science," encompassing learning of all sorts, including what we might today call arts and humanities along with the natural sciences. But the writings of Müller and his contemporaries make it quite clear that they saw themselves as constructing something more akin to what we would today call one of the "natural sciences" or "hard sciences." [12] Müller regularly used analogies with such sciences to describe the "Science of Religion": [13]

> My endeavour has been ... to yield to no presumptions, but to submit to facts only, such as we find them in the Sacred Books of the East, to try to decipher and understand them as we try to decipher and understand the geological annals of the earth, and to discover in them reason, cause and effect, and, if possible, that close genealogical coherence which alone can change empirical into scientific knowledge. This *genealogical* method is no doubt the most perfect when we can follow the growth of religious ideas, as it were, from son to father, from pupil to teacher, from the negative to the positive stage. But where this is impossible, the *analogical* method also has its advantages, enabling us to watch the same dogmas springing up independently in various places, and to discover from their similarities and dissimilarities what is due to our common nature, and what must be attributed to the influence of individual thinkers. [14]

Here, Müller invokes analogies from both geology and biology to frame the study of religion. That Müller should make such connections is not surprising. He lived through an age of rapidly changing ways of understanding and classifying the natural world, from the development of evolutionary taxonomy in the 1860s to the formalization of the periodic table of elements in 1871. A drive toward comparison and classification was in the air, and Müller framed both the "Science of Language" and the "Science of Religion" as a part of this general movement: "All real science rests on classification, and only in case we cannot succeed in classifying the various dialects of faith, shall we have to confess that a science of religion is really an impossibility." [15] Much of Müller's prodigious corpus of writing about religion sought to carry out this kind of classification and systematization. The results of his labors and those of other early practitioners were summarized by Jordan, who assured readers that by 1905 the "Science of Religion" had indeed met the most demanding standards:

> By "Science" we mean, in brief, not only ample knowledge, but systematised knowledge. In addition to the multifarious facts which have been collected and verified and then assorted into classes, we must be able to discover and verify some at least of the *laws* which link these facts together, and which demonstrate that they are in reality integral parts of a coherent whole.[16]

Jordan thus suggested that the "Science of Religion" could operate in the same way as physics or biology, observing facts and generating laws with explanatory and predictive force. The idea that the study of religion should be expected to engage in the same kinds of processes and produce the same kinds of results as the natural sciences has had a mixed legacy. Over the course of the twentieth century some practicing scientists themselves began to argue that the natural sciences are not simply a set of disembodied laws but rather a cluster of social practices.[17] Viewed from this angle, the "hard sciences" are a discourse (the sum of what scientists do and say), and not the transparent window on nature that many of Müller's contemporaries imagined that the natural sciences could be. Today, then, many scholars of religion see no reason at all to attempt to model the study of religion strictly on the natural sciences. On the other hand, a significant segment of the academic field of religious studies continues to look to the natural sciences, especially cognitive science, as the most promising direction for the study of religion.[18]

I turn finally to the ongoing role of comparison in the study of religion. Müller's generation of scholars were intent upon describing the world as they thought it actually was and then organizing this knowledge. Religions existed in the world and needed to be accurately understood. Such understanding of religions was best achieved through *comparison* of characteristics. Some in the field today embrace a similar approach to comparison.[19] The now time-honored practice of introducing university students to the study of religion by teaching them sets of facts about "World Religions" would be a prime example. Other scholars, however, have attempted to use comparison in a rather different way. Jonathan Z. Smith, for instance, has made the following case:

> Comparison does not necessarily tell us how things "are." ... Like models and metaphors, comparison tells us how things might be conceived .... A comparison is a disciplined exaggeration in the service of knowledge. It lifts out and strongly marks certain features within difference as being of possible intellectual significance, expressed in the rhetoric of their being "like" in some stipulated fashion. Comparison provides the means by which

we "re-vision" phenomena as *our* data in order to solve *our* theoretical problems.[20]

Recognizing that no specific items or characteristics of items naturally *demand* comparison requires us to direct our attention to which items a given scholar *chooses* to compare and how that scholar goes about the act of comparison. As we have already noted, Müller took for granted that religions were simply there in the world, waiting for competent scholars to accurately describe and classify them. For Müller, the means of comparison of these religions was obvious. To compare religions was to compare *texts*: "In order to have a solid foundation for a comparative study of the religions of the East, we must have before all things complete and thoroughly faithful translations of their sacred books."[21] To this end, Müller undertook the monumental task of overseeing the publication of a fifty-volume set of English translations of ancient "sacred" literature, *The Sacred Books of the East*, published between 1879 and 1910. Cultures without writing (and hence without scriptures) were simply not a part of this comparative undertaking. Müller was happy to have the input of modern practitioners from various traditions, but the point of reference for him was always texts: "Nothing can be more welcome for our purpose than that learned natives also from eastern countries should give us their individual views of their own religions. But it should be a condition *sine qua non* that they should always support their statements by references to their own sacred and canonical texts."[22] In addition to neglecting those cultures that lacked written scriptures, the choice (both by Müller and many of his predecessors and contemporaries) to focus strictly on comparison of texts also tended to "textualize" those groups that they did study. European scholars who mastered the ancient languages tended to judge contemporary practitioners against the idealized religious systems they extracted from these ancient texts. For instance, Müller had this to say about the modern Parsis (followers of the Persian prophet Zoroaster) in India: The Parsi priests "would have to admit that they cannot understand one word of the sacred writings in which they profess to believe ... . A Parsi, in fact, hardly knows what his faith is."[23] Such scholars thus effectively made themselves the arbiters of what counted as "good" religion and "bad" religion. Again, this is a role that many scholars of religion still wish to play.[24] For our purposes, the point is that choices about what to study and compare have consequences.

Thus, one lesson that can be taken away from Müller is this: When *we* make comparisons, we should take care to be acutely aware of our own choices: Why are we comparing *these particular* items and not others? How and why have we chosen the *criteria* by which we will compare our chosen items? Making these choices explicit allows others to subject them to analysis and criticism, which, at the end of the day, is what scholarship is all about.

Müller's approach to the study of religion as reflected in the opening quotation is thus perhaps not so distant from the practice of religious studies today as it might at first appear. As we have just seen, Müller's comparative impulse finds different forms of expression among contemporary students of religious studies. And even Müller's obvious Christian biases may be understood as simply saying out loud that which is only just whispered or implicit in much current scholarship on religion in North American and in some European contexts: Even the most seemingly objective comparative studies of religion are, simply by using the concept of religion, inflected with (Protestant) Christian assumptions, even those studies of religion that are still couched in terms of "science."[25]

2

William James

Emily Suzanne Clark

The individual's religion may be egotistic, and those private realities which it keeps in touch with may be narrow enough; but at any rate it always remains infinitely less hollow and abstract, as far as it goes, than a science which prides itself on taking no account of anything private at all.[1]

Psychologist and theorist of religion William James (1842–1910) was interested in individuals' religious feelings and experiences. He defined religion as, "the feelings, acts, and experiences of individual men in their solitude, so far as they apprehend themselves to stand in relation to whatever they may consider the divine."[2] James's emphasis on religious experience led him to the conclusion that there was something authentic and true about religion, even if it was only the experience and not necessarily the theology behind it. That realness lay within the interiority of the religious subject in their experience. With the language of egotistic and private realities, we can see that James emphasized the inner states of religion, private to the individual. By being "less hollow and abstract" than other components of religion, he contended that there was something solid and real about the inner life of religious emotions and experiences. James argued that those private realities of religion should be the main focus, that an approach that emphasized them would always be fuller than one that neglected the private side of religion. Implied in this quotation, and more broadly in James's larger work, *The Varieties of Religious Experience*, are assumptions as well as challenges to the field worthy of our reflection. It is instructive to both think against James as well as think with him in regards to the religious interiority and its ramifications for the larger study of religion. As a final note of introduction, at times in this essay I'll be thinking about the implications of the quotation in light of James's other writings, but at other times, I'll take the quotation out of its context and reflect solely on it.

James presumed that religion's *true* place of residence was the interiority of the religious subject, namely in their experiences. While difficult for a scholar to access, this quotation suggests that the religious interior was more authentic and real than any other facet of religion. Religion at its center is egotism. Its core is personal and not social. It is private and not public, let alone political. Just one page before this chapter's focus quotation in *The Varieties of Religious Experience* James wrote, "*As soon as we deal with the private and personal phenomena as such, we deal with realities in the completest sense of the term.*" He admitted that experience might be "sneered at as unscientific," but he contended that it was "the one thing that fills up the measure of our concrete reality."[3] Not only was religious experience, and thus religion in general, a private matter for James, it was solitary as well. In other words, it was not just that religion existed in the interior experiences of being human, those experiences occurred in solitude, as his definition put it.

James conceded that the interior element of religion was "narrow," but still, a study that centered it would be fuller than one that discounted its significance. This would seem to suggest an assumption that experience was more pure, more authentic than other religious modes, such as practice or institutional structure. Religious interiority was beyond the purview of scientists or those who sought to reduce religion to some other force, like economics. But emphasizing the interiority of religion can risk overlooking the significance of religion and materiality. The study of material religion entails more than just examination of material culture, or stuff, but rather considers religion to be embedded in the materiality of the cultural, social, political, gendered, racialized world. Scholars of material religion argue that "the appeal of and concerns about religion today can only be fully grasped if the materiality of religion—the modes through which religious concepts and beliefs sediment and become tangible in social and political settings—is taken into account."[4] Religious experiences, even those located in the interiority of the individual, do not take place outside of the material world. On the obvious level, the bodies of the religious subjects ground them in the material world and furthermore, their understanding and experiences of reality are also based in the material world.

As an experience is recounted and narrated, the reactions of others might prompt the experiencer to shift or change their account, consciously or unconsciously. Additionally, providing an account of an inner experience is inherently a social process. When a UFO abductee describes their physical, emotional, and psychological experiences aboard the alien ship, they might tell listeners, "I know what I sound like, but this really happened." However, the more people question their story, the less they may come to trust their experience. Or, conversely, when there is evidence and conversation disproving the veracity of one's experience, they might refuse to discount their own experience. When nineteenth-century spirit photographer William Mumler was exposed as a fraud, there were those who sat for him and received a photograph of themselves and the spirit of a deceased loved one who continued to trust in their experience over the news. "Sure," they said, "he might have created fake photographs for some, but my photograph, my experience, the comfort and love I felt in his studio was genuine." Experience is a tricky business.

Still, the private realities of religion are certainly important components in the study of religion. Religious experience and religion and emotion are huge areas of focus in the discipline. James's emphasis on the private realities of religion as being rich for analysis ring true for many scholars of American metaphysical religions: a vague term for certain, but a useful one. Catherine Albanese defined metaphysical religion as ideas and practices that emphasize "an individual's experience of 'mind.' "[5] A range of traditions fit this category, including some investigating by James in his research of psychical phenomena. Also included in that category are Spiritualism, the practice of communicating with the spirits of the dead, and mesmerism. In the nineteenth century, many Americans believed their internal realities could be altered through mesmerism. Mesmerism, named for German physician and scholar Franz Anton Mesmer, could influence one's consciousness and physical health. Mesmer's 1766 doctoral dissertation, "On the Influence of the Planets on the Human Body," examined the power of planetary magnetic fields and what he called "animal gravity." These invisible forces permeated all living beings, and harmony and health depended on those forces. Knowing how to manipulate those invisible forces allegedly allowed a mesmerist to place someone in a trance as well. Charles Poyen, who popularized mesmerism in the United States, encountered it as a means of controlling enslaved laborers in the Caribbean. Industrialists in the northeast United States used it to manage the health and productivity of mill and textile workers, thus using mesmerism to alter their workers' interior states.[6] One of the foremost theologians of American Spiritualism was a mesmeric trance speaker named Andrew Jackson Davis. Davis traveled vast distances first through the natural splendor of upstate New York and then to the realms of the spirit world while in trance, showing that the private realities of religion are hardly small. He later dubbed this experience his "first flight through space," but it was a flight that did not require him to leave his home.[7]

Private realities can also be made external reality, according to some. The New Thought Movement, another tradition considered metaphysical religion, first emerged in the mid-nineteenth century, and a version of it still quite popular today in the world of self-help authors and life coaches. Norman Vincent Peale's *The Power of Positive Thinking* (1952), Rhonda Byrne's *The Secret* (2006), and entertainment mogul Oprah's vision boards are three of the most famous iterations of the metaphysical ideas of the New Thought Movement. The New Thought Movement argued that action within and right thought could alter the world around oneself. In this way, a private reality could become external reality.

Many of these examples have involved historical subjects, and centering interiority can be difficult when working with historical subjects, especially those from marginalized communities. In *Wayward Lives, Beautiful Experiments: Intimate Histories of Riotous Black Girls, Troublesome Women, and Queer Radicals*, Saidiya Hartman employed literary theory and "pressed" the limits of the archives in order to recreate the interiorities of the turn-of-the-twentieth-century Black women she studied.[8] Considering her temporal focus, her subjects were not directly accessible and archival politics meant she could not access written materials from her subjects. After all, not everyone's writings make it to secure archives. To try to access their interiority, emotions, and experiences, Hartman combined intellectual work with imagination. This prompts the question: whose interiority is accessible to scholars? Silence in the archives often means a silent interior of silenced subjects, and damage can be further perpetuated in that silence. Scholars of marginalized communities often have to read sources "against the grain" to discern the religious lives of their subjects. For example, studying nineteenth-century New Orleans Voudou presents a challenge for historical sources. Most of the sources from that era are newspaper accounts, which were often sensationalized. Others come from white outsiders to the tradition who frequently demonized it for its West African heritage. Sources from the early twentieth century can be helpful, like anthropologist Zora Neale Hurston's 1935 study *Mules and Men*, but this requires some of what historians call "upstreaming," or using known sources to try to extrapolate the earlier unknown. If these materials are not carefully and critically employed, especially the writings of white outsiders, attempts to recreate the religious interiorities of Voudou practitioners can inadvertently further colonialist damage.

In light of these material and historical challenges, affect theory[9] offers helpful commentary on James's privileging of the interior.[10] Affect is quite hard to define but can be described as "feelings, emotions, enthusiasm, energy, and matter" that "move through flows, affix in structures, spread by contagion, and circulate selectively."[11] Developing at a nexus of queer theory, postcolonial theory, and feminist theory, affect theory questions the private/public binary and argues that regimes of power have ramifications for the private and vice versa. Donovan Schaefer defined affect as "the propulsive elements of experience, thought, sensation, feeling, and action that are not necessarily captured or capturable by language or self-sovereign 'consciousness.'"[12] Affect theory, Sara Ahmed argued, "clearly challenges any assumption that emotions are a private matter, that they simply belong to individuals, or even that they come from within and *then* move outward towards others."[13] Rather, affect theory encourages scholars to read the social energies that move and flow through cultural and political forces and then how those affects shape how we feel and how we interact with the world around us. Oddly reminiscent of mesmerism, affect permeates through our private interior, rendering it not so private after all. While James defined religion as "the feelings, acts, and experiences of individual men in their solitude," many scholars have questioned that solitude.[14]

Though, an emphasis on private realities does not require us to ignore the connections between internal states and larger cultural systems. In *Medusa's Hair: An Essay on Personal Symbols and Religious Experience*, anthropologist of religion Gananath Obeyesekere employed psychoanalysis to explore the religious experiences, cultural meanings, and personal symbols of Sinhalese Buddhists, such as the importance of matted hair or fire walking, as a mode of "interdigitation of deep motivation and public culture."[15] Ecstatic states, or what he labeled "hypnomantic consciousness," created innovative, subjective imagery, or protoculture, that were sometimes accepted into the larger group thus becoming culture.[16] What began as a private reality of an ecstatic priest or priestess became a public understanding. Trance states and spirit possession regularly enfold the private and the public, and private realities are not divorced from the larger material world. After all, as Obeyesekere wrote, "ecstasy and trance are modes of knowledge of both mystical and pragmatic reality." Through trance, one of his subjects came to know "the truth about the gods" that then helped him withstand a local economic downturn.[17]

Early scholarship on trance and spirit possession among African diasporic communities reveal that not all inner states were taken seriously. Historical white authors, be they missionaries, enslavers, or travelers, regularly concluded there was nothing "rational" in the ecstatic experiences of spirit possession and shouting of Black communities in the US South and elsewhere around the Caribbean. This was part of a wider trend, where Christian discourses on demons and the "heathen other" located possession in the bodies of the vulnerable, the questionable, the troubled, and, even, the outright evil. The possessed allegedly had no control or autonomy of their own bodies, and in the eyes of the "modern," Christian West, that lack of control derived from a moral failing. While most scholars today do not characterize spirit possession with such a judgmental frame, that trend has a deep history in the field.[18]

24   FIELDNOTES IN THE CRITICAL STUDY OF RELIGION

However, more important for this reflection than the field's problematic past with spirit possession is what spirit possession suggests about the presumed privateness of inner states. In the 1930s, Katherine Dunham, an African American modern dancer, studied dance and ethnography in Haiti and completed initiation ceremonies, such as becoming a servant of the *lwa* (deity), Damballa. As she progressed through the initiation ceremonies, alongside others, she watched another woman first experience spirit possession. When Damballa entered her, Dunham described "cataclysmic tremors" overtaking the woman followed by speaking the language of the spirits. The priestess mentoring them and facilitating their initiation told her to "open up" and let the *lwa* "talk to us."[19] The woman later danced and received other revelation from the *lwa*. Here, spirit possession was clearly a private but also a very communal experience. The priestess requested the spirit to talk to the community, "us," through the possessed woman. Her words and her dance movements were those of the spirits. Similarly in Brazilian Candomblé, another African diasporic tradition, those undergoing initiation ceremonies to become a medium for the *orixás* (spirits) first prepare their consciousness for the experience of spirit possession. In Candomblé, spirit possession is a powerful, internal reality, but its larger meaning is derived in public. It is in the larger community that the priestesses and priests become possessed by the *orixás* and dance and move as them, sharing knowledge for the community. Those private realities are often not so private.

Some scholars who pivoted to experience and interiority did so in ways that set religious experience apart sui generis, as a special class of experience that cannot be analyzed in any way other than one that takes into account its "true," ontological nature.[20] These scholars seem to see religious experience as something that could even proof the veracity and realness of a religion's claim to truth. James did not do that. He felt that experience and inner states were the way to approach the study of religion but also felt these states could be analyzed in psychological terms. Still, there was something about inner states and private realities that struck him as pivotal to investigating religion and its meaning in human life. James's comments that attention to the private realities of religion provide a better study, one "less hollow and abstract" than a study of religion that ignores the private, raises the specter of authenticity. I have no desire to pursue authenticity or authentic religion in this essay (or any other, for that matter), but I mention the issue here because it seems to be a possible assumption of James's. Inner, private states yielded more fruitful and accurate accounts of religion because there was something more real to them. James believed there was a higher power that worked through people in those interior states to prompt a desire for self-transformation and self-improvement.[21] While his own religious pejorative is outside the abilities of this essay, considering that his reflections in the conclusion of *The Varieties of Religious Experience*, wh ch is where this essay's focal quotation resides, they warrant further attention.

Just two sentences before this chapter's quotation, James wrote that any science that ignores the individual's "feelings" and "spiritual attitudes" would be "like offering a printed bill of fare as the equivalent for a solid meal."[22] This seems to be a commentary on method and on religion itself. Reading about food was not as *real* as eating it. Experience provided something more. Additionally, the choice of comparison, including the materiality of food and the tangible experience of consumption, suggested that religious experience had had an authenticity to it. Just a bit further back in *The Varieties of Religious Experience*, in the paragraph before this chapter's quotation, James discussed the subjective and objective parts of religious experience. The objective part was "the sum total of whatsoever at any given time we may be thinking of" and the subjective was the "inner 'state' in which the thinking comes to pass."[23] The thinking or objective part included "the cosmic objects" about which we might think, presumably the divine entities or spiritual beings of a religion. Those cosmic objects would always be abstract, and while the subjective part, the personal experience, was only a "small bit" in comparison, it was "solid" and "*full.*" The cosmic only engaged the "symbols of reality," rather than reality itself.[24]

James argued that people should trust their own experiences. In one of his essays on researching psychical phenomena, such as alleged telepaths and spirit mediums, he wrote that "one has to follow one's personal sense."[25] In his pursuit of psychical research, James rejected the classical dualism of natural/supernatural and normal/paranormal and instead sought to "reconcile" those binaries.[26] Though James investigated psychical phenomena, it would be inaccurate to call him a debunker. Debunkers approached mediums and séances with the assumption that everything they witnessed was chicanery. Their goal was to discover the methods of trickery and expose the people behind it. Though his goal was explanation too, James did not assume that all mediums were charlatans. He had some trust in psychical phenomena and in his experiences of it. James wanted to discover the causes of psychical phenomena. While that was fraud in some cases, James held out the possibility that natural or even supernatural forces enabled mediums to do the seemingly unexplainable. In the most fantastic cases the science behind the phenomena continued to elude him, leaving him, as he put it, baffled. When he could not explain the experiences that left him in awe, he concluded that there must be "something in these phenomena."[27] These experiences hinted at the truth behind the nature of reality and the potential of reconciling the natural and supernatural as mutually at work in our world.

James found himself confounded by the medium Lenora Piper in particular. He and his wife, Alice, visited Piper shortly after the death of their infant son,

Herman. James had not planned to see her, and certainly not while grieving his son, but his mother-in-law encouraged him to do so after her sittings with Piper. When Alice's sister, Margaret, went to see Piper, she brought a sealed letter containing her mother's handwriting in Italian. Despite not knowing Italian and keeping the letter sealed, Piper was able to describe the letter and its author. It was this experience in particular that convinced Alice's mother that her grieving daughter and son-in-law should have a sitting with Piper. James kept his connection to Alice's mother and sister a secret, and presumably, with the different last names, Piper did not know that Margaret and Eliza Gibbens were related to Mr. and Mrs. William James. While entranced, Piper began to speak about family members and shared details that made James "uneasy."[28] Finally, before coming out of her trance, she asked about a dead child. Considering medical care and the ubiquity of illness at the time, James could explain this as a good guess, until she first claimed she clairvoyantly heard "Herrin" as the boy's name, before correcting herself and relaying that it was "Herman."

James's work encourages contemporary, critical scholars of religion to take seriously the experiences our subjects describe as real, even if the ideas behind those experiences cannot be proven true. Whatever may be the ontological *Truth* is less significant than what was true to the experiencer. Even if the religious ideas communicated in that experience were not real, the experience had observable effects in the experiencer's life. When it comes to studying Spiritualism, or the practice of speaking with the dead, I do not focus in on whether or not the spirits of the dead *actually* communicated with those at séances or worked through mediums. My work emphasizes the materials used to enhance those communications, how people responded to séances, and what their understanding of the spirit world revealed about the material world. For those convinced that the spirits of their deceased loved ones came to them through mediums, the spirits were as good as real. James certainly thought private experiences had real effects in the broader world, and here actor-network theory can be helpful.[29] Rather than think of humans as unique actors in the world, actor-network theory draws the scholar's attention to the "assembling collectives" that make up the world around any one person, collectives that include nature, society, people, objects, and implied religious entities.[30] Whether we think it's real, our subjects' assumption of its realness matters.

James also challenges us to recognize that the scholar is not divorced from the worlds they study. We all have interior experiences and know how tricky, powerful, and confounding they can be. And, James engaged in psychical research at the same time he wrote *The Varieties of Religious Experience*. His defense of the private realities of religious experience likely formed, at least in part, because of his own inexplicable experiences. James investigated mediums who demonstrated mental abilities as well as physical. He was particularly interested in telepathy but found many examples of "*baffling*," psychical abilities.[31] He struggled to come to clear conclusions about whether spirit "raps" and clairvoyant mediums were genuine. While his research allowed him to conclude that some of what he witnessed was natural, there were experiences that he considered supernatural. Even if the majority of Spiritualist demonstrations were the result of "swindling," he presumed that mediumship originated from "some originally genuine nucleus."[32] His experiences studying psychical phenomena, and especially his sittings with Piper, revealed to him the fuzzy line between scholar and religious subject. After delivering a public lecture on Spiritualism in New Orleans, I received a business card from a medium, just in case I ever wanted to talk to the dead. I never contacted him, but I also still have his business card. It is in the desk drawer beside me, right underneath where my copy of *The Varieties of Religious Experience* currently sits on my desk.

3

Edward B. Tylor

Mitsutoshi Horii

While anthropology, as regards the collection of materials for study of the religions of the world has gained of late vastly, the time has come for a more thorough criticism of these materials, so as to separate in the religions of the lower races the genuinely early and native part from the accretions and transformations due to contact with civilized foreigners.[1]

The above quotation is from Sir Edward Burnett Tylor's article "On the Limits of Savage Religion" published in 1892 in the *Journal of the Anthropological Institute of Great Britain and Ireland*. Tylor was born in London in 1832 and died in 1917 in Wellington, Somerset, in England. He is often known as "the founder of social anthropology."[2]

This short essay unpacks the idea of "savage religion," more accurately, the two categories "savage" and "religion" as well as the ideological similarity between these two concepts. The argument that follows is inspired by Michael-Rolph Trouillot's critique of anthropology as "Savage slot."[3] The capitalized "Savage" refers to "the abstract category, rather than to a specific and historical subject or group of individuals."[4] It is the West's Others, which have been subject to anthropological gazes. By the word "slot," Trouillot means a category which is used to filter knowledge and meaning. When anthropology is specializing in the study of "Savage," meaning the West's Other, "Savage" becomes the category of understanding through which the West conceptualizes its Others. What Trouillot problematizes here is that the ways in which the West analyzes and conceptualizes its Others universalize the West.

My argument is that the same critique can be made against the category "religion." Since the Renaissance and the European Enlightenment, the term "religion" meant Christian civility as opposed to the "pagan" barbarity of non-Christians. By the time Tylor was writing his "On the Limits of Savage Religion," however, a different notion of religion had become prevalent. This new category "religion" is conceptualized as modernity's Others. In this discourse, modernity is assumed to be "nonreligious" or "secular" as opposed to "religion." Importantly, the idea of "secular" modernity consists of ostensibly non-religious realms of "politics," "economy," "science," and the like. This is what I call "Religion slot." The capitalized "Religion" refers to "the abstract category, rather than to a specific and historical subject or group of individuals," and it normalizes Western modernity by unmarking it.

In the twenty-first century, the category of savage has lost its legitimacy in the academic discourse. In contrast, "religion" is still widely used as a "slot" for modernity's Others. Thus, this essay aims to problematize "Religion slot." The first section briefly discusses the idea of savage. The following section problematizes the projection of the category "religion" upon non-modern or "indigenous" communities.

The Idea of "Savage"

Twenty-first-century readers will notice that Tylor's anthropological works were written in a language that would be unacceptable in the twenty-first century. It is characterized by "ethnocentric and disparaging depictions of indigenous and non-Western peoples."[5] In the Anglo-American English-speaking public arena today, including academic scholarship, Tylor's language would be rejected as "racist."

In the quotation above, the native people in colonized territories of Euro-American empires are called "lower races" as opposed to ostensibly "civilized" people in metropoles. It is clear that Tylor identifies himself as belonging to the latter category of people. In Tylor's article quoted above, not only are indigenous people called "lower races," but they are also referred to in many other derogatory ways. As the title of the article suggests, for example, Tylor uses the term "savages." He also uses the terms "low tribes" and "barbaric races" as well as "rude races" and "barbarians."

Importantly, Tylor is not an exception. The use of such terms was very common in late-nineteenth-century academia. Tylor's language reflects a particular worldview that was shared by his contemporaries in the late nineteenth century. According to Ter Ellingson:

The "savage" and the "Oriental" were two great ethnographic paradigms developed by European writers during the age of exploration and colonialism; and the symbolic opposition between "wild" and "domesticated" peoples, between "savages" and "civilization," was constructed as part of the discourse of European hegemony, projecting cultural inferiority as an ideological ground for political subordination.[6]

In his "On the Limits of Savage Religion," Tylor refers to indigenous people in North and South Americas and Australia as "savages." Twenty-first-century scholarship seems to agree that such classification is not acceptable and it is "a myth that should long ago have been dispelled."[7] In contrast, what has not yet been dispelled by twenty-first-century scholarship is the idea of "religion." It has been widely recognized that the category "religion" was constructed as part of the discourse of European hegemony, naturalizing "secular" modernity and authorizing its domination over non-modern lifeways. Yet, the analytical use of the category "religion" is still common.

Problematizing "Religion Slot"

In his "On the Limits of Savage Religion," Tylor examines a variety of belief systems of indigenous communities in North and South Americans and Australia. Thus, what Tylor groups together as "savage religion" includes the multitude of belief systems of indigenous people in these parts of the world. It seems that the designation of beliefs of indigenous people as "savage religion" was a norm for nineteenth-century intellectuals. My argument is that the norm that governs the usage of the term "savage religion" is still widely shared by twenty-first-century scholarship. This is because, although the word "savage" is no longer acceptable, the term "religion" is still widely used by scholars as an analytical category. The following part of this essay discusses the two problematics of "savage religion" and "indigenous religion."

"Savage Religion"

First, for a long time in the history of the colonial encounters of Europeans with indigenous people in non-European parts of the world, European explorers regarded the natives in their colonies as people without "religion." For example, Jonathan Z. Smith's (1998) "Religion, Religions, Religious" introduces a couple of the earliest examples of this kind of usage. It quotes the occurrences of "religion" from two sixteenth-century colonial-era travel journals.[8] First, Smith refers to an example from *A Treatyse of the Newe India* (1553), which is Richard Eden's English translation of part of Sebastian

Müenster's *Cosmographia* (1544). The quotation goes: "At Columbus first coming thether, the inhabitants went naked, without shame, religion or knowledge of God." The second example is from Pedro Cieza de León's *Crónica del Perú* (1553). In this book, Smith reports, the North Andean indigenous people were described as "observing no religion at all, as we understand it." The apparent absence of "religion" was believed to be the sign of barbarity of natives. In this sixteenth century context, the apparent lack of "religion" in indigenous populations, for example, made European colonizers think that indigenous people were not full human beings.

It must be noted that Müenster was Lutheran, while de León was Catholic. In the light of this confessional difference between them, it is important to stress that whereas "religion" was conceptualized as Christian civility, as opposed to the "pagan" barbarity of natives, in the Protestant usage, "religion" was often used as opposed to "Catholics."[9] At the same time, the term "religion" was also applied to categorize various beliefs and practices that colonial explorers encountered all over the world. This kind of use imagined the plurality of "religions" and the world and developed into what is in the present day called "world religions paradigm."[10] Historically, however, the application of "religion" to non-Christian traditions was "ironic," because it still implied that the true religion was Christianity, while other "religions" were in fact all fallen ones, essentially regarded as "paganism" or "idolatry."[11] The hegemony of "the Christian religions" over other parts of the world was naturalized and authorized in the language of plural "religions."[12]

In this light, Tylor's idea of "savage religion" is an example of "ironic." By referring to belief systems of indigenous people as "religion," Tylor's discourse locates indigenous beliefs in the same category as Christianity. However, by calling the former as "savage" kinds, they assumed to be inferior kinds to the imagined "civility" of Christianity. This indicates his evolutionism. Like his contemporaries, Tylor believed in the three stages of human collectives: "those of savagery, barbarism, and civilization."[13] This modern fiction of the evolution of human collectives goes as follows:

> In savagery humans subsisted by hunting and gathering and had an extremely limited technology. The stage of barbarism was reached when agriculture became available. This development led to settled villages and town life and great improvements in knowledge, manners, and government. Civilization began with the development of writing.[14]

For Tylor, "religion" as a universal property of human beings follows the same stages of development. He believed that "religion" in savagery was "animism" and it evolved into different forms as human collectives move up the stages.

To summarize, "this evolution was from a belief in souls to that of spirits, then on to a polytheistic pantheon of gods, and then finally to monotheism."[15]

Tylor's theory of animism as the elementary form of religion was, however, contradictory to another influential theory of the origin of religion in his time, the theory of primitive monotheism. One of the main advocates in primitive monotheism was Andrew Lang, who had initially been a follower of Tylor but became committed to the theory of primitive monotheism. In general, the theory of primitive monotheism claims that the belief in one God is the primordial form of religion, whereas religions of indigenous communities are degenerated from the original monotheism into forms of polytheism or even "lower" expressions such as animism.

Although it is clear that Tylor takes the opposite position to the theory of primitive monotheism, he did not enter the debate for a long time. It was not until the publication of "On the Limits of Savage Religion" that Tylor directly critiqued the theory of primitive monotheism. "On the Limits of Savage Religion" starts with the following sentence:

In defining the religious systems of the lower races, so as to place them correctly in the history of culture, careful examination is necessary to separate the genuine developments of native theology from the effects of intercourse with civilized foreigners.[16]

Tylor's argument is that what is often regarded as the supporting evidence of primitive monotheism is actually the influence of Christian missionaries. Tylor argued that the Christian idea of one almighty God had already been brought to many indigenous communities and incorporated into their belief systems. According to Tylor, what his contemporaries thought to be the evidence of primitive monotheism was actually reminiscent of Christian influences in the previous time.

Analyzing the debate between Tylor and Lang, James Cox problematizes both positions.[17] He argues that both Tylor's and Lang's claims are limited by their lack of understanding of the communal context in which a specific belief exists. Cox states:

What was lacking in each case was a concern for the actual communities of believers that comprised the subject matter on which their debate proceeded. In the process of attempting to establish convincing arguments in support of their opposing conclusions, they ignored indigenous agency.[18]

In other words, what Tylor and Lang were observing was indigenous responses to colonialism. What Tylor saw as missionary influence, on the one hand, and what Lang believed as primitive monotheism (namely, indigenous people's beliefs in "Supreme Being"), on the other, were likely to be a product of struggles and negotiations of indigenous communities with the powerful force of colonialism. These are deeply interrelated into indigenous ways of life and communities' sovereignty.

Cox's argument for indigenous agency is a valuable step forward for a more nuanced understanding of beliefs in indigenous communities. This perspective was originally developed in his 2014 monograph, which examines the ways in which the idea of "Supreme Being" or "God" was "invented" in four different indigenous communities in New Zealand, Zimbabwe, Australia, and Alaska.[19] Importantly, he warns that the beliefs in "Supreme Being" or "God" must be understood in the specific context of the lifeways in each indigenous community. Thus, he is critical of the nineteenth-century approach to belief systems of indigenous people as it tends to separate beliefs from other aspects of indigenous people's lifeways.

In my view, however, Cox's approach carries the similar limitation to Tylor and his contemporaries in the late nineteenth century. Although Cox does not regard the indigenous people he studies as "savages," he frames their beliefs, practices, and their relations to other aspects of life as "religion." Thus, he employs the term "indigenous religion." What is not explicit in the discourse of "indigenous religion" is that the very categorization of specific aspects if indigenous people's ways of life as "religion" functions to undermine their claims for self-governance and sovereignty. In other words, the category "religion" functions to marginalize and disempower indigenous communities while sustaining the hegemony of Western modernity. This is what I call "Religion slot."

"Indigenous Religion"

Now I would like to problematize the projection of "religion" upon indigenous people's ways of life. As for Tylor's term "savage religion," this essay has already argued the problematics of the idea of savage. However, it must be noted that "religion" is equally problematic. My contention here is that unlike "savage," the term "religion" continues to be widely employed in twenty-first-century scholarship as if it is an innocent category. In order to problematize "religion," the following paragraphs refer to some recent studies of the category "religion" in Native American communities.

In his study of the Navajo people, Leland Wyman states: "There is no word or phrase in the Navajo language that can be translated as 'religion' in the sense of the term in European languages."[20] Wyman, however, does not completely abandon the term "religion" as he recognizes that "this word [religion] is the most convenient label for Navajo belief." Nevertheless, "to use a more accurate term," Wyman argues, Navajo "religion" should be conceptualized as "a ceremonial system."[21]

More recently, Tisa Wenger's study of Pueblo Indians and Brandi Denison's study of the Ute people employ similar terms as their preferences to "religion": for example. "Pueblo ceremonialism,"[22] "tribal system of governance,"[23] "Ute ceremonial practices,"[24] "Ute ceremonial life," and "Ute cosmology."[25] Rather than framing ceremonial systems of indigenous communities as "religion," these studies examine the ways in which these communities have historically negotiated with the category "religion" in their struggle for sovereignty.

The ceremonial system of Native Americans was for a long time *not* regarded as "religion" in the colonial context of the United States. They had been classified as "heathenry" or "infidelity"[26] as well as "paganism,"[27] supposedly, as opposed to the older notion of religion in the sense of Christian civility. Native Americans were regarded as "barbarians" without "religion," who should be "civilized" through conversion to the Christian religion and modernity.

This perception continued well into the late nineteenth century. In the case of the Ute people, for example, Denison explains:

In the late nineteenth century whites perceived that Utes did not have a religious system. This perception dovetailed with white aspirations to remake the Ute from superstitious, savage hunter-gatherers into civilized Christian farmers.[28]

Native American tribes did not regard their own ceremonial practices as "religion" either. In her study of Pueblo Indians, for example, Wenger states,

"Religion" is a product of European cultural and colonial history that has no direct translation in Native American languages … Pueblo Indians began to use the Spanish word religion to refer to Catholicism, and most of them adopted under Spanish rule in the seventeenth and eighteenth centuries, speaking of their indigenous ceremonial traditions simply as *costumebres* (customs).[29]

Native Americans' ceremonial practices are more encompassing than what the term "religion" tends to imply. Wenger explains, for example:

Pueblo Indians had long understood their tribal ceremonies as a kind of community work, in the same category as maintaining the irrigation ditches and cleaning the public spaces—all of which provide mutual benefits and must therefore be shared in one way or another by all members of the tribe.[30]

Similarly, Denison explains the Ute people's lifeways as follows:

Ute lifeways encompassed conceptions of *puwa* [the life force of the universe], resource collection, leadership, and notions about the individual. This all-encompassing worldview located the Ute in place, giving meaning to the struggles of living in a harsh yet bountiful environment.[31]

However, once the indigenous population stopped resisting colonial rule, their ceremonial practices became gradually regarded as "religion." By the 1920s some Native American communities started utilizing the constitutional concept of religion as a private belief, in order to legitimize and defend their identities and ways of life by classifying them as "religious" and protect them under the constitutional principle of "religious freedom."[32] Nonetheless, the same constitutional notion of religion was actively utilized by the US government authorities in the late nineteenth and early twentieth centuries "to delegitimize indigenous patterns of social and political organization."[33] For example, Pueblo Indians were governed by "multiple leaders of ceremonial societies,"[34] and participations in ceremonial activities such as dances were "just as essential as agriculture and ditch work to the survival and integrity of the community."[35] In this context, the US government's classification of Pueblo Indians' ceremonies as "religious" functioned to "delegitimize indigenous systems and undermine tribal structure of authority."[36]

In the case of the Ute people, the construct of "Ute Land Religion" was used by white settlers to justify their land appropriation. Denison documents that by early twentieth century the Ute people had managed to have non-Ute allies.[37] And it was in this collaborative effort for indigenous sovereignty and reconciliation that the so-called Ute Land Religion was invented. According to Denison it was "evolved from academic studies and popular cultural representation" as "a caricature of Ute ceremonial practices."[38] This claim of Ute ceremonial practices as "religion" was a discursive strategy of the Ute people and non-Ute allies to put the Ute traditions under the constitutional protection of "religious freedom."

This had a similar consequence for Pueblo Indians. As their ceremonial practices were classified as "religion," they became conceptualized as separate from what moderns call "politics" and "economy," for example. In the Ute's lifeways, however, their ceremonial practices were not separated out from their reliance on the land, and what moderns call "political boundaries," or "economic exchange." Thus, "it was difficult for Utes to gain ground for their desire for unlimited hunting and fishing access to their ancestral grounds;

resource collection and land ownership have no place in articulation of Ute Land Religion."[39] In the discourse of Ute Land Religion, hunting rights and land ownership of the Ute people are not prioritized as it falls outside the boundary of "religion," or the Anglo-Americans' view that Utes had a "religious" engagement with the land.

Conclusion

The starting point of this short essay was Edward B. Tylor's notion of "savage religion." Both "savage" and "religion" are modernity's Others. Historically, the idea of "savage" naturalized and authorized the ostensible "civility" of modernity. In almost the same way, the category "religion" functions to sustain the hegemony of ostensibly "secular" modernity. It unmarks modern realms of "politics" (the nation-state) and "economy" (market capitalism) as if they are the natural order of things or the bedrock of reality. In the twenty-first century, it is no longer acceptable to describe non-modern ways of life as "savage." It is also clear that the evolutionism that the term "savage" provokes is not methodologically useful to analyze the multiplicity of human lifeways on Earth. In contrast, "religion" is still widely used as an analytical category in scholarly discourse. My contention is that "religion" is as problematic as "savage." Rather than projecting "religion" upon non-modern lifeways, we must critically examine the ways in which such projections have transformed non-modern ways of life, and importantly, how it universalizes Western modernity. "Religion" should come down from the list of analytical categories, in the same way that "savage" was deleted from it decades ago. "Religion slot" must be avoided.

4

Joseph Kitagawa

Christopher M. Jones

[The history of religions'] aim is to study the nature and structure of the religious experience of the human race and its diverse manifestations in history, such as the manner in which humankind has perceived and developed various models of the universe. In other words, the task of the history of religions is to delineate the religious meaning cf humankind's religious experience and its expressions through the integration and "significant organization" of diverse forms of religious data.[1]

Joseph Kitagawa is the most consequential scholar of religion that you likely have never heard of. Kitagawa (1915–1992) taught and researched at the University of Chicago Divinity School from 1951 until 1984, and during his time there he was perhaps the single most important figure in establishing the history of religions as an academic discipline in the United States. He was hired by his mentor, Joachim Wach, as an instructor at the University of Chicago Divinity School n 1951, the year he completed his degree. Only four years later, in 1955, Kitagawa had to step into the role of his mentor when Wach unexpectedly died. As the head of the program in history of religions, Kitagawa cofounded the journal *History of Religions* and oversaw the hiring of two immensely important figures in the field's development, Mircea Eliade and Charles H. Long. In 1970, Kitagawa became dean of the Divinity School, a position he held until 1980, during which time he helped to develop the Hyde Park consortium of theological schools and participated in the process of reimagining the role of the Divinity School as a vital part of the broader university.[2] Kitagawa also published widely in the field and mentored a generation of graduate students.

Why, then, have you probably never heard of him? There are several reasons. In his own lifetime, Kitagawa's work was eclipsed by that of the man he hired to replace Wach, Mircea Eliade, and Eliade's work has continued to be an essential part of the history of our discipline. Kitagawa's scholarship is significant, but it is easy to overlook because so much of it focuses on thorny questions of disciplinary identity and method, rather than on the sorts of grand, sweeping claims that define Eliade's. Kitagawa's most important contributions to our discipline, moreover, weren't in publications and lectures. They were his quiet, often invisible work as an administrator and as a mentor. In these respects, as I will argue, Kitagawa proves a better model than Eliade for a more cautious and collaborative future for our discipline. Finally, Kitagawa was a Japanese immigrant, and we cannot overlook the reality that our discipline has always been more interested in studying people from outside of Euro-American civilization than in hearing from them. This essay is an attempt to rediscover Kitagawa and to reimagine the discipline of religious studies by using the quotation at the top as an interpretive lens.

The quotation, taken from the end of Kitagawa's essay "Religious Studies and the History of Religions," ends with the word *data*, and that is where I would like to start discussing it. Data is the one thing that pretty much every scholar of religion agrees upon. Our discipline distinguishes itself from its nearest disciplinary kin, fields like theology and philosophy of religion, by its emphasis on data. Where theologians can cite doctrines and traditions as authoritative, and philosophers can work within the world of logical abstraction, scholars of religion are always beholden to the things that they can observe within the field of human expression and experience: sacred texts, human subject interviews, material artifacts, ethnographic reports. We do not study gods, spirits, devils, or the ultimate nature of cosmic reality. We do not have empirical access to these things. Instead, we study people: what they say, what they do, and what they leave behind. Nearly every scholar of religion from the early twentieth century until today would agree that we focus on the human side of religion in our study.

Debates in the field of religious studies have often centered on two questions: (1) what constitutes "religious" data and (2) what should we do with it? Both questions have been subject to debate for well over a century. The first question, about the nature of religious data, has typically fallen into two camps. There are those who have argued (and still argue) that religion is sui generis, literally "of its own kind," incomparable to anything else. They have typically understood the elements that we associate with religion (e.g., belief in spirits or deities, myths, rituals, the sacred, transcendent realities) as constituting a distinct and universal dimension of human experience. In their way of thinking, all human cultures have religion, and all religions are constituted by similar categories. Religious data are data that fall into those religious categories: myths, rituals, sacred texts, mystical experiences, and the like. It almost necessarily follows that scholars in the sui generis camp assume that there is a transcendent reality that underlies human religious expressions and experiences, and they generally engage in at least some speculation about the nature of that reality.

On the contrary, there have been those who have argued that religion is a socially constructed category with a distinctly Eurocentric and Protestant genealogy. From their perspective, religion is not a universal human category. Rather, the term religion (as it is used today) was invented first by Europeans as they explored (and colonized) other parts of the world during the Early Modern period. As the story goes, Europeans "discovered" things that looked like Christianity in the cultures of sub-Saharan Africa, South Asia, East Asia, the Americas, and Micronesia, and they used the term religion to invent a genus to lump all of these different species into. Europeans of this era, however, never doubted that Christianity was the right and true religion, so the term religion has always had a Eurocentric and Christian-centric bias baked into it. That is why, scholars in the second camp argue, we cannot simply use the term religion to define our field of study. Instead, we have to devote time and energy to theorizing the term, examining its roots, its development, and its contemporary usage. Some would even advocate for eliminating the term entirely, or at least avoiding it when we study non-European cultures. Though scholars of this camp may be personally devoted to a religious tradition, they avoid any speculation about the nature of ultimate reality in their academic work.

Where would we situate Kitagawa in relation to this debate? In order to consider that question, we need to first understand what Kitagawa means by "the history of religions." That term gets thrown around a lot in scholarly literature on religion, particularly in work from before 1990, and it still shows up in the name of one major professional society, the International Association for the History of Religions. As a student of religion, you might get the sense that it's one of those terms you're just expected to know, but let me reassure you that its meaning is not at all self-evident. The term itself originates as the English translation of the German phrase *allgemeine Religionswissenschaft*. It is not a literal translation, however; that would be "General Science of Religion." Why the loose translation? In German, "science" refers to any sustained critical study; in English, by contrast, it connotes images of lab coats, vials, microscopes, and specimens, things rarely associated with humanistic studies.[3] But why, then, "history"? To understand that, we have to understand where the German field of *Religionswissenschaft* ("the science of religion") originated. The term was coined by Friedrich Max Müller, a philologist. Philology, in the specific sense, was a discipline that aimed to show how modern languages developed historically from shared root languages. Philologists like Müller, for example, show that modern languages as geographically disparate as English and Hindi developed from a common root language, Proto-Indo-European. They did this by comparing the modern languages, developing general theories about how languages change over time, and then using those theories to work their way backward.[4] Müller thought he could do the same thing with religions. He thought that, by reconstructing the historical development of the world's religions, he could identify the shared, common root of all human religion.[5]

Let's now look at how Kitagawa uses the term history of religions. In what sense is it historical? Is religion a sui generis phenomenon, something incomparable and irreducible? In the quotation that starts this chapter, Kitagawa argues that the history of religions is the study of "the nature and structure of the religious experience of the human race and its diverse manifestations in history."[6] For Kitagawa, the history of religions is historical insofar as it studies historical data. But what do these data reflect? Notice the work that the definite article is doing in this quotation: "*the* religious experience of the human race." That singular experience, like a Platonic form, asserts itself in "diverse manifestations" throughout human history, in all of the "historically given religions."[7] Note also that Kitagawa is interested in the "nature and structure" of this singular experience by studying data related to its manifestations. By "nature," however, Kitagawa does not seem to be referring to essence, a singular, defining feature of religion, ala Otto's numinous or Eliade's sacred. Indeed, pairing "nature" with "structure" suggests instead that "the religious experience of the human race" lacks a singular essence—it is, in fact, inseparable from its "diverse manifestations." Kitagawa's emphasis on the uniqueness of religion is disciplinary: he believes that religion can be most profitably studied as religion, and not as something else. He argues that religious phenomena demand particular methodologies, and while they can be included in the work of other disciplines they will never be properly understood by those disciplines. Kitagawa, then, is not too far from the famous dictum of J. Z. Smith that "there is no data for religion. Religion is solely the creation of the scholar's study."[8] He would agree that religion, insofar as we study it critically, is a heuristic, a constructed analytical term whose correspondence with Ultimate Reality is beyond the reach of our disciplinary tools. Religion may be a universal human experience, but as an academic discipline the history of religions is no different in kind from any other: it delineates a particular subject matter, and it has a distinct methodology that has been developed to study that subject matter, just like psychology, sociology, or biology.[9]

There is another crucial (and prescient) way in which Kitagawa breaks from quintessential scholars in the sui generis camp like Otto and Eliade. Let us circle back again to the phrase "diverse manifestations in history." Unlike Eliade, who has been duly chastened by his successors for the ways that he imposed his own understanding of "the sacred" on other cultures with little regard for local contexts, Kitagawa everywhere insists on situating religious data within their particular lifeworlds. This is not simply methodological rigor on his part. Kitagawa was among the earliest and most persistent critics of Eurocentric bias in the academic study of religion. As early as 1959, he wrote:

> It is apparent that from the time of the Enlightenment *Religionswissenschaft* has been operating with Western categories in the study of all religions of the world, in spite of its avowed principles of neutrality and objectivity ... Even those (scholars) concerned with Eastern religions have asked, unconsciously if not consciously, "Western" questions and have expected Easterners to structure their religions in a way that was meaningful to Westerners.[10]

Kitagawa went so far as to argue in the same essay that the search for religious essences and universals betrays a Western bias about the nature of religion and its role in society.[11] When Kitagawa talks about "diverse manifestations in history," he seems to imagine something much closer to Jonathan Z. Smith's polythetic definition of religion than to the sort of universalizing schema characteristic of other sui generis thinkers, and his strident critique of Western bias places him on the path to more radical scholars like Talal Asad and Russell McCutcheon who would like to abandon the use of religion as a scholarly category altogether because it is too closely aligned with Protestant Christianity.[12]

As prescient and insightful as Kitagawa is about the impact of Western power and colonialism in our ways of defining religion, however, he is also very much a scholar rooted in his places and times. One of the most important developments in the past few decades, spurred in part by the work of scholars like Tomoko Masuzawa and David Chidester, has been the realization that so-called primitive, archaic, and indigenous religions are not fundamentally different in practice from the so-called world religions (e.g., Christianity, Hinduism, Taoism) that have spread beyond their places (and cultures) of origin. These traditional religions, moreover, are often wildly different from one another and should not be lumped together under a common rubric. This, however, is precisely what Kitagawa does throughout this scholarly career. In an early essay, he explicitly defends the label "primitive" to describe humans both in the distant past and in traditional societies in the modern world.[13] In his final book, *The Quest for Human Unity*, he presents a sweeping survey of

44   **FIELDNOTES IN THE CRITICAL STUDY OF RELIGION**

human religious history, from the origins of our species to the present moment, and he devotes a total of three pages to discussions of religions outside of the so-called World Religions.[14] They are simply not part of the purview of religious studies in his mind. Kitagawa also repeatedly makes reference to "genuine" religions. With this nomenclature, Kitagawa probably means to distinguish religion from sociopolitical phenomena like Maoism, which he labels (with scant justification) a "quasi-religion."[15] It is conspicuous, however, that despite Kitagawa's resistance to essentialism he is still very much interested in protecting the boundary between "religion" and "quasi-religion."

On the question of what constitutes religious data, then, Kitagawa is remarkably complex and prescient. He questions the received tradition of sui generis historians of religion in his own time, and he anticipates some major developments in the field of religious studies in the decades following his retirement from public life in the mid-1980s. We will see a similar sort of complexity and prescience in Kitagawa's approach to the second question of what we should do with religious data. In the field today, there are essentially two answers to this question. There are those who would argue that our primary task is to interpret the meaning that religious data have for the people who practice that religion. For interpretive scholars, religious studies is a humanistic discipline similar to the study of art or literature. Scholars in this camp have typically subscribed to a sui generis understanding of religion, or at least to the idea that religion is a universal category that can be identified in any human culture.[16] Since, for them, religion is a universal and irreducible human phenomenon, our task as scholars is to serve as intercultural translators who make the practices of people around the world intelligible to an educated public. In the process, we make the world's religious symbols available to people to incorporate into their own personal searches for ultimate cosmic meaning.

There is a growing community of religious studies scholars, however, who argue that the purpose of the critical study of religion is ultimately to explain religious phenomena, and not merely to interpret them. Whereas interpretation is about the meaning of religious phenomena, explanation is about the prior causes of these phenomena. Explanation necessarily entails reduction, since religion cannot be used as the cause for religious phenomena without engaging in circular argumentation. Scholars who seek to explain religion, then, analyze and reduce religious phenomena to their prior social, psychological, cognitive, and biological causes.[17] Those scholars generally explain religion in terms that religious practitioners would not accept.[18] In explaining religion, however, scholars do not by any means dismiss what people say about their own religious experiences. On the contrary, the starting point of all explanatory work is an accurate description of religious phenomena that religious people would themselves accept.[19] Explanation also incorporates careful, culturally embedded interpretation of the meaning of those phenomena for the people who experience them. Finally, it involves an explanation of what caused those phenomena to occur. In practice, interpretation and explanation are complementary and mutually informing.[20]

Where would we situate Kitagawa in this conversation? Based on the quotation above, does he advocate for an interpretive or an explanatory approach to religious phenomena? On a cursory examination of Kitagawa's words, the answer seems obvious. Notice the emphasis on *meaning*: "The task of the historian of religions is to delineate the religious meaning of humankind's religious experience."[21] Kitagawa would appear to be entirely in the interpretive camp. He regards the religious dimensions of human experience to be self-evident, and he considers it the scholar's task to interpret the meaning of that experience to the reading public. Note, too, the repetition of the word "religious" in the quotation. That is not incidental. For Kitagawa, as for other scholars in the sui generis school of thought, religious experiences can only be interpreted *as religion*. The lens through which particular religious data should be interpreted, then, is the entirety of human religious experience "through the integration and 'significant organization' of diverse forms of religious data." A historian of religion interprets individual data in light of all that which is known about human religious experience. Each individual datum, meanwhile, changes what we know about the whole, and each time that the whole changes, we must go back and reevaluate the individual data that constitute it.[22] The historian of religion's task is a never-ending hermeneutical feedback loop. Kitagawa's vision for the historian of religions is staggering in its ambition: a bona fide historian of religions is expected to have sufficient facility in religion to be able to study any particular religious phenomenon from the perspective of the "priority of the whole," that, to be able to integrate the particular into a "comprehensive methodological framework."[23]

Despite his clarity and vehemence on the interpretative (and distinctly religious) nature of the history of religions, Kitagawa's thought once again displays a complexity that anticipates subsequent developments in the field of religious studies. In the essay that contains the quotation, Kitagawa rightfully recognizes that the term religious studies is little more than a placeholder, a shorthand way of designating whatever can be taught about religion at public or otherwise non-sectarian (or post-sectarian) colleges and universities.[24] Religious studies implies neither theory nor method, just domain. These are the same problems that lead McCutcheon, twenty years after Kitagawa, to call for a reductionist, redescriptive, explanatory approach to the study of religion—the exact opposite of Kitagawa's agenda for the history of religions.[25] McCutcheon is right, in my view: religious studies, like any other academic discipline, cannot assume that its domain of study is self-evident. We have an obligation to define our terms. Definitions imply reduction, and reduction in turn implies causality. It is absolutely within the purview of religious studies to examine the ways in which prior causes (e.g., social, cognitive, economic) produce phenomena that we subsequently come to regard as religious.

What, then, of the history of religions? I must confess a few things about my biases at this point. Like many scholars of religion, I was first introduced to the academic study of religion by the history of religions. It was not Kitagawa, however, whom I first read. It was Mircea Eliade. Like many scholars of religion, I was drawn to Eliade not because his work promised a critical perspective on religion, but because it was in many respects a new religion in its own right.[26] His vast forays into the world's sacred texts showed common patterns (the Sacred, the center, the axis mundi, a deep yearning to connect with eternal realities that transcend the illusory march of history) suggested to me that all religions were valid and that none was fully right. As somebody on the cusp of being post-Christian, that was a message I wanted very badly to embrace. You can imagine, then, my disappointment when I took my first graduate class on religion and discovered that Eliade was wrong about nearly everything, largely because he ignored the particular sociocultural contexts of his data in his rush to impose his own quasi-theological schemata on them. I have spent much of my subsequent career confronting (and deconstructing) Eliade's legacy, pushing for a critical, reductionist, and explanatory framework for the academic study of religion. Until I was asked to write about Kitagawa, I had all but dismissed the history of religions as a legitimate field of study.

I must confess something else as well: before I was asked to write this essay, I had never heard of Kitagawa. Eliade and Kitagawa died relatively close to one another (1986 and 1992, respectively), and in the subsequent decades Kitagawa's profile has dropped significantly while Eliade's has remained very high. I think there are two reasons for this. First, Eliade was famous in his own lifetime, with substantial impact on culture far outside of the field of religious studies (or even outside of academia). Kitagawa had arguably as great an impact on the field as Eliade, but his impact was not tied up primarily in publications that bear his name. Rather, Kitagawa influenced the field by mentoring his students, by hiring important faculty (including Eliade himself), and by serving as dean of the University of Chicago Divinity School.[27] Second, Kitagawa's scholarship itself was more modest than Eliade's, largely because he remained committed to careful, contextual treatment of individual data. Kitagawa's work, unlike Eliade's, is hesitant about identifying parallels between disparate religious traditions and humble in its overall aims.

So, I would like to end this essay with a plea and a suggestion: we should reread Kitagawa's work, and we should look to him, rather than to Eliade, as an exemplar for how to do scholarship in religion. Despite his flaws, Kitagawa embodies much about the best future for our discipline. Kitagawa's dual identity as an Episcopal priest and as a historian of religion captures the discipline's ongoing struggle to manage the insider/outsider divide, and Kitagawa arguably was more successful than Eliade in acknowledging the boundaries between religious studies and theology. Likewise, Kitagawa's persistent and extensive reflections on disciplinary history and methodology give his scholarship a clarity that is often lacking in Eliade's speculative (and context-deficient) examinations of unrelated religious phenomena. Kitagawa lays out a clear vision for the methods and goals of the history of religions. Finally, Kitagawa's own biography offers a better trajectory for religious studies, particularly in the twenty-first century as we grapple with our discipline's dark (and ongoing) history of racism and colonialism. Kitagawa was born and educated in Japan (as part of the Christian minority in that country) and spent his career cross-pollinating scholarship in religion in both Japan and the United States.[28] He fled to the United States in the late 1930s as Japan's militarism increased, and he spent 1941–5 in an internment camp, an experience that left him traumatized years ater.[29] Kitagawa thus bore in his own body the marks of Western racism and colonialism, and he devoted significant energy in his later years to advocating for refugees. If our discipline has a future, it will depend on the degree to which people from all over the world have a voice in shaping it.

5

James G. Frazer

Krista N. Dalton

Hence every inquiry into the primitive religion of the Aryans should either start from the superstitious beliefs and observances of the peasantry, or should at least be constantly checked and controlled by reference to them. Compared with the evidence afforded by living tradition, the testimony of ancient books on the subject of early religion is worth very little.[1]

In the preface to the first edition of *The Golden Bough* James Frazer (1854–1941) attempted to solve a "difficult problem."[2] He was puzzled by the public festivals of European peasantry. The kindling of bonfires on certain days of the year and the burning of effigies recalled to Frazer the ancient rituals of human sacrifice. Ceremonies of springtime conjured far more than "any sentimental wish to smell at early violets."[3] They resembled magical acts for ensuring the revival of plant life following the throes of winter. These rites were to him a kind of time capsule of primitive atavism. As a folklorist at the turn of the twentieth century, Frazer assumed that the superstitions of "savages" from time out of mind were preserved in the European peasant.[4] The continual presence of these myths in the seasonal rituals concerned with fertility and agriculture suggested to him that the customs of provincial Christians were still pagan at their core. By analyzing the rural population of Europe, Frazer argued, anthropologists and folklorists alike could uncover the origin of these practices. He theorized that these myths were the remnants of antique Aryan

50   **FIELDNOTES IN THE CRITICAL STUDY OF RELIGION**

religion, allowing researchers to glimpse the timeless mentalité of the ancient past.

Frazer was not alone in his scholarly obsession with the Aryans. As British imperialism encroached upon India, European scholars noticed an affinity between Sanskrit and the old languages of Europe.[5] Theories that these languages had originated from a common Indo-European source emerged, most prominently professed in 1786 by Sir William Jones at the annual celebration of the Royal Society of Bengal. Philologists soon sought to reconstruct the earliest form of this alleged root language and trace the cultural links between its descendants. What began as a study in philology soon became a preoccupation of anthropology. Scholars of this time believed language was an extension of cultural development and that linguistic studies offered a window into the origin and early history of humankind. This idea inspired Sanskrit scholar Max Müller to take the philological theory a step further. In 1861, during his "Lectures on the Science of Languages," Müller declared that this common linguistic source originated in the prehistoric Aryan race from whom Indians, Iranians, Greeks, Romans, Celts, and Germans all descended. He advocated using ancient Sanskrit texts to trace the development of Aryan culture to these descendants. Undertaking an immense translation project of the Rig Veda, Müller argued that studying these ancient Sanskrit hymns would shed light on the historical development of religion.

While Müller studied ancient texts in order to illuminate the trajectory of belief-systems tied to linguistic development, Frazer turned to contemporary peasant practice. Drawing upon the work of Wilhelm Mannhardt, who had chosen fieldwork over philology, Frazer argued that Mannhardt's collection of oral superstitions and myths were the "fullest and most trustworthy evidence we possess as to the primitive religion of the Aryans."[6] Here Frazer made an important juxtaposition between living tradition and ancient texts. If the peasantry were the preservers of the past, would not their everyday practice and popular myths enlighten scholarly understanding far more than etymological reconstructions from ancient books? Ethnography rather than philology could provide the superior portal to the past, as Frazer insisted that "the primitive Aryan, in all that regards his mental fibre and texture, is not extinct. He is amongst us today."[7]

When Frazer published the *Golden Bough* he shocked the British public.[8] He brought Christianity into comparative study with ancient myth in order to argue that it was simply a perpetuation of primitive animistic beliefs. The crucifixion of Jesus was yet another sacrifice of a scapegoat, and the resurrection a mythic drama designed to capture the imagination. The presence of antiquated myth-ritualism in Christianity was to Frazer a ruinous indictment, writing elsewhere that advanced societies still derived much from systems of taboo, from the "empty husks of popular superstition on which the swine of modern society are still content to feed."[9] By 1915, Frazer had expanded the initial two volumes into twelve, with each volume consisting of hundreds of pages filled with speculation about a perceived evolutionary path from primitive magic to civilized religion and finally to the enlightened era of science.

Frazer's work is now largely regarded as a relic of a fraught, and frankly racist, colonial era. His own field of anthropology increasingly sought to distance itself from his "misapplication of Darwin's theory of biological evolution to human history." [10] His imperial gaze stigmatized the rituals of the poor and the colonized, and he grossly speculated without suitable evidence. Yet one important methodological insight endured. Frazer's ultimate goal was to reconstruct Aryan religion using the oral interviews and ethnographic observations obtained from European peasants, even though he did not actually care what those interviews revealed about the practices of the people themselves. As Jason Josephson-Storm writes, Frazer "betrayed some ambivalence about superstition, making it simultaneously valuable as the remnant of the ancient Aryan religion, and yet also a sign of the primitive savagery in the heart of modern Europe." [11] Peasants were at once both the useful bearers of authentic timeless Aryan practice and damned by the very persistence of "primitive" myths. Nevertheless, Frazer's insistence upon studying the practices of ordinary people rather than the institutional elite was a groundbreaking insight. His work demonstrated that when scholars looked outside the boundaries of organized religion, they could discover myths and practices that confounded the neat boundaries between religious traditions. Christianity, in his case, was rife with hybridity. [12]

While scholars have long set aside Frazer's misplaced Aryan teleology, the impulse to prefer living tradition to the beliefs and ideas preserved in ancient texts reflects a growing disciplinary preference. This impulse surfaced in a different iteration in the late 1990s with the study of lived religion. Lived religion contends that the everyday practices of ordinary people do not simply imitate the norms of religious institutions; rather, they are themselves the meaningful site of doing religion. [13] While scholars historically focused upon institutional history and theology, they knew "precious little about the everyday thinking and doing of lay men and women." [14] This focus upon the everyday emerged amidst a widespread debate over whether the modern world was secularizing into a post-religion age. [15] Lived religion scholars challenged this thesis by examining how religiously inflected habits continually manifest in ordinary, even "secular," spaces. Whether seeking out traditional Jewish foods or purchasing children's toys, as the recent work of Rachel Gross examines, [16] or transgressive performance art rooted in Catholic forms that Anthony Petro explores, [17] the perspective of lived religion demonstrates that religion is very much alive if you know where to look for it. [18]

52 FIELDNOTES IN THE CRITICAL STUDY OF RELIGION

The turn to lived religion resembled in Frazer's preoccupation with the practices of those at the institutional margins, but with the analytical shift came the specter of an old dichotomy. Religion was divided along a high-low binary that juxtaposed organized religion against popular practice. Yet with lived religion's appeal to privilege the everyday, it at times overcorrected the discipline's focus. Everything associated with institutional religion, especially books and beliefs, was cast as somehow less authentic and less desirable of a study than that of kitchen religion.

The early forebearers of the study of lived religion were quite wary of this potential resurgence of the high-low binary. Professor David Hall convened a conference later published in the edited volume *Lived Religion in America* (1997) in order to rethink the term "popular religion." The term had come to signify the behaviors of parishioners who occupied a liminal space between the theologians and elders of the church (or its religious equivalent) and the blasphemous habits of common folk. In this space lay people fashioned their own religious practices inflected with their local superstitions and culture— such as building a shrine for the dead or using herbal medicines and spells with the name of God. These practices ran counter to the intellectual side of religion, whose priests and scholars would decry such habits as distortions of "true" religion. While the study of lived religion took up a similar call to recognize the agency of lay people, it intended to take a step further and break down "the distinction between high and low that seems inevitably to recur in studies of popular religion."[19] Clergy could be just as complicit in bending sacramental theology, folk customs just as resonate of institutional ideas. Rather than preserve a division between the clergy and laity, theology and practice, lived religion saw everything as fair game for analysis. As Nancy Ammerman insists, "Religion is not more or less real or worthy of study based on where it is practiced or who is in focus."[20]

In his 2003 plenary address for the Society for the Scientific Study of Religion, Robert Orsi echoed this early call for the study of lived religion to avoid a high-low binary. He insisted,

> The study of lived religion situates all religious creativity within culture and approaches all religion as lived experience, theology no less than lighting a candle for a troubled loved one, spirituality as well as other, less culturally sanctioned forms of religious expression. Rethinking religion as a form of cultural work, the study of lived religion directs attention to institutions and persons, texts and rituals, practice and theology, things and ideas-all as media of making and unmaking worlds.[21]

All forms of cultural work inform religious ideas and impulses. Texts and doctrines are not static vessels of the institutional but are another assemblage of religion. To privilege one set of idioms over another would be to mistakenly narrow the scope of religion as lived.

Despite these warnings the high-low binary persisted. The intervention of lived religion urged scholars to change their definitions of religion from a composite of institutional texts, beliefs, and doctrine to the day-to-day practices, behavior, and rituals of non-elite adherents. As illustrated in a recent monograph offering an updated theory of religion, Christian Smith argues that "we need to put on hold our interest in *ideas and beliefs* of religious people, and concentrate on their re igious *practices*, that is, on repeated, religiously meaningful behaviors. The common bias toward an 'intellectualist' view of religion needs to be corrected with a primary focus instead on people's reiterated actions."[22] Similarly, David Chidester in his new monograph devoted to the materiality of religion writes, "By focusing on the materiality of objects, we expand the study of relig on beyond the limited scope of beliefs, doctrines, and texts."[23] In these two examples, a litany of things associated with institutional religion—beliefs, doctrines, texts, and/or ideas—are continually drawn as a recurring warning of outdated or limited analysis.

There is much to value about these calls to elevate practice and materiality. For so long the discipline of religious studies and the definition of religion itself was informed by a Protestant orientation toward belief rooted in canonical texts.[24] See E. B. Tylor's definition of religion as "belief in spiritual beings" and Frazer's "a belief in powers higher than man" and consider the disproportionate emphasis. However, the binary that inevitably emerges when positioning belief versus practice is also misleading. Practices are not divorced from beliefs. It has become commonplace in the discipline to characterize certain religions, such as Judaism, as religions of "practice" contra Christianity as a religion of "belief." And while this is a helpful corrective, it is also wrong. It is not as if Jews do not believe things when they do things. Nor is it the case that Christians never do things animated by beliefs, even if unorthodox ones. I suspect that the impulse to privilege practice over belief, akin to Frazer's own preference for peasant tradition over ancient books, is in part rooted in a frustration with Christian hegemony. Looking beyond belief became a shorthand for looking beyond the looming lens of religion defined by Christian roots and biases. But in framing the future of the discipline as oriented toward practice *rather than* belief, the high-low binary reemerged in a different light.

With the turn to the ordinary came a stigmatization of things associated with organized religion, in particular their sacred texts. This shift had consequences. First, the study of ancient texts was deemphasized. Ancient texts—the Bible as exemplar—became the punching bag for critique of outdated analysis of religion. I was once at an orientation for new college students where different faculty members stood up to introduce religious studies and their individual areas. One faculty member emphasized the close-reading skills developed from reading texts in her classes on ancient religion, but another faculty member quickly interjected that the study of religion was about "much more than texts." His classes would examine practices of "real" people. In this example, ancient books were juxtaposed with living tradition, pointing to an enduring perception of texts as sacred relics of inflated import. This stigmatization is not without some point. Not only were these texts largely written and preserved by an elite class of men, but they also often reflect the institutional concerns of their makers. Women do not fare well in the pages of these texts. Nor do the lives of enslaved people or the poor. These texts do not outright tell us about the lives of everyday people, nor do they seem all too concerned with representing their stories. They are rich with ideology and laws but lacking details of the ordinary. It is fair to ask what value they could have for the new directions in the study of religion, but the answer is not nothing.

Additionally, the scholars of those ancient texts (i.e. "text scholars") are often contrasted against the relevance of modernists who study "living tradition." This opposition is silly—it is not as if scholars of antiquity do not study people who lived. They are not so immersed in philology and textual meaning that they need be ignorant of those outside of the text. As much as the author may be "dead," ancient books are not divorced from the lives in which they inhabit.[25] Texts retain their connection to communities, material substance, and transmission. But this opposition also assumes that the study of antiquity is therefore less compelling than that of modernity. With the urgency of questions facing the modern world, it is expected that scholars can offer knowledge that speaks to the present and it is unfairly presumed that the study of antiquity precludes relevance. This perception has immediate costs in departments that might shy away from offering too many courses focused on ancient religion. Small liberal arts colleges, for instance, can often only afford to hire one person in "Buddhist studies" or "Islamic studies." While these positions are theoretically open to scholars working in any time period or region, the expectation is that candidates must be able to teach courses primarily on the modern. "Students won't find it relevant" and "all you do is read texts" are oft-repeated rationales against leaning too much toward antiquity.

It is not necessary to set up a division between "living tradition" and "ancient books," as Frazer suggested so long ago, in order to analyze religion as it is lived. A growing number of premodern scholars have resisted frameworks that describe ancient religion as a belief system modeled after an elite Christian theological template.[26] Religion in the ancient world was both regional and temporal. It was enmeshed in ethnic and civic ties, inflected by the strength of empires and contact with neighbors. Elites and non-elites alike stepped over the boundaries of religious affiliation with ease. Antiquity scholars seeking to move beyond the scope of gods and doctrine have sought to examine the ordinary, largely illiterate, people on the margins of the canon. In doing so the doctrinal and institutional portrait of the ancient world derived from texts has been questioned, complicated, and enriched by the evidence afforded from analysis of the everyday lives of ancient people.

This move, however, was not intended to eschew sacred books but to bring them into conversation with other sources of evidence—such as archaeological findings, material objects, inscriptions, and receipts. The sacred books themselves have been increasingly scrutinized. No longer seen as a simple reflection of how religion was actually lived, they nevertheless provide different kinds of evidence by reading against the grain and comparing with other materials. Take, for example, the Babatha archive. Found in a cave in Wadi Hever in 1961, these thirty-five legal documents—largely bills of sale and marriage contracts—provide a window into the life of an ordinary Judean woman and her family that complicates normative (i.e., rabbinic) standards of Jewishness. While the authors of these documents write in Aramaic and in some places use similar clauses proscribed in rabbinic law, in other contracts they swear "by the genius (*tyche*) of the Lord Caesar" and employ Greek scribes. No mention of a Jewish court appears, but the authors register their contracts with local roman authorities. Babatha's *ketubah* (marriage contract) was written in Aramaic and contained the promise that she would be a wife "according to the law of Moses and the Jews," but in her stepdaughter's marriage contract, the groom promised to feed and clothe her "in accordance with Greek custom." Examining the ways these documents do and do not align with the normative rabbinic texts offers a window into the fluidity of legal habits and traditions of Jews in antiquity. As Hannah Cotton, scholar of the Babatha archive, writes, "These documents are the raw material of which life is made, and on which the rabbis wished to put their own stamp."[27] This method of reading against doctrinal and ideological rhetoric of ancient texts with an eye toward the lives of ordinary people does not privilege practice over belief, the everyday over the institutional. It situates those texts amidst a vast ancient landscape of idioms and considers the matrix of connections therein.

The study of ancient texts has further expanded to include their material substance. Since the 1980s "new philology" has replaced the quest for linguistic origins with an embrace of the material lives of texts. Liv Lied and Hugo Lundhaug explain that this new approach centers "the fact that a literary work does not exist independently of its material embodiment, and that this physical form is part of the meaning of the text."[28] If, as Chidester writes, "studying religion focuses attention, not on religion, but on the material conditions of possibility for regotiating the human,"[29] then a turn to materiality does not preclude texts but rather recognizes them as material objects of use in their own right. Prior to the advent of the printing press, and with it the standardization of the printed page, books existed as manuscripts. Each manuscript was unique. Marginalia littered the edges, scribes annotated and edited lines, and the words themselves could vary between the pages. The physical page varied in form, words written upon grooved papyri, processed animal skin parchment, or the rough side of stone. They've been found buried in dirt, stashed in caves, or stored in dormant rooms.

Texts are not abstract or timeless entities; they are physical artifacts produced by social and economic contexts. They circulate among people and in so doing live lives of their own intersecting with the communities that possessed them. Kathryn Rudy, for example, has examined "signs of wear" upon medieval Christian prayer books, "including dirt, fingerprints, smudges, and needle holes, which index some of the physical rituals they have witnessed."[30] Some owners kissed certain illuminated miniatures so often that they rubbed the countenance away.[31] The choice to kiss one over another when compared to their correlated written prayers attests to the diverse practices, anxieties, and preferences of lay believers, as Rudy notes, "The images that are uncharacteristically undamaged can be as telling as those that are heavily rubbed."[32] In this example taking the text's materiality to account enhances the sense of everyday practice. Nor are texts confined to the page. Pieces of texts, including sacred words, were inscribed upon a range of objects: devotional art,[33] incantation bowls and amulets,[34] monumental pillars and statues,[35] receipts and bills of sale,[36] graffiti,[37] and so forth. The premodern world was alive with words that testified to the lives of those who deployed them. By incorporating these material texts into the study of religion, the everyday lives of people in the past emerges in more corporeal form.

Anyone attempting to read ancient texts is faced with an enormous task. They must learn languages, many of which have long gone the way of death, or grapple with the insufficiency of translation as the "preliminary way of coming to terms with the foreignness of languages to each other."[38] Here we might return to Frazer's initial disparaging claim about ancient books and expand what they might signify in the philological pursuit of knowledge that he was so quick to disregard. While we no longer think that philology will unlock the origins of cultures and the mysteries surrounding those origins, the study of ancient texts can illuminate much about religion when approached from a different frame. Sanskrit scholar Sheldon Pollock offered the following defense of the enterprise in response to the perception that philology had lost its relevance: "Philology is, or should be, the discipline of making sense of texts. It is not the theory of language—that's linguistics—or the theory of meaning or truth—that's philosophy—but the theory of textuality as well as the history of textualized meaning."[39] There is no unfiltered access to the lives that leave their traces in ancient texts, but interpretive choices were made in their composition and use, and it is the study of those choices that expands our knowledge of the world

To do so is not to apply a transtemporal reading that funnels antiquity into the guise of modernity in order to be relevant. Readers of ancient texts must reckon with the distance of the past. I often have to pause and remind myself that the ancient romans did not have tomatoes. The rabbis who authored the Talmud never heard the refrain of *lekha dodi*, a now essential liturgical component of a Friday night service. Early Christians would be astounded by the presence of Bibles—a book that could be held in the hand and read in the vernacular. The religious subjects of the past are not us. This distance is why the stories and practices recorded in ancient texts are often strange. The plot of Tobit is hinged upon a bird that poops in his eye and blinds him, healed only when the angel Raphael advises to smear upon his eye "the gall of a fish," whose heart and liver were already burned to expel a demon. To analyze the religious lives of people illuminated by ancient texts requires what C. Michael Chin calls an "imaginative stubbornness" or "a determination to remember that people living in past worlds were not always very much like us, but that we should pay attention to them anyway."[40] This is a different kind of empathy than that in a focus on the modern. There self-reflexivity and individual knowledge are ready implements since the present moment is continually being refracted through personal experience. Attention upon the past, by comparison, necessarily fractures a steady sense of what "we know." It requires an empathy not built upon the modes of being that we might share but on the common sense that the world always unfolds in strange ways.

Such a longstanding juxtaposition between living tradition and ancient texts suggests that the scholarly pursuit for authentic religious practice has long grappled with the contrast between elite and folk religion, uneducated and educated practice, and superstitious and rational belief. The resolution of these tensions, however, is not to feed into a reconstituted high-low binary by siloing ancient texts from living practice. With declining enrollments and the shrinking of tenure lines, religious studies might seek to stave off its demise by sacrificing its links to the pre-modern. But to do so would be a mistake. It is precisely the foreignness of the past that makes the study of ancient books so valuable to the present moment. Modern notions of religious identity are unsettled as religious traditions believed to be timeless are exposed as porous in the past in ways they are not in the immediate present. To ask what constitutes a Jew or a Christian in antiquity, for instance, is to immediately confront the inadequacy of the question.[41] Readers are forced to erase the boundaries of nation-states and redraw their map of the world as the landscape of religion crosses different ethnic and imperial lines. The past and the present are not seamlessly connected, as Frazer believed, but studying them on their own terms—with their varied sources and particular limits—and tracing the transmission links between them provides a fuller portrait of religion.

To illustrate this point, I close with an anecdote from my own teaching. I teach a course focused on the development of religious charity and philanthropy from the ancient to modern world. In one of the early weeks of the semester, I assigned portions of the book of Exodus. Because the Hebrew Bible's agricultural portions for the poor are framed as a perpetual memory of the enslavement of the Israelites in Egypt, I wanted students to analyze the story. A senior American studies major in the course came to class that day with sheer astonishment at what she had read. "That is the same story told by enslaved persons during antebellum America!" she declared. This student had never read the Exodus story or connected its reception to the slave rows of the American South. When she had heard the refrain "Go down Moses," she did not hear the echo of voices across millennia who drew on the biblical narrative in their moments of struggle. Her study of the habits of enslaved persons in America was enriched with an awareness of the reception of the biblical text.

Religion is an accounting of the connections made between people and things, objects and texts, habits and customs, that inform our interpretations of life. It is always situational. It is always entangled. Perhaps the future of religious studies is not a setting aside of beliefs and texts in order to examine practice, but rather an appreciation of how living tradition animates them all. Making sense of texts requires scholars of antiquity to adopt much of the insight brought by the study of lived religion. Disrupting normative institutional frames, expanding canons, and looking toward the margins enhances textualized meaning. Likewise appreciating the diverse lived experiences of religious subjects is not to set aside texts but to change how we read them. Appreciating the materiality of texts is to situate them back into the hands that held them and to trace their links to the hands that could not. Ancient books live lives and inhabit lives in ways that illuminate living tradition.

6

Wilfred Cantwell Smith

Edith Szanto

We should be able to arrive at a point where we can understand, not with complete assurance but with reasonable confidence, and not fully but in significant part, what the faith of other persons, other groups, even other ages, is and has been. This becomes the new and challenging business of "Comparative Religion" studies—a task that is just beginning at this level and is assuredly difficult but assuredly rewarding.[1]

The above quote summarizes the philosophy of the famous Canadian Islamicist and scholar of comparative religion, Wilfred Cantwell Smith.

Wilfred Cantwell Smith (1916–2000), a decorated early Canadian scholar of religion and especially of Islam, was one of the first to critically examine the category of religion. For this reason, Smith continues postmortem to be celebrated in Canada as well as in the United States as a mid-twentieth-century scholar, who had a hand in shaping the contemporary study of religion at several major institutions influencing a generation of scholars, and leaving behind several books that are still read today, even if only as artifacts from a history that produced religious studies as a discipline today.

As a young man, when he was still pursuing his undergraduate degree at the University of Toronto in 1938, Smith became the president of the Canadian Student Christian Movement, which called for "think[ing] about contemporary society in the manner of the Hebrew writing prophets, such as Amors and Jeremiah, to express judgement on corruption, and to call for a transformed future."[2] Smith also sympathized with Marxist critiques, especially of colonialism, and indeed the Canadian Student Christian Movement had strong socialist leanings.

It was high hopes for a better future, especially in light of the horrors that were going on in Germany at the time and the poverty and deprivation preceding and especially following the Second World War that led Smith to pursue a graduate degree at Cambridge and from there he decided to go to South Asia, which at the time was still under British control. In the South Asian city of Lahore, Smith taught Islamic history at the Forman Christian College for five years. Most importantly, however, he "took part regularly in discussions with a group of young Indian intellectuals—Hindu, Sikh, Muslims, and Christian—they shared his hopes for the future."[3] Many of these were either colleagues from other colleges, or civil servants, and had studied abroad, in Britain, before returning. Several of these friendships lasted till the end of their lives. When Smith later wrote on the pleasure and satisfaction he derived from colloquy, it was these conversations with educated friends in India that he must have been reminded of.

Smith left South Asia before partition, but the violence and communal riots that accompanied the partition of India and Pakistan in 1947 left Smith greatly disillusioned. This was not the only source of disappointment for him. Wilfred's brother had been observing what was going on in the Soviet Union, serving there as the Canadian ambassador. Soon, Smith abandoned many of his Marxist convictions. Yet, judging from his academic work, it is obvious that Smith never completely gave up hope for a "brighter future" and this greatly impacts his legacy. Indeed, he developed his vision for a brighter future as elaborated in his writings on world theology, as well as other concepts. For this, he drew on both his theological education as well as his education in Oriental languages and cultures.

He also founded and led several academic programs some of which continue to thrive today and follow his vision. Specifically, Smith founded programs of religious studies at Dalhousie University in Halifax, Canada, and the Islamic Studies Institute at the University of McGill, and he became the second director of the Center for the Study of World Religion at Harvard University.

While Smith saw himself as a scholar of comparative religion, he was not the kind of scholar of religion Aaron Hughes calls for, that is, someone who helps us understand "the messy business of religion and the manifold ways various groups appeal to it for legitimation."[4] Instead, Smith was engaged in "the creation of ecumenical preconditions necessary for interfaith dialogue."[5] Hence, Hughes describes Smith as a scholar with an "overtly liberal Protestant theological program... [that is] getting different religions talking to one another."[6] This program also makes sense given that Smith was a theologian, a Presbyterian minister, and a missionary married to a daughter of missionaries.

In *The Meaning and End of Religion*, the same book from which the above quote is taken, Smith wrote a critique of the term "religion" as a concept that is both a modern Christian and Western-centric notion. Note that "religious," as an adjective, was acceptable to Smith.[7] Smith stated that his telos was to further the comparative study of religion, or more specifically to promote a theology of comparative religion. For Smith, comparison should not be done as critique, but as a form of dialogue or rather "colloquy."[8]

Smith called for "colloquy" instead of "dialogue" in his relatively late work *Towards a World Theology: Faith and the Comparative History of Religion* (1981). Smith wrote:

> At best, dialogue designates a transition through which one moves to something new. (If dialectic in Hegelian mode suggests—too much, to my ears—antithesis, does one none the less envisage synthesis? In any case, one is changed by serious conversation, otherwise it was not genuine.) As a term I prefer "colloquy"; partly for its multilateral connotations but chiefly to suggest a side-by-side confronting of the world's problems (intellectual or other) rather than a face-to-face confronting each other.[9]

Colloquy, unlike dialogue, assumes a speaking together, assumes give-and-take, conceptual equality between the participants. Moreover, Smith set an example for this, for how to engage or at least how to think about engaging "the other." He claimed that we have entered a new phase of "comparative religion," the role of the investigator has also changed. The investigator no longer retrieves information from books as an "armchair anthropologist" reading others' travelogues but traveling and interacting with informants or interlocutors personally. By speaking directly to "others" elsewhere in the world, a scholar of comparative religion ought to be learning as well as contributing to interfaith dialogue.

In a 1959 chapter written for Mircea Elia's and Joseph Kitagawa's edited volume, *The History of Religions: Essays in Methodology*, Smith wrote on "Comparative Religion"—in the singular. Smith begins his account by explaining that a new era is upon us, not only within but also outside of academia. He noted that in the past, scholars contented themselves with describing what he refers to as the "externals." In particular, he claims that European scholarship (until that time, in the 1950s and 1960s that is) was predominantly concerned with describing "externals" such as ceremonies, deities, object used in temples, and the like.[10] In the new era, scholars no longer simply study ancient texts and lifeless objects, but they also encounter people belonging to foreign religious communities.

This has two-fold consequences for Smith: first, scholars ought to recognize that they are now writing for a global audience, rather than simply for their own constituents, and secondly, academics' work is now being read by members of those "foreign" (or "Other") religions. Anthropologist Talal Asad echoed this point decades later writing about how English as the new lingua franca has impacted writing, for example, in the Arab world, leading to changes is grammar, diction, and even story lines.[11] Given this global impact, Smith argues that scholars ought to be more careful in thinking about their responsibility towards Others. In other words, he is urging scholars to become "caretakers" rather than "critics."[12] While Smith acknowledges that outsiders can attain great insights into the externals and history of religious communities they are not part of, he reserves a special place for insiders. Note that he points out that recognizing historical change within one's tradition is rather difficult and might be easier for an outsider to outline and describe. Yet, Smith's emphasis on faith, which is ultimately inaccessible to outsiders, means that he privileges insiders. Academic accounts for Smith ought to be measured by the extent to wish insiders recognize themselves in such portrayals.

For Smith, the common goal of interfaith colloquy is getting to know one another and coexistence more generally. But do people need to get to know one another to live as peaceful neighbors? Can't they just be friendly to each other without knowing about the other's beliefs and practices? This is what Grand Mufti Shaykh Kuftaro's representative at Syrian interfaith dialogue events argued.[13] But for Smith, getting to know one another, which he also termed as the acquisition of humane knowledge, rather than just describing the "externals," was central to that vision as well and was in the service of peaceful coexistence.

In the academic world, there are still those who follow in Smith's footsteps. These include, for instance, the current vice-president of the American Academy of Religion, Amir Hussain. Like Smith, Hussain holds that the work of comparative religion should "serve humanity."[14] In a recent interview, Hussain explains that his most recent work has been dedicated to showing that Muslims have contributed to the growth and development of America.[15] He thinks it is important to reach a general audience and this may well have been a reason behind his choice of the publisher, that is, Baylor University Press, a Christian private university press in Texas. He says he wants to change the world and make things better through mutual understanding—whatever that means.

Outside of the academy, however, this idea—that dialogue and learning about certain features of one another's thought—has flourished. The notion is simply that "talking with" and getting to know the beliefs of another can pave the path to peace and prosperity. It echoes the supposedly commonsensical assumption that diplomacy is always a good and that, given enough time and effort, diplomacy will succeed in creating freedoms and peace. This is the purpose of the UN, which was created after the end of the Second World War, the precise years that shaped and informed Smith as a young scholar.

On the webpage of the United Nations, the self-portrayed history reads as following:

> As World War II was about to end in 1945, nations were in ruins, and the world wanted peace. Representatives of 50 countries gathered at the United Nations Conference on International Organization in San Francisco, California from 25 April to 26 June 1945. For the next two months, they proceeded to draft and then sign the UN Charter, which created a new international organization, the United Nations, which, it was hoped, would prevent another world war like the one they had just lived through.
>
> Four months after the San Francisco Conference ended, the United Nations officially began, on 24 October 1945, when it came into existence after its Charter had been ratified by China, France, the Soviet Union, the United Kingdom, the United States and by a majority of other signatories.
>
> Now, more than 75 years later, the United Nations is still working to maintain international peace and security, give humanitarian assistance to those in need, protect human rights, and uphold international law.
>
> At the same time, the United Nations is doing new work not envisioned for it in 1945 by its founders. The United Nations has set sustainable development goals for 2030, in order to achieve a better and more sustainable future for us all. UN Member States have also agreed to climate action to limit global warming.
>
> With many achievements now in its past, the United Nations is looking to the future, to new achievements.
>
> The history of the United Nations is still being written.[16]

In short, the goals are to prevent a world war, promote peace, provide aid, protect the human rights spelled out by the UN, "and uphold international law."[17] The message is that only in cooperation will nations, and implicitly humanity, survive. This is also an assumption that carries a communitarian bias. It is communitarian, not individualistic. The divide between communitarian and individualistic is not an absolute divide, but rather a spectrum. Different cultures have at different times emphasized different approaches to survival, both in the short- and the long-term.

In recent years, American films have often celebrated individualistic or small-group survival strategies. These films tell stories about individual or small groups of preppers who prepare for a number of apocalyptic events in the high forest planes of Arizona, Utah, and Colorado, as well as in the mountains and forests of Montana and North Dakota. One such film that narrates the story of an individualistic heroic prepper and the consequences of his acts of altruism is *10 Cloverfield Lane* (2016). In this film, a man has prepared for an apocalyptic event by building a large underground bunker. On his way to the bunker, he accidentally hits a woman with his car and decides to have mercy on her and take her with him. Spoiler alert: the woman is not exactly lovingly grateful and ultimately kills her rescuer-cum-captor. What do we learn? The audience learns that individualistic survival strategies have higher chances than altruistic or even communitarian survival strategies.

On the other end of the spectrum, there are those—and this includes Smith as well as the UN—who think that "we"—that is, humanity—can only survive if "we" conduct peaceful negotiations together. But are these two "we-s" the same? Whether or not the survival and thriving of humanity, however defined, is tied to the longevity and stability of nation-states, is not questioned. Also, it is not questioned whether all will even be able to survive. Perhaps only a few will survive and maybe even cooperation won't be able to save everyone. The assumption is that "unity is good"—no matter what. We don't know whether the many that ideally make up this international unity are themselves individually "good." Who measures that and how? The same group that constitutes the group. Such an approach does not allow for outliers unless they have leverage because they are major funders.

The UN not only encourages but also requires mutual recognition of sovereignty by the member states. What about communities that are not represented? The Islamic State of Iraq and Syria (ISIS) might be an example. What about ethnic minorities who wish to claim sovereignty but aren't recognized by neighbors and the international community? Such groups have no seat at the table. So does not having a seat at the table automatically label a group "bad"?

Why aren't groups such as ISIS invited to the negotiation table? The sensational violence they broadcast was a major factor. Yet, as Giorgio Agamben argues, no state is born without what he calls "foundational violence."[18] This violence is later forgotten. As Ernest Renan argued in 1882, the process of nation-building, and its accompanying nationalism, requires forgetting. To build a sense of belonging, foster identity, and promote unity, a nation must not only remember certain foundational victories, as for instance, the American Day of Independence, but also forget the violence leading up to these events. Another example is Thanksgiving in the United States. Americans know about the violence Native Americans have suffered at the hands of European immigrants to the New World. Yet, this is something people don't focus on when they "go home for the holidays." It is precisely the cognitive dissonance of Americans generally knowing that there was a lot of violence in American history, particularly against Native Americans and African Americans, and the impulse to celebrate Thanksgiving as a feast of friendship, peace, love, and joy, which makes Wednesday Addams' speech so uncomfortably funny in the

1993 film *Addams Family Values*. Agamben would agree that the foundational violence, and the subsequert omission of that violence from memory despite the commemorative display of the holiday itself, are necessary for group identity formation.

The UN similarly misrecognizes the violence not only surrounding and preceding its founding, as well as the violence it perpetrates when keeping peace. For instance, when thinking about the Bosnian War that lasted from 1992 to 1996, outrage is usually focused on the Serbian fighters who raped and murdered civilians during what became known as the Srebrenica massacre. However, "in the peacetime that followed," as Victor Malarek explains, "thousands of women and girls—abducted from Eastern Europe and forced to work as sex slaves in the bars and brothels that dot the mountainous Bosnian countryside—became fair game for the tens of thousands of UN peacekeepers and international aid workers who poured into the region."[19]

In Syria, where yours truly spent some time volunteering with two different UN agencies, projects were often a waste of money and occasionally potentially harmful. For instance, internet cafes that were funded by UNDP in the early to mid-first decade of the twenty-first century did not overwhelmingly benefit the intended audience: poor farmers in the countryside. Small loan projects to uneducated rural women often ended up tying these women into cycles of debt, rather than initiating them into prosperity. How does one even measure successes in development? One possible answer would simply be that the UN tries—whether successfully or not—to improve people's lives everywhere in relative terms. Nominal successes are held up as showpieces on websites and in promotional pamphlets and magazines. What trumps above actual outcomes is simply the stated goal of global peace.

This goal, which resonates with Smith's ideas, is stated in the UN Charter of 1945, specifically the first article, which reads as follows:

Article 1
The Purposes of the United Nations are:

1. To maintain international peace and security, and to that end:
   to take effective collective measures for the prevention and
   removal of threats to the peace, and for the suppression of acts of
   aggression or other breaches of the peace, and to bring about by
   peaceful means, and in conformity with the principles of justice and
   international law, adjustment or settlement of international disputes
   or situations which might lead to a breach of the peace;
2. To develop friendly relations among nations based on respect for
   the principle of equal rights and self-determination of peoples, and
   to take other appropriate measures to strengthen universal peace;

66   FIELDNOTES IN THE CRITICAL STUDY OF RELIGION

3. To achieve international co-operation in solving international problems of an economic, social, cultural, or humanitarian character, and in promoting and encouraging respect for human rights and for fundamental freedoms for all without distinction as to race, sex, language, or religion; and
4. To be a centre for harmonizing the actions of nations in the attainment of these common ends.[20]

This charter shows that the signatory states implicitly accepted "peace" as a universal good, that acceptance of others is a universal value, and that survival can only occur through international cooperation. It does not ask whether this is in fact in everyone's interest. A famous social theorist and philosopher Michel Foucault held that "politics is the continuation of war" through other, that is, "peaceful," means.[21] In other words, Foucault casts doubt on the absolute distinction between war and peace, especially in the sense of "peaceful politics."

In Iraq, after the situation settled post the withdrawal of troops under the American president Barak Obama in 2011, two UNESCO chairs were established at Iraqi universities. The first was the UNESCO chair on the Development of Inter-Religious Dialogue Studies in the Islamic World established at the University of Kufa in 2015. The second UNESCO chair was the Chair on Genocide Prevention Studies in the Islamic World. It was established in 2019 at the University of Baghdad following the killing of Yezidis in the aftermath of the rise of ISIS in 2014.[22] The website of the UNESCO Chair for Inter-religious Dialogue Studies in the Islamic World at the University of Kufa states:

The Kufa University UNESCO Chair aims to produce multi-disciplinary academic knowledge on aspects of Sunni-Shi'i relations, and to contribute original research to the study of non-Muslims in Muslim majority society. The focus of the Chair is on Islam and Iraq past and present, however within a comparative perspective that considers other world religions, and other multicultural societies characterized by alternating periods of conflict and accommodation between communities. The Chair will bring together a diverse team of Iraqi professors, researchers and public intellectuals to share in research projects. A regional and international network of universities and scholars will support the developments of the chair's research and teaching capacities through program of visiting lectureships, joint PhD supervision, and collaborative research. On the basis of the knowledge product, the [UNESCO Chair] will develop educational initiatives and engage with civil society, and religious and political actors to foster understanding, dialogue and reconciliation between sectors and religious communities and help rebuild social cohesion in Iraq.

[O]bjectives

- develop the knowledge and skills of lecturers, researchers, and students in research methodologies and theoretical and conceptual approaches for the study of religion and interreligious relations;

- produce jointly with partners, quality research on comparative religion and interreligious relations in Iraq and the Islamic world from different disciplinary perspectives (religious sciences, humanities, and social sciences);

- provide a platform where professors, students and other intellectuals from Iraq, the region and beyond can meet and work together across sectarian and religious divides;

- promote gender equality and empower women by targeting at least 25 % female participation in academic and dialogue promotion activities;

- contribute to the public debate and policy decision-making to improve interreligious relations, governance and social cohesion in Iraq and the Islamic world at large;

- foster networking and the sharing of knowledge notably through the development of a dedicated website, publications including newsletters, the organization of conferences and workshops; and,

- cooperate closely with UNESCO on relevant programmes and activities, and with relevant UNESCO Chairs.[23]

The UNESCO chair is precisely the kind of researcher that Smith had in mind. He or she (but most likely a "he" in Iraq) will be involved in interfaith exchanges, not only as a scholar but also as an actor. Could the UNESCO chair talk with absolutely everyone? Theoretically yes, but not in practice. For instance, he did not enter into dialogue with delegates from ISIS, nor did he cultivate with scholars in the region but who were not classified as Arabs. Is strengthening a previously emerging network that also encourages the status quo an act of charity or even goodwill?

Smith promises that the effort put into learning about other religious traditions and trying to understand the faith of other persons will be rewarding. Again, this is problematic, if for no other reason than the impossibility this presents to scholars wanting to write about hostile or militant groups.

Today, many scholars of Religious Studies, especially those subscribing to social scientific versions of Religious Studies, no longer see it as their main task to make students understand "with reasonable confidence, and not fully but in significant part, what the faith of other persons, other groups, even other ages, is and has been."[24] Yet the ideas, the undergirding assumption, that sitting at common table is an unquestioned good found in institutions other than academia, such as in the world of humanitarian aid and development, the UN. There, these ideas reverberate. They echo Smith's sentiment: Smith's notion of colloquy expects various parties to speak with another and then come to a consensus, but not as a way of forcing or bullying individual parties involved. In short, Smith assumes goodwill and a common goal. Similarly, the UN also assumes and expects a general belief in human goodwill. Moreover, the UN portrays itself as the protector of common goods and values, including human rights, and it insists on being authorized based on ideals and not on actual results. Like Smith, the UN calls for a "brighter future for all" as something that ought to be achieved through communication, through colloquy. Both are activist in outlook and are dedicated towards a particular course of action to achieve an envisioned but uncertain outcome.

7

Sigmund Freud

Robyn Faith Walsh

First of all, it must be said that it is useless to question savages as to the real motivation of their prohibitions (es habe keinen Sinn, die Wilden nach der wirklichen Motivierung ihrer Verbote) *or as to the genesis of taboo* (Genese des Tabu). *According to our assumption* (Voraussetzung) *they must be incapable* (unfähig) *of telling us anything about it since this motivation is "unconscious" to them* (denn diese Motivierung sei ihnen "unbewußt ").[1]

Compiling "field notes' on Sigmund Freud (1856–1939) is specifically difficult because it is nearly impossible to navigate scholarship, or even our day-to-day lives, without encountering the remnants of his thought.[2] This is not because Freud was or continues to be particularly influential in the study of religion[3] but because he has managed to achieve something few do—he has become "a name."[4] To some extent, the fine detail of his work has been glossed over thanks to a combination of translation, time, and the colloquial ubiquity of his terminology.[5] Freudian slip. Oedipal complex. Cathartic. Subconscious. Penis envy. Blaming your "id." Ego. Libido. All thanks to Freud. All in need of clarity or outright revision.

To approach the work of such a "canonical" figure and systematically untangle the language and thought represented by an unmoored quote like the one above requires a great deal of contextualization. While it is always important to consider an author's historical milieu, Freud in particular was a product of certain trends n academia in the nineteenth and early twentieth

70   FIELDNOTES IN THE CRITICAL STUDY OF RELIGION

centuries that created a permission structure for him to present hypotheses about psychology—that is, the subconscious processes of a human subject or subjects—as observable "facts." Moreover, his choice of terms like "savages" (*Wilden*), and his colonialist and demeaning description of certain peoples as "incapable" (*unfähig*) of possessing even basic awareness or rationality for their actions, is indicative of discourse in the Romantic era that functionally viewed those outside the purview of the contemporary, elite, European male as less-than, "primitive," child-like, uncritically prone to "wonder," to myth, to superstition. It is important to understand this intellectual history because, without that knowledge, we are at risk of repeating the same mistakes.

And, unfortunately—sometimes unwittingly— we do. This is evident, for example, when scholars in the field use terms like "primitive" to describe peoples and social movements (e.g., "primitive" religions, "primitive" Christianity) and inadvertently import any number of assumptions about the rationality, comprehension, relative capital, and organization (or lack thereof) of these groups. We also find it in the study of history, with unsupported claims that "the ancients" were cognitively distinct from modern human beings in some fundamental way or were innately naïve. Similarly, when we reduce the complex social practices of our objects of study to often ill-defined terms like "magic" or "taboo" (*Tabu*), we risk reinforcing false dichotomies of civilized/uncivilized, Western/non-Western, religious/not religious, and so forth.[6] Even the use of terms like "world religions" or comparative approaches built on the concepts of "monotheism" and "polytheism" can invoke colonialist paradigms or carry implicit ideas about what constitutes "true" religion.[7] And studies—even whole disciplines— that invoke hierarchies of culture are in need of significant reassessment; Freud's own penchant for privileging the ancient Greeks in his analogies, allusions, and clinical terms stands out as a prime example. As Hughes and McCutcheon caution in the introduction to this volume, "for many scholars today the past of our field is a series of problems from which we feel that we are luckily distanced or even insulated today"[8] but, as they clarify, this is a stance that comes with a cost.

Thus, in order to evaluate the quote above we must begin by contextualizing Freud's place within the historical trajectory of the field of religious studies. In so doing, we establish the intellectual trends and institutional structures that authorized his psychoanalytic and phenomenological approach to religion.

Key to this undertaking is recognizing that academia in the nineteenth century was dominated by the intellectual shifts and politics of Germany. Freud, based in Vienna for the majority of his life, was steeped in these movements and their consequences, often publishing in German and employing the terminology of the guild.[9] The decade in which Freud was born (1850s) was a postrevolutionary era that gave rise to both increased nationalism and a shift within scholarship that privileged "empirical experience" in the study of ethnography, myth, and folklore. Sometimes referred to as an era of "Romantic positivism," the work of intellectuals like Jacob and Wilhelm Grimm focused on amassing and amalgamating the oral stories and inherited myths of a given peoples (*Volker*), including so-called savage peoples (*wilder Völker*), in order to draw conclusions about their unifying language and "spirit" (*Geist*).

The field of "comparative mythology" also emerged in this period, established through scholars like Adalbert Kuhn (1812–1881) and Friedrich Max Müller (1823–1900). As the historian George S. Williamson explains, Kuhn and Müller are particularly notable in that they sought to locate "the Indo-Germanic ("Aryan") roots of both Germanic and Greek mythology" through the study of collected folklore and philology.[10] This effort signaled, among other things, an increasing methodological concern for identifying the concrete "origins" of religions and peoples—an approach to histories, ancient societies, and literatures, which arguably continues to this day in certain corners of the field of religious studies.[11] Among *historians* of religion in particular, extant texts, objects, and so on are often treated as reliably representative of entire peoples and movements; a bit like the ethnographers of old, the notion that there is an essential and holistic group or "community" that can be identified, evaluated, and meaningfully compared to competing entities is often built upon the slimmest of data. But more on this point in a moment.

In the mid- to late-nineteenth century the twin concept of "folk psychology" (*Völkerpsychologie*) proposed that the "intellectual life of nations" could be retrieved through analysis of their myths, fables, and customs.[12] What was sometimes framed as a search for origins was more often than not allied with notions of cultural evolution and implicit hierarchies of "civilized" and "uncivilized" or "primitive" peoples; the latter end of this scale included both peasant classes and autochthonous groups. Among the goals of this movement was to "establish a 'science of religion' " that could, via comparative methods, demonstrate the founding, development, and exchange of ideas between cultures. For Kuhn and others, this entailed revealing the "origins [of] the primitive mental apparatus of ancients unable to fathom the most basic notions of causality."[13] By the latter half of the century, "psychological ethnology" materialized through the work of psychologists Heymann Steinthal (1823–1899) and Mortiz Lazarus (1824–1903). Agitating against certain forms of idealism, they viewed nations and peoples as holistic, "biological [entities]" for whom collective thoughts—expressed through myths and action—could be evaluated through the tools of psychology and psychoanalysis.[14]

Put simply, psychological approaches to religion and sociology existed well before Freud. So, too, did comparative methods linking seemingly disparate elements between cultures for the purpose of painting grand schemes of human history and knowledge. Freud managed to parlay his medical training on (so-called) hysteria and the interpretation and significance of dreams, impulses, neuroses, and desires into an eventual "Freudian revolution" by virtue of his application of the same principles to humanistic subjects.[15] With the benefit of hindsight, this was perhaps not so much a revolution as a confluence or a consequence of the intellectual movements that came well before his personal rise to popular prominence—including the false notion that invoking conclusions on the basis of "science" signals subjective-free interpretation.[16] Moreover, as the historian Suzanne Marchand correctly assesses, Freud—like Friedrich Nietzsche, Max Weber, and Carl Jung—had a "knowledge of ... cultures [that was] not very deep and rather idiosyncratic."[17] While one might dispute the value and efficacy of his therapeutic work, Freud's engagement with historical and ethnographic analysis was amateurish and, to the extent to which it was even accepted by his peers, was perhaps feasible only by virtue of reductive and colonialist frameworks.

Indeed, Freud ranks among those Hughes and McCutcheon term "armchair" anthropologists;[18] although his theoretical claims about the unconscious and neuroses are grounded in work with patients in a clinical setting, his observations about the beliefs and practices of any number of religions are at best impressionistic. In contemporary judgment they are also manifestly colonialist and racist. Toggling freely between "prehistoric man" and what he has gleaned about the indigenous peoples of Australia, Polynesia, Malaysia, and Melanesia, his stated thesis in *Totem and Taboo*, for instance, is that the simplistic "mental lives" of these "primitives," "savages," and "half-savages" offer "well-preserved" *comparanda* for evaluating the fundamental elements—the "early stage"—of "our own [psychological] development."[19] "Our" in this construction meant those whom Freud deemed "civilized"— that is, people who shared his same relative background, education level, and privilege. Indeed, elsewhere he explicitly names "the white peoples of Europe and America" and their "*civilized* communities" as a foil to his anecdotes from various ethnographic sources.[20] What he establishes, then, is a tautological project by which his observations about the psychology and neuroses of his clinical patients are ostensibly manifested—and thereby confirmed—through comparative and sweeping claims about the traditions, laws, and actions of peoples he considers evolutionarily closer to a "primitive" human subject.

Revisiting Freud in this manner demonstrates, among other things, that phenomenology and psychoanalytic methods in the study of religion should be treated with (at best) extreme caution. So, too, the theory that—like the dreams of an individual—art, myth, literature, folklore, and so forth are the key to understanding the collective "mind" of a given people. Such approaches deny agency to a subject insofar as the "unconscious" is ultimately what shapes reality. In part, this is why Freud can posit that "savages" are "incapable of telling us anything about" their "unconscious" motivations— they are subject to, not authors of, their thoughts and actions.

SIGMUND FREUD

Freud's emphasis on the "unconscious" also permitted any number of comparisons across time, space, and subject without much regard for concrete historical, technical, or practical contexts. The religious studies scholar Daniel Pals explains:

> To Freud and his followers, it seemed at times as if he had found an explanatory golden key. Analysis of the psyche opened a door on the innermost motives of human thought and action, from the stresses placed on the individual personality to the great forces that drive and shape civilizations. It could uncover the smallest secret of a single, troubled self while at the same time offering a new perspective on the great endeavors of human history, among them society, morals, philosophy, and—not least—religion.[21]

As it concerns the study of religion, for Freud the irrational impulses that fueled the manifest neuroses of his patients (e.g., compulsive behaviors, phobias, antisocial actions) were akin to the irrational demands of religion (e.g., belief in unseen beings, self-mutilation, and deprivation). Simply observe, identify, and describe the neuroses and whether through free association, personal experience, or common sense, you will eventually determine cause.[22] While certain aspects of this theoretical work arguably prefigure later questions from cognitive anthropology and evolutionary theory on religion as a counterintuitive commitment, these fields would not accept the view that an entire group of people can be reduced to a single, uniform subject.[23] In contrast to the holism of *Völkerpsychologie*, the dynamic reasons that human beings select for certain behaviors or beliefs cannot be explained through broad observations or ethnographic generalizations—"[c]ultures and religions are not ontological y distinct 'superorganisms.'"[24] Rather, what we call religion can only be explained through the study of a complex ecosystem of overlapping cognitive, social, embodied, and environmental interests.

In Freud's own time there was awareness that many of his theses and conclusions were, to quote Simone de Beauvoir, "strange fictions."[25] Beyond his brand of speculation about indigenous peoples, their cognition, and religion already discussed, he frequently drew conclusions about human psychology directly from his own personal experiences. Even contemporary scholarship on Freud—including this piece—can find itself in the curious position of having to pepper critical analysis with anecdotes from his life, so seemingly formative are these biographical elements to his theoretical claims.[26] Was his childhood sexual attraction to his niece Pauline the basis for his clinical theory of ambivalence?[27] Is it even conceivable that an entire theory of human consciousness—the so-called Oedipal complex—is the unlikely consequence of a young Freud being forced to translate Sophocles in school?[28] How much did his own experimentation with pharmaceuticals—including cocaine—fuel his conclusions about the therapeutic nature of dreams and free association?[29] Was his alleged affair with Lou Andreas-Salomé (1861–1937) a motivating factor in his analyses of "narcissistic women"?[30]

These and related questions not only function to spackle over lacunae in Freud's argumentation, but they smack of a greater penchant for elevating certain thinkers into the stratosphere of opinion—much like the Romantic "genius" and "poet" who speaks for an entire movement or age.[31] Why one representative figure emerges over another is due to numerous social factors of class, race, gender, reception, location, and utility—not the nebulous category of "genius." Indeed, Freud's universalizing tendencies gave credence to certain established power dynamics of race, empire, and gender; he offered an authorizing strategy to naturalize these social hierarchies, which made him a particularly useful tool across a number of fields.

Relatedly, some of Freud's more obvious tendencies toward "strange fictions" appear in his analyses of women. One particularly illustrative example is his claim that young biological females, at the developmental point of realizing they are physiologically distinct from biological males, develop what he terms "penis envy"—the neurotic expression of extreme "jealousy … [and] body narcissism" over their lack of this allegedly apex appendage. This "castration shame" thus explains for Freud why women as a whole are "less individualized, more narcissistic, and lacking in a sense of justice" than their male counterparts. Despite this pitiable state, Freud judges that there is at least one "good cultural outcome" from penile cupidity: some women will aspire to, and obtain, university professorships.[32]

I confess I struggle to find much of anything that is redemptive in Freud's work, insofar as it has had so much pernicious influence.[33] There are, however, three aspects related to his life and work that I will highlight that are largely external to his oeuvre.

The first is that some credit Freud for his more critical-minded approach to the study of religion in that he does not assume the "divine" is the source of religious knowledge or behavior, but rather looks to "human projection of complex developmental issues and unconscious wishes"—what Paul Ricoeur in his *Freud and Philosophy* (1970) deemed Freud's "hermeneutics of suspicion."[34] Given the degree to which Freud's evaluations are nonetheless based upon observation and speculation about human consciousness, however, it is difficult to champion him as a forerunner of a realist tradition. He is perhaps more securely located along the track of European Romanticism that found later expression in phenomenology and structuralism.

Likewise, in the quote under consideration in this chapter, Freud arguably signals an important methodological issue when it comes to the terms, testimony, and discourses of the peoples, groups, and practices that we study—namely, that in order to describe accurately our "objects of study" we cannot uncritically adopt and reproduce their own understandings of the world. As the sociologist Rogers Brubaker explains, we "take vernacular categories and participant's understandings seriously, for they are partly constitutive of our objects of study. But we should not uncritically adopt the engaged categories of ethnopolitica practice as our categories of social analysis."[35] To illustrate through example, if one were to accept without question the theological statement "the Apostle Paul was a Christian" and begin reproducing that terminology (i.e., Christian) in a historical description of Paul, it would at minimum be a demonstrable anachronism (the term "Christian" did not yet exist in Paul's day) and, more problematically, it would effectively erase that Paul was an established member of another religion (Judaism), an ethnicity (Judean), not to mention the significance of his social location as a Pharisee. So, while the notion that Paul was a "Christian" may seem intuitive to a practicing Christian given Paul's later status as a founding figure of the religion, to adopt uncritically that terminology is to reinforce fictive ideas about the development and cohesion of what is later known as Christianity, not to mention processes of so-called conversion.

To be clear, however, what Freud is assessing is not the uncritical adaptation of the terminology of, say, the Dayak people. He engages in armchair psychology, effectively dismissing entire ethnic and social groups as incapable of self-awareness, articulation, or communication based on his assumption that what he calls "taboos" are at turns instinctual, unconscious, or reducible to paradigms of neuroses. Immediately following his quote on taboo and the subconscious cited above, he speculates that taboos are "prohibitions of primeval antiquity," "[violently] imposed by primitive men," and then inculcated from generation to generation until rendered "innate" in the minds of those incapable of rational discernment. He continually and uncritically adopts terms and concepts of his own making and reifies them in a tautology premised not on sociological principles of inquiry, but on the colonialist and dehumanizing notion that he can speak for his subject better than they can for themselves.

Second, one can contend that Freud's interdisciplinary interest in coupling the sciences (e.g., observations in a clinical setting) with the humanities (e.g., history, religion) was innovative for the academy and made new lines of collaboration and conversation possible. The arguable consequences of these efforts range from an increased understanding and acceptance of sexuality outside of heteronormative paradigms, to the development of new methodologies (e.g., affect theory) that combine neuro and related sciences with the study of literature, media, politics, sociology, so-called material culture, embodiment, disability, and so on. But Freud is not an avatar for a new era of scientific modernism for all the reasons of method, terminology, and so forth emphasized throughout this chapter.

Finally, and crucially, we should not forget that Freud was forced into political exile during the Second World War. Although he vehemently maintained that he was a "natural atheist" throughout his life, Freud was born into a Jewish family, often discussed Jewish texts and figures in his work, and associated in his early career with Jewish institutions.[36] He was thus driven by the Nazi regime from Vienna as an elderly man, at a time of significant ill health, living out the last year of his life in asylum in England. While I have cautioned against approaches to Freud that treat his personal biography as data or lionize him as a solitary Romantic genius, on this detail of his life, I advocate for awareness. To the extent that the effects of war and the struggles of refugees are often sadly anonymized, here Freud's significant profile in contemporary cultural imagination offers one corrective.

8

Gerardus van der Leeuw

Tenzan Eaghll

For the "primal experience," upon which our experiences are grounded, has always passed irrevocably away by the time our attention is directed to it. My own life, for example, which I experienced while writing the few lines of the preceding sentence, is just as remote from me as is the "life" associated with the lines I wrote thirty years ago in a school essay, I cannot call it back again: it is completely past. In fact, the experience of the lines of a moment ago is no nearer to me than is the experience of the Egyptian scribe who wrote his note on papyrus four thousand years ago. ... The immediate, therefore, is never and nowhere "given"; it must always be reconstructed.[1]

Before I discuss the above quotation from Gerardus van der Leeuw (1890–1950) I would like you to also consider the following quotation from Friedrich Nietzsche (1844–1900):

God is dead. God remains dead. And we have killed him. "How shall we comfort ourselves, the murderers of all murderers? What was holiest and mightiest of all that the world has yet owned has bled to death under our knives: who will wipe this blood off us? What water is there for us to clean ourselves? What festivals of atonement, what sacred games shall we have to invent? Is not the greatness of this deed too great for us? Must we ourselves not become gods simply to appear worthy of it?"[2]

FIELDNOTES IN THE CRITICAL STUDY OF RELIGION

What do these two disjointed quotes by Gerardus van der Leeuw and Friedrich Nietzsche have in common? In my mind the answer is strikingly simple: both are discussing the philosophical "death of objective experience" as an evidentiary source of knowledge claims. For many students today this "death of objectivity" is such an ancient occurrence that it may not register historically right off the bat, but around the turn of the eighteenth century, philosophy underwent a major shift, which is often called the "Copernican turn in philosophy," and after that point the search for the source of knowledge claims and truth with a capital "T" began to radically transform. Prior to this Copernican turn, when philosophers made truth claims they either turned to objective experience to show how their knowledge conformed to objects in the world or turned to trusted sources like Aristotle or the Bible to show how their claims conformed to authorities that were regarded as true. However, after the Copernican turn in philosophy the external world came to be seen as dependent upon the faculties of perception within the human mind. Henceforth, the focus of philosophy became more and more the very modes of perception that the human mind imposed upon experience in order for there to be a world of objects to experience in the first place. All this was made possible by the eighteenth-century philosopher Immanuel Kant because he convinced many that the mind shapes our experience of the world, not the other way around. As he questioned in the preface to *The Critique of Pure Reason*,

> Hitherto it has been assumed that all our knowledge must conform to objects. But all attempts to extend our knowledge of objects by establishing something in regard to them *a priori*, by means of concepts, have, on this assumption, ended in failure. We must therefore make trial whether we may not have more success in the tasks of metaphysics, if we suppose that objects must conform to our knowledge ... We should then be proceeding precisely on the lines of Copernicus' primary hypothesis.[3]

Kant's subsequent proofs in his three Critiques destroyed the classical methods of knowledge verification by arguing that knowledge was dependent upon the a priori categories of the human mind—categories like quantity, quality, relation, and modality—not the objective experience of things or dogmatic metaphysical truths. Importantly, Kant never claimed that these categories of thought provided knowledge about objects, but simply that they provided the necessary characteristics for individuals to experience the world in the first place. Building upon Kant's arguments, subsequent thinkers have developed this idea in various ways, some to make the role of cognition more scientifically precise (e.g., cognitive studies), some to emphasize the cultural origin of the categories themselves (e.g., structuralists and poststructuralists), and some who do a little bit of both. For our purposes, what is important is the ways in which method and theory in the study of religion is tied up with this philosophical development, because what we find in the quotes by van der Leeuw and Nietzsche are two ways this Copernican turn in philosophy has impacted the field. In what follows, I will start by unpacking the quotes in relation to their philosophical context and then close by connecting them to contemporary theory in the study of religion.

Van der Leeuw's opening quote is a perfect example of a phenomenological solution to the Copernican turn in philosophy. The quote comes from *Religion in Essence and Manifestation*, which was first published in 1933 under the German title *Phänomenologie der Religion*. The larger chapter this quote is extracted from begins by discussing the nature of experience from a phenomenological perspective, and then builds up toward a theory of religion. Like a good post-Kantian, van der Leeuw rejects the immediate givenness of experience and affirms that all we know is based on the rational structures we impose upon sensory phenomenon. As he writes, "the immediate, therefore, is never and nowhere 'given'; it must always be reconstructed." Van der Leeuw's point is that *no* experience, whether it be his own writing in the present moment or that of an ancient Egyptian scribe from some dead religion, takes place in the "living present." All we ever have, he claims, are the sensory images that present themselves to the understanding in the form of phenomenon, and all the rational structures we use to reconstruct this phenomenon are secondary.

Critically speaking, what makes this quote by van der Leeuw so intriguing is that it puts him in line with a long list of critical thinkers, from G. W. F. Hegel to Jacques Derrida. For instance, in the early nineteenth century Hegel famously quipped that "the owl of Minerva flies at dusk." By this, Hegel was implying that philosophy comes to understand history only *after* it passes away. Philosophy cannot be prescriptive because the view it offers is always one of hindsight:

> One more word about giving instruction as to what the world ought to be. Philosophy in any case always comes on the scene too late to give it … When philosophy paints its gloomy picture then a form of life has grown old. It cannot be rejuvenated by the gloomy picture, but only understood. Only when the dusk starts to fall does the owl of Minerva spread its wings and fly.[4]

Hegel's basic point here: historical rationalization is always post hoc. We never encounter the living present but only memories we have of past occurrences.

A similar point was also made by Derrida in "Violence and Metaphysics" when he argued that the question of our historical origins—precisely our "jewgreek" origins—should not be understood as "a chronological, but a pre-logical progression."[5] That is, all decisions about history, whether ancient or modern, are decisions that are made before we turn to our "data." We don't study the chronological progression of history but the difference that presents itself as history relative to our cultural/linguistic perspective.

Having noted this important critical element of van der Leeuw's work, it is also important to take issue with how he develops his phenomenological method in problematic ways. After all, if we wanted to critique Gerardus van der Leeuw it would not be too difficult. As numerous critical scholars of religion have argued, van der Leeuw doesn't pay attention to the historical or cultural context of "religion" and his ideas about the subject are as theological as they are anthropological. Moreover, he presents man as a site where religious experience takes place and doesn't question the assumptions that underlie this supposition. In fact, I even critiqued van der Leeuw in a chapter I wrote about the influence of phenomenology upon the academic study of religion.[6] In that chapter, I merely mentioned van der Leeuw in passing alongside his contemporary Rudolf Otto, as I critiqued the phenomenology of religion more generally. I pointed out that early-twentieth-century thinkers like van der Leeuw and Otto can best be understood as Protestant theologians because they used phenomenology to argue that religion can be defined according to mystical experiences of "the holy" (*Das Heilige*). Although van der Leeuw will argue that the immediate is nowhere given and must be rationally reconstructed, he also argues that phenomena are "gradually revealed" in experience and can function as a form of "testimony" for the phenomenologist, and it is upon this notion of gradual revelation and testimony that he builds his phenomenology of religion.[7] It is for this latter reason that van der Leeuw is usually critiqued alongside other theological and phenomenological theorists of religion who try to present religion as evidence for some holy or sacred dimension of experience. Critical theorists find this problematic because it implies that phenomenological definitions of religion describe some unique, distinct, or sui generis domain of experience that cannot be historicized or subject to critique.

Nietzsche's quote that I mentioned at the start of this chapter is an example of a far more critical wing of thought that developed in light of the Copernican turn in philosophy. Of course, Nietzsche himself would scoff at the notion that he inherited anything from Kant, as he savagely critiqued him, but scholars generally agree that Nietzsche's incendiary critique of Western metaphysics undoubtedly has some element of a Kantian trace. Some scholars even go so far as to suggest that Nietzsche's entire philosophical project takes place within a Kantian horizon.[8] For instance, in the preface to *The Critique of Pure Reason* cited above, right before Kant calls for a Copernican turn in philosophy, he argues that the metaphysical edifice of Western culture (i.e., Christian theology) is a dogmatic wasteland that has never been able to prove its own foundations:

> Time was when metaphysics was entitled the Queen of all the sciences; and if the will be taken for the deed, the pre-eminent importance of her accepted tasks gives her every right to this title of honour. Now, however, the changed fashion of the time brings her only scorn; a matron outcast and forsaken..[9]

For Kant, the passing away of classical metaphysical structures was a cultural crisis that required a new philosophical approach to save the Western world from oblivion. In his preface he speaks of this urgency when he states that his philosophical work is necessary to stop the Western world from being swallowed up by more "intestine wars," "ancient barbarity," and "complete anarchy."[10] How can we not see in this intense language a portent of the far more iconoclastic and spellbinding prose of Nietzsche?

This genealogical point of similarity being noted, Nietzsche's criticism of Western metaphysics and of religion also stands in stark contrast to Kant's approach to the problem and his methodology. The fact of the matter is stark indeed, as Nietzsche hated what he saw as idealism of not only Kant, but also that of Hegel and his followers. In fact, Nietzsche argued that Kant gives us nothing but a covert Christianity, and that Hegel is just a Swabian theologian. To understand Nietzsche's statement that "God is dead," therefore, one must understand this relation of his to Kant and others, and at the same time go beyond them. This is because by announcing that God was dead Nietzsche was not really critiquing the idea of the "supernatural," making some proud atheist proclamation, or even providing a new philosophical system to replace that of the philosophers who preceded him. Rather, what Nietzsche was describing was the death of Truth with a capital "T," or what philosophers often call "true worlds theory." Examples of true world theories would include some of the stories found in the Christian bible, Catholic theology, or the work of philosophers who present grand universal narratives about existence. As we saw above, it is precisely these types of theories that Kant critiqued as well, and this is the element of the Copernican turn in philosophy that Nietzsche carries forward. However, Nietzsche goes much further than simply challenging the immediate givenness of objective experience as a source of evidentiary knowledge claims. Nietzsche wasn't interested in establishing any a priori categories of cognition within the human mind or uncovering some obscure experience of "the Holy" that lay just beyond the reach of objective experience. Rather, Nietzsche sought to understand how people were shaped by the traditions, cultural norms, beliefs, and habits of European culture, and subsequently, how they were affected by the dissolution of old truths as a new modern world began to emerge. In a way slightly similar to Hegel but with an entirely different methodology and result, Nietzsche looked for the categories of experience in cultural and historical fragments all around him.

Hence, by emphasizing the death of God Neitzsche was not simply talking about a religious idea but emphasizing how all the old truths that used to guide the world were passing away. A subsequent quote from *Twilight of the Idols* may help prove the point, as Nietzsche used the words "God" and "idol" in similar ways: "What is called idol on the title page is simply what has been called truth so far. Twilight of the Idols—that is: the old truth is approaching its end." [11]

The precise passage from which the opening quote by Nietzsche is taken is the "Madman" in *The Gay Science*. In the passage Nietzsche describes a man who runs into a busy marketplace in the morning and says frantically, "I am looking for God, I am looking for God." The people in the marketplace mock this madman by asking him how he lost God and if God is hiding, but the madman isn't fazed by this mockery and responds to their jokes with somber seriousness: " 'Where has God gone?' he cried. 'I will tell you. We have killed him—you and I. We are all his murderers.' " [12]

With this strange narrative Nietzsche is not describing the waning of religion or the disappearance of the belief in God per se but the way in which preceding centuries had exposed God to be a fiction, and the gravity of this situation for knowledge claims and truth. Moreover, he is doing so by appealing to the cultural construction and destruction of the idea of God. For example, in his writing he regularly documented how the concept of God had slowly been removed from the center of European thought and replaced with doubt and skepticism, and how this exposed a nihilist void at the heart of Western culture. In one of his early publications titled *Dawn: Thoughts on the Presumptions of Morality*, for instance, he notes how the death of God can be evidenced in the way that atheistic arguments have triumphed over theological arguments.

In preceding centuries, when scholastic theologians like Thomas Aquinas put forth proofs *and* counter proofs for the existence of God it was because belief in God was a foregone conclusion. The role of intellectuals like Aquinas was therefore to explain the logic that lay beneath the pervasive cultural belief in God. In contrast, in the nineteenth century when intellectuals like David Straus traced out the historical origins of Christian belief in Christ it was because skepticism and doubt were the new methods of scientific inquiry. The role of intellectuals was therefore to show how the idea of God developed and took hold of culture in the first place. As Nietzsche writes in *Dawn*,

In former times, one sought to prove that there is no God – today one indicates how the belief that there is a God could arise and how this belief acquired its weight and importance: a counter-proof that there is no God thereby becomes superfluous. When in former times one had refuted the "proofs of the existence of God" put forward, there always remained the doubt whether better proofs might not be adduced than those just refuted: in those days, atheists did not know how to make a clean sweep.[13]

This is what Nietzsche means when he says that the "holiest and mightiest of all that the world has yet owned has bled to death under our knives." The knives of reason had exposed the idea of God, and all the meaning and truth that came with it, to be a human fiction and historical creation.

For Nietzsche this idea that god is dead is therefore not news. In fact, the specific phrase "God is dead" had previously been uttered by Martin Luther, Blaise Pascal, and Hegel. What is news is Nietzsche's statement that *we* have killed him. As Nietzsche writes in the opening quote, "How shall we comfort ourselves, the murderers of all murderers? What was holiest and mightiest of all that the world has yet owned has bled to death under our knives: who will wipe this blood off us?" What is "news" is therefore the task at hand in light of God's death, and in light of the blood left on our hands. After all, what can possibly come after God? What will provide the meaning, value, and purpose to human life after this death? Moreover, what value is the will to truth at all in a world that has no foundation for truth? This is the central question for Nietzsche after recognizing that God is dead, "What is to come next?"

Nietzsche's answer to this question is that each of us has to take the place of God in our own lives to fill the void of divine absence. As he writes in the final line of the opening quote, "Must we ourselves not become gods simply to appear worthy of it?" Formerly the role of God had been to provide meaning and value for life but now all that needed to be filled by the strength and courage of each individual—what he called the Übermensch ("Overman," "Uberman," or "Superhuman")—or else the whole world will be swallowed up in the nihilist void of our empty beliefs.

Nihilism was the arch nemesis of Nietzsche's thought—the kryptonite to his Übermensch, so to speak—as everything he wrote was aimed to help overcome the nihilism that he thought infected European thought. Importantly, however, Nietzsche had a very different understanding of nihilism than is typically given to the term, as he thought Christianity and the belief in God was itself nihilistic.[14] The reason for this is that belief in God is belief in an empty signifier, it is a belief in grammar *as* divine and an attempt to find meaning and morality through a submission to grammar. As Nietzsche writes in *Twilight of the Idols*: "I am afraid we are not rid of God because we still have faith in grammar."[15] Nietzsche thought Western religious thought was nihilistic because it grounded the world upon nothing (nihil)—the idea of an all-powerful being who is absent from his own creation.

Unlike Kant and Hegel, therefore, Nietszche's practical solution to the death of God was not to appeal to Christian morals as imperatives for a modern secular world or to seek out some sort of manifestation of the spirit within the world, but to call upon the courage of free spirits to make the world anew right here and now. His affirmation of life, sense, music, Dionysian festival, and dithyrambs is an attack on those who might wish to reify their pithy ideas into abstract universals and those who want to return to nature as if it were a self-reflective organism. Nietzsche argued that he belonged to a new type of "free spirit" that cannot be returned to ethical wholeness or cornered with dialectical reasoning. These free spirits are homeless and they live life without ontological ground nor moral foundations.

Nietzsche's literary method for achieving all this critical work was genealogy, which was a radical historicizing of concepts and values. As Foucault notes, Nietzsche's methodology was so effective because he used historical analysis against entrenched ideas to expose how cultural notions are constructed in a piecemeal fashion:

> The genealogist refuses to extend his faith in metaphysics, if he listens to history, he finds that there is "something altogether different" behind things: not a timeless and essential secret, but the secret that they have no essence or that their essence was fabricated in a piecemeal fashion from alien forms.[16]

Nietzsche didn't philosophize by developing logical arguments and philosophical positions in the traditional manner of his predecessors. Rather, he philosophized much like a doctor diagnoses a patient. Nietzsche would often begin his writings by noting an intellectual or cultural problem and discussing examples of how it operates in literature or history. After this he would trace out the historical construction of this problem by taking it apart, piece by piece. In this way, he didn't argue for philosophical positions per se but tried to demonstrate how certain cultural traditions, beliefs, ideas, and habits were constructed in the first place.

In the study of religion, one of Nietzsche's influences has been through the rise of constructivism. Constructivism is a broad sweeping term that encompasses a wide array of critical methods that employ literary, political, and social analysis to show how cultural products are manufactured. Hence, much like how Nietzsche showed how the death of God had occurred in *The Gay Science*, or how Christian morality had emerged in *The Genealogy of Morals*, contemporary constructivists are interested in showing how the category of religion and its related terms emerged in relation to European colonialism in the early modern period.

It has taken some time for the study of religion to catch up with Nietzsche but since Joseph Kitagawa's *The History of Religions*, constructivism of the 1990s has grown with increasing prominence in the field. In fact, Richard King argues that this rise of constructivism in religious studies constitutes a Copernican turn in the study of religion. King points out that the primary result of this emergence of constructivism has been the "denaturalization" of religion—or if I may play with the implications here for Nietzschian purposes, death of religion. This rise of constructivism is associated with the development of postmodernism, poststructuralism, postcolonialism, critical race theory, feminism, and queer theory within the humanities and social sciences. As King writes, "the constructivist position has established itself as a truism of sorts within the academy."[17]

This critical development being noted, constructivism has in no way eclipsed the prominence of phenomenology within the field. After the work of van der Leeuw and his contemporaries like Otto, phenomenology only grew in influence and ultimately dominated the study of religion throughout the twentieth century. As William Arnal writes in a recent chapter on the subject, phenomenology still dominates the field today:

> Nearly all modern theories of and approaches to religion therefore have tended to take for granted the givenness, and the cultural universality, of religion, even when, as with, for example, Marx or Freud, religious phenomena are reduced to aspects of other (universal) human processes … the dominant approach to religious studies today (at least as it affects the teaching and the organization of departments and professional associations) remains phenomenological in its orientation.[18]

As we saw with van der Leeuew, despite the philosophical death of objectivity as a source of evidentiary knowledge claims, sui generis theories of religion continued to develop undaunted up into the twentieth century. Even if a theorist has a very nuanced understanding of how experience is never given in a direct and immediate manner, they will often still posit the "given" nature of religious experience and protect the category "religion" from critical analysis by deeming it wholly other, or suggesting that it is given only in obscurity.

Taken together, these two remnants of the Copernican turn in philosophy have come to influence most of the discourse on method and theory in the study of religion over the past hundred years. Thinkers like van der Leeuw and Otto, as well as their more contemporary manifestations like Mircea Eliade and Jean-Luc Marion, constitute the theological wing of the Kantian influence upon the field. Though they might be easy to critique for their treatment of the category of religion, these thinkers are nuanced philosophers who are roundly aware that there is no direct access to immediate experience after Kant. However, like van der Leeuw they still posit some way in which religion can be identified as a unique and distinct experience of the sacred. Constructivists like Nietzsche and all the contemporary scholars in the study of religion who have risen to dominance in the preceding decades, such as Jonathan Z. Smith, Russell McCutcheon, and Tomoko Masuzawa, represent the more critical wing of the Kantian influence upon the field. Though less dominant than phenomenology at the popular cultural level, this latter critical wing is increasingly becoming the backbone of advanced academic studies of the subject, and will undoubtedly play an even greater role in the study of religion in the future. Like Nietzsche, the thinkers who belong to this critical wing may be a little bit ahead of their time, as they constantly have to battle entrenched phenomenological narratives about religion in the media and academia, but perhaps that is the task of all "free spirits" who wish to throw off the yoke of past dogmas.

9

Rudolf Otto

Martha Smith Roberts

Nature can only be explained by an investigation into the ultimate fundamental forces of nature and their laws: it is meaningless to propose to go farther and explain these laws themselves, for in terms of what are they to be explained? But in the domain of spirit the corresponding principle from which an explanation is derived is just the spirit itself, the reasonable spirit of man, with its predispositions, capacities, and its own inherent laws.[1]

Very few terms are as recognizable in the study of religion as Rudolf Otto's (1869–1937) vocabulary from *The Idea of the Holy*. The *numinous* and *mysterium tremendum et fascinans* that so accurately describe the indescribable for Otto rely on his subtly novel formulations of the concepts of holiness and sacrality in the supernatural forces of spirit. In one sense, Otto is a phenomenologist and essentialist par excellence. His notion of the *numinous* is taught in many an introductory course as a prime example of substantive, essentialist definitions of religion. This is of course, an important concept for students of religion to grasp, as it offers insight into the ways in which religion has been constructed and set apart as "wholly other," not only by Otto, but also by many scholars and practitioners alike. Otto's essentialism is also tied to the category of experience in ways that anticipate and evoke affective notions of religious "feeling" as a vital part of the religious experience. Das Heilige, or "the holy," represents the ineffable and irreducible element of religion for Otto, it is a clear overplus of meaning, one that is simultaneously a priori (prior to experience) and sui generis (entirely irreducible, a distinct category of meaning); the holy is the sine qua non, the essential substance of religious experience.

These are the key words we use when we teach Otto and essentialism in the religious studies classroom. And they are actually quite important examples for students. This type of study and definition of religion connects with the feelings, personal experiences, and insider accounts that students are often most familiar with as they try to understand the role of religion in everyday life. Many introductory students are comfortable talking about experiences with religion as personal, feeling-based, and individual. And this is where Otto shines. The best way to begin thinking about Otto is to start with an overview of his work and the ways in which his theory of religion is presented to new students via the descriptions that come from introductory volumes.

Otto's Legacy

The point of agreement in all of these descriptions of Rudolf Otto's theory of religion is that it is unarguably essentialist. Walter H. Capps, in *Religious Studies: The Making of a Discipline*, describes Otto's *Das Heilige* as "the most compelling portrayal" of the search for the sine qua non, the irreducible and unique essence, of religion.[2] In *Studying Religion: An Introduction*, Russell McCutcheon notes that "Rudolf Otto's contribution to the study of religion has been tremendous and enduring; it can be attributed to his strongly argued thesis about the internal, participant-only, spiritual, non-empirical nature of religion."[3] In Ivan Strenski's edited reader, *Thinking about Religion*, he notes that Otto "can be included under the general rubric of phenomenology of religion because he exemplifies at least two cardinal features of classic phenomenology of religion: the emphasis upon religious *experience*, especially as grasped from the believer's point of view, and its *autonomy* from other modes of experience."[4] Daniel Pals's *Introducing Religion* similarly highlights the "intrinsically independent and autonomous" nature of religious sensibility in Otto's work, noting that while many weird or uncanny experiences may "faintly resemble the sense of the numinous … Otto maintains, religious experience is of a kind unlike any other."[5] Otto's emphasis on the unique nature of religious experience is key to any discussion of *Das Heilige*. Bradley Herling's *A Beginner's Guide to the Study of Religion* reminds students that while other German Enlightenment thinkers were interested in defending religion as rational, Otto was interested in the nonrational parts of religion.

The individual experience of the holy was so central to Otto that he begins *Das Heilige* by asking readers who have never had a religious experience to "read no farther." The experience that is inspired by the holy is "an ineffable, nonrational experience" that "can only arise in response to something that is radically distinct from ordinary experience … which first takes shape in consciousness as a feeling of absolute reliance on a creating power."[6] Thus, the feelings created by the numinous are "nonrational experiences that exceed the human ability to express them and appear to be unique to religious contexts."[7] John Lyden's *Enduring Issues in Religion* textbook has an aptly titled chapter on Otto, "Religion Is an Experience of Awe and Mystery," which sums up precisely this sentiment.[8] Those people who experience the numinous have a feeling he termed *mysterium tremendum et fascinans*, a simultaneous attraction and repulsion to this external power. In *Studying Religion*, Gary Kessler sums it up nicely. This external power, *mysterium*, or wholly other "is something utterly different from anything else we might encounter and beyond all normal moral and rational categories that we frequently use to help us understand the world." Contact with it results in the *tremendum* experience "of dread, awe, urgency, and majesty." But also, this "encounter with a mysterious and awe-inspiring Wholly Other also leaves us fascinated. Fear is involved, but fascination is involved as well, and this fascination draws us toward the mysterious, holy object."[9]

Lest we think that Otto's theory of religion existed in a vacuum, separate from the political and economic systems of his time, Craig Martin's *A Critical Introduction to the Study of Religion* reminds us of the structures of power at work in Otto's theory. While Otto's definition of religion "as a sensing or feeling of 'the Holy' " may seem quite benign, Martin notes that "his definition was designed to present Christianity—and, more specifically, Protestant Christianity—as the most 'rational' religion and 'unsurpassable.' "[10] Although the experience of religion is non-rational, for Otto, "Christians sensed or felt 'the Holy' and put that feeling into rational terms better than any other religion."[11] Religion also became "a tool for ranking cultures and putting his favorite at the top" and Otto was thus "reinventing the definition of words to serve his interests, thereby presenting his culture as superior to all other cultures."[12] Martin's work is a reminder that no scholar or theory exists outside of the social and cultural power relations of their time. With that in mind, it helps to contextualize Otto historically.

Rudolf Otto (1869–1937) was himself a Protestant theologian, a scholar of Indian religions, and a philosopher. A German researcher and teacher, Otto spent time in India in 1911–12 learning Sanskrit and studying Indian religions. He was also a professor at two universities in Germany: Breslau and Marburg. He published his most famous work, *Das Heilige* (The Idea of the Holy) in 1917. His theology pushed back against both orthodox Christian dogma and the rationalists that tried to explain religion in other terms. He found himself both defending Protestant Christianity as the superior religion and simultaneously challenged by what he learned through his study of religions outside of the Christian tradition. Gregory D. Alles has argued that "in his best-known writings Otto developed an apologetics not of Christianity, but of religion."[13] While Martin's critique focuses on the hierarchical classification of religion in Otto's work, Alles sees a more nuanced grappling with the possibilities for pluralism within this classification. He agrees that "Otto always presumed the superiority of Christianity."[14] Though he notes that for Otto, Christian experience had parallels in other "religions of high spiritual rank."[15] While I would not go so far as to classify Otto as a pluralist in the sense that we use the word today, he did see the possibility for religious experience outside of Christianity, though Christianity remained, for him, the best system for apprehending that experience. For Otto, religion of any type, Christian or otherwise, was a unique category of experience. He distinguished between naturalistic and religious worldviews, and he posited that religious feeling was something that could not be reduced to the material world.

Contemporary Resonances

With this foundational understanding of Otto's essentialism, we should turn back to the quote that began this chapter:

> Nature can only be explained by an investigation into the ultimate fundamental forces of nature and their laws: it is meaningless to propose to go farther and explain these laws themselves, for in terms of what are they to be explained? But in the domain of spirit the corresponding principle from which an explanation is derived is just the spirit itself, the reasonable spirit of man, with its predispositions, capacities, and its own inherent laws.[16]

Otto's notions of nature and spirit are described here in a chapter titled "The Holy as an *a Priori* Category."[17] The larger goal of this chapter, as we can anticipate after reading the various introductory descriptions above, is to posit that the holy, the numinous, is something that cannot be fully grasped through rationality or natural sense-perception. Rather, the numinous "issues from the deepest foundation of cognitive apprehension that the soul possesses, and, though it of course comes into being in and amid the sensory data and empirical material of the natural world and cannot anticipate or dispense with those, yet it does not arise *out of* them, but only *by their means*."[18] While feelings are the way in which humans perceive of the holy, the numinous experience reveals itself to be outside of the natural world of sense-perception. It is made up instead of "beliefs and feelings qualitatively different from anything that 'natural' sense perception is capable of giving us" in fact, "they are not perceptions at all, but particular interpretations and valuations" of "posited objects and entities" that supplement and transcend the natural or perceptual world.[19]

The quote from Otto that is central to this chapter is an example of his essentialist notions of religion. The self-referentiality of "spirit" in this passage reminds us that for Otto, there was no outside system or concept that could be used as a reductionistic explanation for the thing in itself. Religion, and the encounter with the holy that could create the *mysterium tremendum et fascinans* for humans, was, simply put, not of this world, and therefore, not reducible to it. However, to dismiss Otto's work as itself a relic of another time would be to overlook the contributions that he did make to the contemporary study of religion, outside of simply a chapter in the introductory course, and the parallels that his work has with the contemporary study of religion as well. Otto's interest in the human feelings created in relation to the nonhuman holy, his need to understand religion as simultaneously nonrational and rational, his fascination with religious meanings as always at once overplus and a priori, interior and yet outside of the self, these tensions that he held in his work are the tensions that resurface again and again in the study of religion. The grappling between the descriptive authority of insiders and outsiders is one of these lingering issues. Another is the way in which scholars grapple with experience on its own terms and in relation to religion.

Religious Experience

Otto's unwavering insistence on the importance of a personal religious experience itself remains central to religious studies scholarship. While few will go as far as Otto did in *Das Heilige* and ask readers who have never had a religious experience to "read no further," the notion that personal experience is an essential part of religion is still quite popular in contemporary scholarship.[20] When we look at contemporary discussions of religious experience we will find that there are both continuities and discontinuities with Otto's work. The focus on the personal, individual, and embodied experience resonates; however, "experience" has also become a category loaded with political relevance.

On one hand, personal experience of religion has been an important area where scholars can observe direct challenges to institutional power structures that have tried to silence minority or dissenting voices. Groups and individuals marked as external to the dominant group, be that by race, sex, gender, sexuality, religion, or any number of other categories of identity, have had their personal experiences of religion erased or categorized as unimportant. Recovering these personal experiences can be a way to challenge dominant power structures and hierarchies both inside and outside of religious traditions. For example, in the study of American religions in the United States, Protestant Christianity was often the center of scholarship and teaching on the topic. Histories of religion in America were basically church histories, and early scholars of religion were Protestant theologians. In the mid-twentieth century, however, we see multiple challenges to those narratives of American religious history. These new histories sought to recover and recenter the voices of those silenced groups. Works like Albert J. Raboteau's *Slave Religion: The Invisible Institution and the Antebellum South* (1978) and Charles H. Long's *Significations: Signs, Symbols and Images in the Interpretation of Religion* (1985) along with several other important historians of African American religion began to reconstruct American religious history by recovering Black voices. Similar scholarship emerged around indigenous and feminist experiences and those of other minority groups. In this sense, personal religious experience was part of a larger shift in power. Christianity's "superiority over religions of other forms and at other levels" was not taken for granted in the way Otto presupposed.[21]

This decentering of Protestant narratives paralleled an interest in decentering institutional histories as well. Scholarship on "vernacular" or "lived" religion surged in the late twentieth century and began to include not just the everyday lives and religious experiences of practitioners, but also emphases on ethnographic methods like participant-observation and new interest in the importance of material cultural in the experiences of religion. David Hall's edited volume on *Lived Religion in America: Toward a History of Practice* (1997) is a foundational volume that highlights this move in religious studies. Personal religious experiences were thus a focus for historians, sociologists, and anthropologists of religion in these myriad ways. Robert Orsi used this model to examine the lives of Italian American Catholics in Harlem in his well-known study, *The Madonna of 115th Street: Faith and Community in Italian Harlem* (1988). Katherine McCarthy Brown experimented with the lines of scholarly participation and conversion in her controversial text, *Mama Lola: A Vodou Priestess in Brooklyn* (1991). Following this "participatory turn" in scholarship, we see the "material turn" as well. In works from David Morgan's *Visual Piety: A History and Theory of Popular Religious Images* (1997) to Manuel A. Vásquez's *More Than Belief: A Materialist Theory of Religion* (2011), scholars began to think of the personal experience of religion as connected to embodied experience and material objects in new ways. The material world and the embodied emotions and feelings evoked through contact with it became rich grounds for studying the religious experience.

Another innovation in the study of religious experience builds upon this naturalistic thinking but connected it to one specific part of the body: the brain. Cognitive science of religion (CSR) began discussing religious experience as a mental process. This includes scholarship that studies the ways in which religious experiences are deemed special or valuable, and religious, by practitioners and/or scholars. In *Religious Experience Reconsidered: A Building Block Approach to the Study of Religion and Other Special Things* (2009), Ann Taves dives into an attribution theory of religion that focuses on exactly this. Her work combines religious experience with ideas from cognitive science, though other cognitive scientists of religion go further, studying mystical experiences in the lab, for instance, M. Andersen, U. Schjoedt, K. L. Nielbo, and J. Sorensen experimented with producing mystical experiences in subjects without the use of psychedelics or hallucinogens. Instead, they "used multiple suggestive components including a home made 'God-helmet' device, verbal suggestions, a hospital setting, equipment for obtaining physiological data, white coats, combined with sensory deprivation in order to elicit mystical experiences in … participants."[22] The researchers found that it was possible to generate feelings of a mystical or religious experience in participants. They concluded that "if the aim is to systematically identify and analyze components that increase the probability of eliciting mystical experiences, our design offers a unique potential."[23] For scholars interested in CSR, religious experience is a combination of identifiable components that can be both isolated in the lab and seen in the "natural world."

In a sense, many of the examples contemporary scholarship explain religious experiences in a very different way that Otto did in his own work. He was not interested in challenging the dominance of Protestant Christianity through recovery of marginalized experiences, and the material world and cognitive components of the experience were merely secondary phenomena that allowed humans to try to make sense of the holy or numinous. However, what his essentialist framework for religious experience does share with these later investigations is the importance of the personal experience, the repeatable nature of this experience, and the necessity of human feeling to apprehend this experience. Investigations into the nature of the feelings unique to religious experience continue to raise questions for scholars of religious studies. This focus on feeling and emotion is most clearly seen in the field of affect theory.

Affect and Feeling

In the foreword to the first English edition of *Das Heilige*, *The Idea of the Holy*, Otto writes, "This book, recognizing the profound import of the non-rational

94   **FIELDNOTES IN THE CRITICAL STUDY OF RELIGION**

for metaphysic, makes a serious attempt to analyse all the more exactly the *feeling* which remains where the *concept* fails."[24] In contemporary religious studies scholarship, there are many scholars who continue to take "feeling" seriously as a way to better understand religious experience. One way we see this is in the so-called affective turn in religious studies. Affect theory emerged out of fields like queer theory, postcolonial theory, feminism and poststructuralist philosophy. Only recently has it become popular in religious studies as well. Affect theory is an area of scholarship that posits that affect, feeling, and emotions are important sites of human identity and power relations. In other words, beyond simply placing power in the linguistic and rational realms, scholars who study affect are interested in the ways in which bodies are sites of meaning-making on their own terms. While affect theory has many different interpretive schools, a few representative examples can help to illustrate how contemporary scholars are still grappling with questions that Otto himself grappled with: What powers are involved in the religious experience? Can we use the tools of the natural world to study the spiritual? What makes humans describe experiences the way they do? And what kinds of feelings are connected to religious experience?

One scholar of religion, Donovan Schaefer, has written extensively on affect and religion. In *The Evolution of Affect Theory*, he discusses two different ways that scholars use affect theory. Both have resonances with Otto's writing. The first example builds upon the work of Giles Deleuze, a twentieth-century French philosopher, and can be seen in contemporary theorists like Brian Massumi. In this interpretation of affect theory, *affect* is a proto-sensation, separate from conscious *emotions* or *feelings*.[25] While affect is not a supernatural or religious power, it is seen as separate from and gestured toward by human experiences of emotion and feeling. In the second example, the terms *affect*, *emotion*, and *feelings* are more entangled, not separate, and thus affect is the "felt emotional textures structuring our embodied experience."[26] This second interpretation is seen in the work of philosophers like Sara Ahmed, Kathleen Stewart, and Schaefer himself. In this understanding of affect, emotions and feelings are the object of study, the locations of identity and power negotiations. Thus, the so-called nonrational elements of human experience become just as central as any rational or cognitive work. While the study of affect is not an exact replication of Otto's phenomenology, which posits that ultimately religion is irreducible to any political, historical, or natural explanation, there are resonances here.

Affect theories are interested in the significance of feeling and emotion in human identity and power relations. The religious experience is one way that humans make meaning in the world, and affect theorists argue that religious experience is not simply cognitive, it is embodied. As Schaefer puts it, religion "is best understood neither as exclusively cognitive nor as exclusively human" and "affect theory offers resources for charting maps of power that are not limited to the plane of language. It proposes that—contra earlier phenomenologists of religion who saw religion as sui generis—the phenomenological is itself political."[27] Affect theory thus offers a powerful corrective to Otto's phenomenology of the holy; at the same time, it utilizes some of the same concepts in a new light. One very important critique that affect theory would have of Otto's work would of course be to challenge the notion of Christian superiority in the hierarchy of world religions. If we think about religion in terms of affect and emotion, there is no way that a hierarchy can emerge based on the "most rational" understanding of the holy, which is in a sense what Otto was arguing for Protestantism. Affect theorists in many ways dismantle those very colonialist hierarchies of religion that motivated Otto's work. If affect, emotion, and feeling are central to religion, they argue, then we do not need texts, sophisticated language and concepts, or even human bodies to experience religion. In fact, Schaefer's own work not only seeks to put non-textual traditions on par with established world religions that rely on textual traditions, but it also places animality and nonlinguistic bodies on par with human bodies as capable of affective experience.

Taking feeling seriously, it seems, may create all kinds of new directions for thinking about religion. While Otto would strenuously disagree with much of Schaffer's work, just as Schaeffer disagrees with Otto's notions of the numinous and his hierarchies, both are interested in looking to feeling, emotion, and affect as the space where religion comes into human awareness. For Otto, religious feeling was very specific: *mysterium tremendum et fascinans*, and it pointed toward an equally specific, irreducible, and ultimately supernatural, power that is the *numinous* or the holy. For affect theorists, emotions also point to power relations that are not necessarily linguistic or rational, but they are not supernatural or ungraspable in the way that numinous functions for Otto.

Conclusions

In many ways, Rudolf Otto's place in the field of religious studies remains a touchstone for contemporary studies. In introductions to the field, his work represents the essentialist, substantive approach to defining religion and religious experience. As a phenomenologist, his interest in the irreducibility and a priori nature of the numinous led him to draw a stark line between the study of religion and all other rational and naturalistic explanations. To study religion as religion, or spirit as spirit, was to understand this phenomenon as mediated through human perceptions, but simultaneously fully set apart from them. Despite this need to set religion apart from the natural world, his focus on religious experiences and the feelings that accompany them have resonances in multiple lines of investigation in contemporary scholarship.

In fact, we might look at many of the works on religious experience as following his lead in proposing that religious experiences are a unique site of human life: but instead of this value being located in the numinous or holy, contemporary scholars saw the value of religious experiences as both personal and historical, private and political; they were often a means to challenge dominant power structures and institutions, not to reinforce them. The value of the individual experience of religious feeling was not in what it pointed to outside of human power, but in the ways in which it lay bare human power relations. In a sense, this is where affect theory most prominently both builds upon Otto's legacy and breaks from it. Reverberations of Otto's need to understand the power behind religious experiences and feelings permeate affect theory. These resonances can be seen perhaps as continuations based on the subtitle to Otto's work: *An Inquiry into the Non-Rational Factor in the Idea of the Divine and Its Relation to the Rational.* While the inquiry into the nonrational continues in the affective, material, participatory, and nonlinguistic turns in the field, the answers seem to no longer point to the numinous or holy, but rather to the body, affect, materiality, experience itself, or cognitive capacity. In this sense, Otto might be disappointed with content of the investigations, but perhaps not their form.

10

Carl Jung

Lauren Horn Griffin

The psychologist has to contend with the same difficulties as the mythologist when an exact definition or clear and concise information is demanded of him. The picture is concrete, clear, and subject to no misunderstandings only when it is seen in its habitual context. In this form it tells us everything it contains. But as soon as one tries to abstract the "real essence" of the picture, the whole thing becomes cloudy and indistinct. In order to understand its living function, we must let it remain an organic thing in all its complexity and not try to examine the anatomy of its corpse in the manner of the scientist, or the archaeology of its ruins in the manner of the historian.[1]

One of my favorite TikToks to share with students begins with the creator, dressed as a vaguely English medieval peasant, behind the wooden screen of a confessional. The viewer occupies the point of view of the priest:

Hi! Forgive me Father for I have sinned. It has been three days since my last confession. I did want to say, based on the feedback I got last time, I *am* a Myers-Briggs INTJ. I don't know if I said that last time. I'm also an Enneagram 3. I'm a Capricorn: sun *and* moon … So, okay. I just wanted to say all that before we get into it. I just think the context is helpful for us both—but particularly you. I'm just saying, I didn't invent these personality flaws. Yeah, yeah, ten Hail Marys—that'll be good. But do you have any, like, Attachment Theory worksheets? That would be really helpful. Or any, like, long-term goal setting? Yeah, an Act of Contrition, I can do that. Alright, thanks so much. See you soon.[2]

I like to use this video in class because, in addition to satirizing the idea that our personality types determine our behavior, it highlights the Catholic Church as an institution of discipline. Visually, the ornate latticed screen of the traditional confessional booth comprises 95 percent of the shot, with only a small glimpse of the creator behind it. The assumed dialogue from the priest, assigning prayers as penance instead of acquiescing to the request for personality resources, highlights the priest (and the Church) as the disciplinary authority. In the end of the video, the penitent leaves the confessional slightly dissatisfied with the interaction and, we can assume, still longing for an analysis of personality type.

Just as Carl Jung (1875–1961) analogizes the work of the psychologist and the mythologist in the above quote, I think using the analogy of personality type and religion can redirect our study of religion from a coherent and consistent "worldview" toward centering the ways in which things we call religious are not separate from their historical, material, and social reality. For (as the TikTok so humorously displays) whatever a personality might be, it is not a consistent "type" separate from social situations and power. In other words, the problem for us is not necessarily whether or to what extent a personality exists, but whether our actions should be represented as something that derives from some interior and nonempirical "type." Using this as an example or analogy might help newcomers to the field rethink "religion," as Donald Lopez put it, "as a state of mind that produces practice."[3] Just as "personality" is not a set of characteristics set apart from social reality, culture is not a set of meanings apart from historical and material conditions.

In the quote above, Carl Jung provides a little disclaimer before he goes on to unpack one of his most well-known concepts: archetypes. He warns against trying to extract the origins, causes, or "real essence" of myth or myths, lest they be ripped from their context and reduced to a social or psychological function. In direct contrast to the functional approaches from Durkheim or Freud that attempt to explain the origin or cause of religion, Jung wanted scholars to, as some might say today, "take myth seriously" by not explaining it away or reducing it to other social or psychological phenomena. He thought myth (and especially the similarities he saw in his comparisons) revealed the existence of a collective unconscious—indeed, myth is the *expression* of the unconscious. Like the penitent who imagines their personality to be a bounded "type" consistent across social situations, Jung reads myth as an ahistorical, interior uniformity that remains consistent across time and space, each leaving behind the situatedness of history and culture. In observing how people behave, we categorize their behaviors—naming the "type" thought to manifest itself in those behaviors—and then proceed to use those very categories to explain the behavior. Using a similar circular framework, Jung's approach to religion categorizes the myth—naming the archetype the myth manifests—and then uses those archetypes to explain the myth. With personality type we imagine the very traits of INTJ (Introverted, Intuitive, Thinking, and Judging)—even if *in* us and part *of* us—as a bounded entity that we can point to that does something *to* us. In other words, we assume the agency of such "carriers" of both personality and religion. The idea being that dispositions/moods and beliefs (or the sacred or something "human" like the unconscious) manifest in our behavior. We can use Jung's analogy to think through not only how universal categories can flatten particulars but also how they are constructed as isolated from social reality.

In the introduction to this volume, McCutcheon and Hughes argue for a "material" approach to religion, or an approach that takes social reality as central. Indeed, they argue that constructions of religion as knowledge about life or belief systems actually isolates myth (or whatever object of study) from social practice and material conditions and, if one hopes to employ a postcolonial framework, social reality should be central to one's approach. How does this quote from Jung (perhaps surprisingly) capture an approach that is still dominant in the field, and how might we push back on that from a critical perspective? In this chapter, I use another concept of Jung's, personality type, to illustrate the importance of analyzing political, historical, and social conditions. Just as we can see that there are numerous factors that inform our behavior in any given situation (as opposed to being dictated by our personality type), we can see that the "sets of symbols" are not the "it" that shapes cultures, but that social and institutional power creates the conditions for our experience. The TikTok satirizes this construction of personality type can thus shift focus toward power and discipline in the formation of religious subjects. While the audio succinctly satirizing the determinist idea, the visual makes it difficult to separate any "meaning" from social reality and power.

"A Purely Phenomenological Point of View": Jung's Legacy

Carl Jung, a Swiss scholar during the first half of the twentieth century, is widely regarded as the founder of analytical psychology and especially the psychological concepts of archetypes, the collective unconscious, and theories of personality (including the central traits of introversion and extroversion).

His ideas about archetypes and the collective unconscious placed personality theory in a cultural context, as Jung proposed that the individual psyche contains universal psychological constructs. Archetypes, according to Jung, are mental images and symbols that recur in the minds of all individuals and thus inform broader cultural themes such as birth, death, love, and the like. This registry of experiences comprises the "collective unconscious," or aspects of unconsciousness experienced by people across cultures. These shared images and symbols are expressed in stories from myths to dreams, from religious narratives to fairy tales. Jung's archetypes are thus innate, underlying forms (i.e., nonempirical things) that are thought to be expressed in all cultures through motifs like the mother figure or the flood narrative. Because these Jungian concepts involve culture and storytelling, they were attractive to experts in a variety of fields. In fact, one of the most famous applications of Jungian concepts for religious studies comes from mythologist Joseph Campbell who, like Jung, also saw this connection between psychology and mythology. He drew on Jung's archetypes to bring together folklore and psychology in his theory of the monomyth, or hero's journey. Campbell claimed that this monomyth arose from a universal structure inherent in the global myths of antiquity, and he traced a broad template in which a hero goes on a journey, prevails amidst crisis, and returns home changed.[4] While Campbell used the monomyth to compare (i.e., find similarity) and deconstruct religions, a significant part of Jung's project more generally consisted of identifying and describing universal patterns that are part of the collective unconscious. They are, of course, but two examples of the comparative method that was dominant across academic disciplines, with the goal of classification to find broader theories that work across time and space.

Indeed, Jung's quotation above appears at the beginning of a piece in which Jung is explaining an archetypal image (the Kore) that can be found in the psyche of all individuals. It comes from Jung's essay, "The Physiological Aspects of the Kore," which was translated by R. F. C. Hull and published in English in 1954 as part of a collection of Jung's work. However, the piece was originally part of a collection of essays on the science of mythology that Jung wrote with his collaborator, scholar of Greek mythology Carl Kerényi. They hoped that this collaboration would elevate the study of myth to the status of a science. Like the anthropologist E. E. Evans-Pritchard, writing at roughly the same time, Jung (and Kerényi, here) hoped that one day there could be a general science of mythology whose theories could be built up once more studies have been completed. In their book, *Essays on a Science of Mythology*, Kerényi analyzes the child-God as a figure in Greek, Norse, Finnish, Etruscan, and Judeo-Christian mythology.[5] Jung's essay (in which the above quote lives) follows, looking at those same divine child and maiden figures as psychological realities that provide meaning for people. Indeed, in the very next line after this quote, Jung says because this project is so complex, "a purely phenomenological point of view is … the only possible one."[6] In the paragraphs that follow, Jung expands on his methodology, explaining that after observing people throughout his career, he has classified them "under certain definite types." Likewise, after hearing a multitude of dreams and fantasies he has noticed patterns in them that correspond with cultural myths and stories whose characters "can be arranged under a series of archetypes."[7] What Jung is doing here—observation and description (purportedly without explanation) followed by an arrangement based on the nonobservable collective unconscious—mirrors the project of the phenomenologists of religion (e.g., Gerardus van der Leeuw) who are writing at roughly the same time. For example, in another essay, Jung analyzes a woman's dream about a moth flying toward the sun and compares it to sun and light symbols in various cultures concluding that the likeness drawn by many religions between light and the deity are all derived from the collective unconscious (1925). Just as many twentieth-century scholars compared disparate symbols and myths in order to make claims about the essence of religion or even "the sacred," Jung tries to get at the collective unconscious by collecting descriptions of its "manifestations," preserving the idea that a universal meaning can be observed in particular cultural myths or moments.

The majority of religious studies scholars today would recognize that this quest for broad patterns and categories relies on an essentialism that erases the particularities of time and space and divorces "myths" from the social actors who produced them, reflecting little more than the prejudices of the observer. Despite aiming to avoid "attempts at explanation," as Jung says, classification is a socially formative act that produces a specific reading of the world. Indeed, it is generally accepted that even broad paradigms like "world religions" are not neutral descriptors but are formed out of a particular history and have real social consequences.[8] We now recognize that category development necessarily involves comparison, which is not a neutral activity; indeed, it says more about the person doing the categorizing than it does about the myths themselves.

"Let It Remain an Organic Thing": Criticizing Functionalist Approaches

Given Jung's legacy, his own description of this phenomenological project, and his placement within a larger late-nineteenth-/early-twentieth-century comparative approach across disciplines, it might strike us as surprising to come across the particular quote highlighted at the top of this chapter. After setting up a collection of essays meant to level specifics in the name of grand abstraction, Jung warns against trying to isolate the " 'real essence' of the picture."[9] While one of his central concepts—archetypes—isolates stories from historical situations in order to demonstrate their transcendence of time and place (as in the sun/light example above), this quotation of Jung's seems to be advocating for just the opposite. Speaking against essentialization, he implores us to "let it remain an organic thing in all its complexity." In the very next line, he explains that rather than providing "untimely attempts at explanation," he will instead *describe* [his] findings and observations and, where possible, classify them—that is, to arrange them under certain definite types."[10] Here, Jung argues against removing myths, stories, and dreams from their cultural contexts and deconstructing them for their parts "in the manner of the scientist."[11]

But Jung is not speaking against phenomenologists like himself, or those hoping to make a science of mythology (after all, this essay was originally published in a book titled *Essays on a Science of Mythology*). Rather, he is arguing against the decontextualization and explanation of intellectualists like E. B. Tylor and the reductionism of scholars like Emile Durkheim and his one-time colleague Sigmund Freud. In direct contrast to their efforts to explain the origin or the cause (or the "real essence") of religion, Jung wants scholars to let it be by not explaining it away or reducing it to other social phenomena. He thinks that myth (and especially the similarities he saw in his comparisons) reveals the existence of a collective unconscious—indeed, myth is the *expression* of the unconscious. Because we cannot observe the unconscious directly, Jung says, we must look where it manifests, that is, in myths and their archetypal images. By explaining religion in terms of social or economic or even psychological causes, Jung seems to be saying, scholars who try to discover the cause or origin of myth are not able to get at its true "meaning."[12] In other words, the intellectualists and reductionists are all trying to explain away that essential feature beneath our empirical evidence, whereas Jung wants to unearth it for what it is: "For years I have been observing and investigating the products of the unconscious in the widest sense of the word ... and I have not been able to avoid recognizing certain regularities."[13] The quotation above, then, argues that the scholar must observe myths and images and stories in their "habitual" context, but if you look at enough of them and get really good at reading them you can start to see evidence of something (nonempirical) that remains constant despite changes in time and place, whether it be termed "the unconscious" or, for other scholars, "the sacred" or "religion." In this way, rather than look for the origins or social causes to explain the "real essence" of religion, Jung will let it lie just as it is.

In this way, Jung might sound very familiar, as many today also argue that functionalists try to explain religion in terms of social causes and thus do not "take it seriously" or, in other words, appreciate its meaning. For Jung, the commonalities he detects in the myths and stories reveal enduring and cross-cultural ideas—ideas that were lived out by individuals and gave meaning to their experiences. Indeed, Jung's approach fits right in with the larger project of comparative religion and. especially given that Jung is trying to illuminate aspects of the psyche, this might even look like what today we call the cognitive science of religion, which sees religion as a neurological phenomenon. After all, Jung's goal is to look at how the unconscious is expressed in myths and stories just as many scholars seek to illuminate, as Ninian Smart put it, "how religion manifests itself."[14]

"Seen in Its Habitual Context": Preserving the Universal in the Language of Context

Of course, if we were given this quote by Jung without context or familiarity with Jung's body of work (if we were to, say, examine it in the manner of a corpse like a scientist), we might leap to applying his warnings to phenomenological projects like his own. After all, is Jung here not warning against decontextualization and an effort to put into tidy boxes something that is fluid and messy? Is he not arguing that we must situate myths as part of complicated systems of meaning? We might use this quote, then, to approach something like what the anthropologist Clifford Geertz advocated: particularity and the rejection of universal explanations. Indeed, Jung's intense criticism of "attempts at explanation" and advocacy of embedding myth in its "habitual context" here might remind us of Geertz's advocacy of "thick description" in order to illuminate not just actions but also their particular context. In this way, they say, we can understand how people are making sense of the world around them. While the methodologies of Geertz and Jung were drastically different, they both saw "myth" (or "religion") as meaning-making in itself and thus not reducible to anything else. Thus, the task for a scholar of myth, or even a whole system of symbols, would be to thoroughly describe and properly interpret them in order to understand their *meaning*.

In many ways, this view of religion as systems of meaning and sentiments remains dominant in the field today. In this approach, it is assumed that religions provide adherents with beliefs about the nature of the world and how it works, thereby constructing a system of symbols that also shape our purpose and actions. Rather than try to present a grand theory of religion or an explanation of what ' it" is, the dominant scholarly approach became explaining how various groups and individuals around the world are making sense of things and how that, in turn, shapes their behavior. In this way, Jung

104   FIELDNOTES IN THE CRITICAL STUDY OF RELIGION

is on track with scholars like E. E. Evans-Pritchard and Geertz, turning away from social or material explanations of religion and toward viewing it as a set of ideas set apart. Placed in this tradition we might take away, at least from a generous reading of this quote from Jung, a nice reminder of the contextual embeddedness of our objects of study and the ways in which religion (or myth) is meaning-making for people. Indeed, this "worldview" approach is often portrayed as given, neutral, or even banal. For example, when I was a student in an introductory course, I was assigned an analysis of Geertz from Daniel Pals's *Nine Theories of Religion*, in which Pals anticipates his readers might wonder "why such a statement should be regarded as particularly fresh or illuminating." After all, he asks, "how could religion be anything *but* a set of beliefs and behaviors that relate to each other?"[15] It is to this question we turn in the final section.

"Something Concrete, Clear": Religion as Consistent and Coherent

I have used Jung's quote to narrate this turn, even in anthropology, away from social explanations of religion toward viewing it as a system of ideas set apart. For all of Jung's warnings against finding some ahistorical essence—even if we (incorrectly) read him here to mean something like a Geertzian warning that all knowledge is "local knowledge" (1983)—this view constructs religion as a coherent and consistent "system of symbols."[16] But what about those social and material conditions we left behind? Scholars interested in these questions take what is called a critical approach to religion, or a focus on issues of social relationships and power.

Using this approach, we might ask how exactly myth "gives meaning" to reality, or how it actively produces "moods and motivations"? For example, Jung says in the above quote that we must let "it" remain in its context to understand its "living function"; in this construction, the archetype (for the psychologist) or the myth (for the scholar of religion), *does* something. Jung believed that a myth left alone will illuminate "something concrete, clear," even if he cannot provide "an exact definition or clear and concise information" for it.[17] In other words, this approach attempts to *describe* something precisely in order to discover it, or, to emphasize the agency assumed, believes the nonempirical thing will show itself to us. In the introduction to this volume, McCutcheon and Hughes describe how this view is, in some ways, still deployed in the field today through studies that read events or material objects as "sites where religion is said to be either expressed or manifested. (It is an approach, we should add, that to us bears some striking similarities to what for many is the already discredited descriptive and interpretive approach known as the phenomenology of religion.)"[18]

Thus, despite the warnings in this particular quote against "examining the anatomy of its corpse," we can imagine Jung would approve of a Ninian Smart-style analysis of religion as a "six dimensional organism" that *produces* "worldviews" for people.[19] Jung, here, is not criticizing the other ways religious studies often "anatomizes" religion by isolating the categories in which religion is thought to be *expressed* (i.e., myth, ritual, text, image, etc.) in order to draw broader conclusions about "religion" itself or even "what it means to be human" (as I recently read on one university's Department of Religion website). While we are more aware than the twentieth-century phenomenologists of the inherent colonialism of their comparative project, a critical approach to religion emphasizes how the field can still take for granted some of those assumptions about a relationship between objects (or myths or symbols) and their "meaning." Even stripped of what we might call the colonial impulse to decontextualize certain myths, rituals, or symbols in order to put them in a category (e.g., light symbols) that ultimately mischaracterizes them, we still approach religion, as Asad said of Geertz, by seeking or displaying the "meanings" of beliefs and practices rather than "the historical conditions (movements, classes, institutions, ideologies) necessary for the existence of particular religious practices and discourses."[20] A critical approach, then, argues that constructions of religion as knowledge about life or belief systems actually isolate myth (or whatever object of study) from social practice and material conditions when that social reality should be central to one's approach.

"The Psychologist Has to Contend with the Same Difficulties as the Mythologist," or How to Leverage This Conceit to Critique Religion's Paradigmatic Status

For a newcomer to the field, this history of definitions and methodologies and theories can be a lot to tackle. In order to clarify these shifts, I want to draw on one final aspect of this Jung quote: the analogy between "the psychologist" and "the mythologist." How can we use the idea of personality type to critique religion's paradigmatic status? The person–situation debate in personality psychology refers to conversations about the role of innate traits versus situation in determining a person's behavior. Even a personality trait psychologist would argue that the consistency is only relative, not absolute, and that traits are not really predictive of cross-situational consistency. In other words, it is pretty clear that personality type is not fixed and stable, and that blaming all our behaviors on it is spurious. Yet, scaling up, religion is still popularly seen as a bounded and cohesive belief system that remains consistent over time and provides the basis for practitioners' actions. To employ a critical approach to religion, we might be able to start with another concept of Jung's (one that does not appear in the quote above): personality type.

In addition to archetypes and the collective unconscious, one of Jung's most enduring legacies is a ubiquitous piece of pop psychology, the Myers–Briggs Type Indicator (MBTI) (1962), based on Jung's description of introversion and extroversion and personality types. Drawing on the binaries identified by Jung, mother–daughter duo Katherine Briggs and Isabel Briggs Meyers fleshed out a theory of personality type and a test to identify it in the 1920s. Nowadays, the test is deployed in a wide variety of contexts from classrooms to churches. It is especially prevalent in the corporate world, and businesses often use the test to make hiring decisions and to determine who might be a "good fit" for a particular role. But as ubiquitous as the MBTI seems, it is also widely criticized as psychologists speak out about the problems with personality tests and the MBTI in particular (e.g., it is a poor predictor of behavior) as well as with the framework of personality types more broadly.[21] Personality types, after all, emerged as a way to conceptualize and classify our *selves*. People want to understand what makes them "who they are." Of course, the question itself rests upon a few assumptions: that we have a static identity, that it is discernible and can be easily "typed," and that our affiliation with this type can be unknown to us until we uncover them through self-reflection or, say, a personality test. Thus, a process of self-discovery is necessary and healthy and will, if successful, lead to self-improvement. Perhaps even more important, though, is the assumption that understanding *other* people's personality types can improve relationships with them. This way we can more fully know "who" the other person is and properly understand their behavior. If I tell you that I am a Miranda or a Ravenclaw or an INTP (Introverted, Intuitive, Thinking, and Prospecting), that presumably tells you something about my core characteristics and you will then infer how best to relate to me based on that knowledge. Analogously, religious literacy assumes that there is a core set of characteristics we can know about, say, my friend "as a Muslim," and once I learn those, I will understand the reasons for his behavior and how I can best interact with him for a harmonious relationship. Just as we view personalities as a set of traits that are stable and consistent across different situations, we view religion as a set of symbols that are consistent and stable across space and time. This framework of core, essential characteristics, it is assumed, can explain behaviors. Just as we must determine our personality type (static and given) to understand ourselves and others better, we must unlock the meaning (static and given) of these cultures or symbols in order to understand ourselves and others better, with hopes of improving relationships (often known as religious literacy). Just as we might imagine understanding someone else's personality type will help us better understand and more harmoniously relate to them, so is the idea that if we properly understand the "inner world" of various cultures we will understand why they see the world the way they do.

Personality tests reduce a wide variety of behaviors and emotions to a shared "type" and offer a decontextualized response to the situatedness of human relationships. I cannot observe my personality type apart from how it "manifests" in what I say and do. Rather than think about how, for example, women might not speak up in certain settings because they do not feel safe or valued, or for fear that they will be read as "angry" or "aggressive" or "ambitious"—rather than asking those social questions—some might determine that they have an introverted personality type and leave it at that. Again, we assume here that there is something intrinsic and immutable about their "personality"—that they *are* introverted—instead of behaving in a reserved manner at work but becoming quite affable and bold in a different social context. Put in the context of religious studies, these same dynamics can make some claim, for example, that Buddhism (seen as a set of symbols, myths, and rituals) is essentially peaceful and thus makes its adherents especially compassionate.

But as common as personality tests are (from expensive corporate tests to a Buzzfeed quiz), it is equally as common not to take them too seriously. For instance, when people ask what made a figure like Steve Jobs so successful, many might point to his unique "personality" and genius, but few would claim that this alone determined his life. Indeed, we are able to point out a host of other factors, including race, gender, geography, schooling, parentage, and patronage. Even though it might be common to imagine behavior emanating from "who we are," as if our actions are products of our personality type, we can also easily articulate the pitfalls of viewing "personality type" as a set of symbols that unlock the "meaning behind" a person's actions and attitudes. Just as someone might behave differently in different social situations, personality characteristics will likely change over time. Some recent studies suggest that people can effect changes in personality even in the short term through targeted action.[22] Other studies show that personality tests, and the ways people proceed to think and talk about their personality type afterward, makes us filter information through the test results. Personality discourse can actually (re)shape our behaviors and attitudes.[23] Thus, whatever a personality might be, it is not a coherent and consistent "type" separate from my social reality. Just as "personality" is not a set of characteristics set apart from social reality, culture is not a set of meanings apart from historical and material conditions.

Conclusion

Returning to the TikTok featuring the medieval penitent's focus on personality type, when I ask students what the video has to do with the study of religion, someone usually says that personality types (from MBTI to Enneagram) are "like a religion" for some people, presumably in that they are providing answers to big questions about how the world works. In a way, they are right: the idea that "personality type" (a nonempirical thing in and of itself) is expressed in an individual's behavior and the analogous idea that "religion" (a nonempirical thing in and of itself) is expressed in myth, rituals, and symbols both make larger (and similar) claims about how the world works. The assumption is that (1) an inner meaning exists and (2) that it is expressed into various situations where it has to be interpreted, explained, or understood by others. In other words, that a correct understanding of them (e.g., of an introvert or of Islam) is the key to interacting with them successfully.

When I ask my students why they chuckled at the video, they quickly and easily articulate the medieval penitent's overconfidence in the idea that our actions can be blamed on personality types. They proceed to critique this idea by identifying many factors that might shape the penitent's behavior—social, political, and more—including their status as a peasant and the Catholic Church that remains a silent presence throughout. They point out how the off-screen priest is also attempting to control (or, more benignly, influence) the penitent's behavior through this very act of confession. Through this example we can see that, as Asad puts it, "it is not mere symbols that implant true Christian dispositions, but power."[24]

When thinking through various definitions and theories, students quickly conclude that "religion" is not easy, or even possible, to define, and that definitions and categories are not neutral and have real consequences. But when it comes time to *apply* this critical analysis, I often find that I have a harder time communicating why a quote like Jung's still does this work of assuming agency and divorcing concepts we call religious from social reality. Thinking through this using another of Jung's legacies, personality types, might help make the leap to challenging religion as a meaning-making mechanism and articulating why that definition, too, is not neutral or given. In other words, just as Jung saw the collective unconscious as manifest in archetypal myths, so the phenomenological approach sees "religion" as manifest in myth, ritual, symbols, and the like. For students or observers new to the study of religion, getting at this critique by way of analogy can be helpful. This quote from Jung works so well because it invites us to make this exact analogy while also serving as a keen example of what it looks like when religious studies preserves universal understandings even while preaching the importance of context. This gap between the personality type and social situation parallels the break we imagine between a belief system and our social reality. For some it might be easier to first wrap our minds around the complexity of individuals and to challenge the ways in which personality type is not a defining, determining, immutable thing. Just as Jung in this quote uses one to shed light on the other, perhaps it might be helpful to use personality types as an analogy to demonstrate these challenges from the critical approach to religion: how thinking of religion in terms of "systems that make meaning" isolates religion from power, assumes the agency of such carriers of religion (e.g., myth, material objects), and universalizes religion as a coherent, cross-cultural thing that exists out there.

11

Bronislaw Malinowski

Brett J. Esaki

But since the moral rules are only one part of the traditional heritage of man, since morality is not identical with the Power or Being from which it is believed to spring, since finally the metaphysical concept of "Collective Soul" is barren in anthropology, we have to reject the sociological theory of religion.[1]

This quotation pains my psyche more than I would like to admit. With it, ethnographer Bronislaw Malinowski (1884–1942) makes a direct takedown of sociological theories of magic. Among the theorists categorized together are Emile Durkheim and Robertson Smith, who place the social as the primary generation site of the sacred. The quotation hurts to my academic core because both approaches—the ethnographer that focuses on individuals who inhabit a society and the sociologist that focuses on society that houses individuals—are equal sides of me as a religious studies scholar. Moreover, it resonates deeply because the debate exists on a plane of scholarship out of which I desperately want to jump. The best way to explain my reaction is through a scene from the movie, *The Matrix*.[2]

Setting up the final act, Morpheus, the human guide of the psyche and the John the Baptist character, is being tortured to divulge his divine knowledge by Agent Smith, the artificial intelligence (AI) Devil who is exasperatingly conscious of his samsaric prison. While Morpheus writhes in pain, Smith utters a soliloquy:

112 FIELDNOTES IN THE CRITICAL STUDY OF RELIGION

Did you know that the first Matrix was designed to be a perfect human world, where none suffered, where everyone would be happy. It was a disaster. No one would accept the program, entire crops were lost [i.e., lots of humans died]. Some believed that we lacked the programming language to describe your perfect world, but I believe, as a species, human beings define their reality through misery and suffering.

This portion articulates the first level of my turmoil. Part of me hopes for a Collective Soul and some Great Power, and instinctively wishes that the sociological school is correct, that religion is central to society and identity and that simultaneously society and identity sacralize moral rules so that one's moral compass feels like it is part of the soul. This hope is like Morpheus, trying to survive on faith alone, even while life is full of doubt and suffering. Meanwhile, another part of me desires a world without suffering, a heavenly realm free of toil. At the same time, I do not want a painless world, because it is through the suffering that I came to understand who I am and found greater purpose. Like Agent Smith observing humans for generations, ethnographers recognize both parts of humanity, the hopes and the existence, even if they contradict each other and even if the research subjects only like to hear about one part and not the other. The first level of my turmoil can be summarized thusly: I, the ethnographer, am crushing the skull of the sociologist (also me), and I am rooting for both.

The second level of turmoil is depicted by more of the soliloquy.

Which was why the Matrix was redesigned to this—the peak of your civilization. I say your civilization because as soon as we started thinking for you, it really became our civilization, which is of course what this is all about: evolution, Morpheus, evolution. Like the dinosaur, look out that window, you had your time, the future is our world, Morpheus, the future is our time.

Smith relates that the Matrix is a virtual-reality delusion of living at the height of civilization, and while suspended in the delusion machines exploit humans. Through this exploitation, the machines will evolve past humans and discard them. To understand this portion's message, we need not to focus on the individual perspectives of Morpheus and Smith. Instead, we are supposed to recognize the irony that the machines are doing no better than humans, who in the human era exploited other beings and natural resources to evolve their civilization. Both struggle for existence and neither has the moral high ground.

Likewise, my turmoil is revealed by taking a step back from the individual academic arguments of Malinowski and Durkheim. In one step back, I recognize that the academic battle takes place within a historical and social context. In two steps back, I understand that problems with the arguments are often less about the particularities and more about the overall ignorance of the era. In three steps back, I make the shocking self-recognition that I participate in the ignorance because the era has not passed. We are stuck in the Matrix; we are invested in its delusion; we are exploiters and the exploited; we are anthropocentric.

Before thinking about anthropocentrism and the Anthropocene, which is a term for the era of human dominance over the world's resources, it is more appropriate first to consider the allure of one aspect of this era: the colonial mindset. Agent Smith alludes to this. He notes that the revised Matrix mirrors "the peak of your civilization," which features suffering and no guaranteed happiness. Specifically, the Matrix was an idealized 1990s world of American dominance through global, unrestrained neoliberal capitalism; this world features ubiquitous images of success while everyone suffers from endless labor within limited career possibilities and identity options to find success.

The analogous larger context of Malinowski's quotation is scientific positivism built upon colonial expansion. Following this context, academia analyzes encounters around the world to build universal truths about humanity—and this is its Matrix. Like the denizens of the Matrix who cannot see the prison construct, the debate of the sociological theory and evolutionary theory of religion (that Malinowski is supporting) can engulf religious studies scholars. We fight to prove that our work contributes to universal truth, all the while laboring in neoliberal institutions of higher learning, and thus we become economically, professionally, and personally embedded in the colonial mindset.

In the next part of this chapter, I will walk through tensions between the sociological and ethnographic theories of religion found in Malinowski's quotation and reveal blind spots of their era. We can do this because we are distant enough from these arguments that we can see some of our predecessors' ignorance.

Two common images of ignorant, out-of-touch scholars haunts the sociological and ethnographic schools: the armchair academic and the "going native" scholar, respectively. For those unfamiliar, the armchair academic is one who, comfortable in his (and almost always "his") library, gathers accounts from around the world into some grand theory, while not having an on-the-ground connection to the referenced people. The "going native" scholar is one who believes that he knows the ways of the indigenous people he researches and identifies as one of them, while he actually sticks out like a sore thumb wearing outlandish European scholars' clothes or indigenous-esque accoutrements. These are two sides of the same colonial project, with the gathering of foreign materials in the West and condescending judgment of all others by Westerners.

Yes, these are stereotypes, but not following these patterns is difficult, if not impossible. To avoid the problematic patterns of the armchair scholar, one needs to see the messy realities of life and to work hard to understand a foreign culture. However, it is extremely difficult to start as an outsider, not raised in a culture, and to learn that culture. First, one carries cultural habits and blind spots. Second, knowledgeable people from that culture may not be willing to share crucial aspects of their culture, sometimes to keep that knowledge secret, sometimes because they do not trust outsiders or you in particular, sometimes because they are not confident that you can understand it, and many other reasons. Moreover, if one dedicates a lifetime to deep cultural engagement, then one would not have time to gather details of many cultures. Last but not least, if one did this, then they would be an ethnographer, and ethnography is a whole field dedicated to the thorny problems of learning cultures.

To avoid the problematic patterns of the "going native" scholar, one needs to step back and recognize how distant one will always be. This is extremely hard for scholars because we dedicate ourselves to expertise, and the expertise of ethnographers is cultural knowledge. Pride, egotism, and professional standing keep ethnographers from admitting the dearth of their knowledge. For ethnographers raised in the cultures of study, this admission is personally painful, because we (and I am speaking as a Japanese American who has done ethnographic work on Japanese Americans) feel like we know our own people. However, we are not solely acting as cultural members when we do ethnographic fieldwork, and as a result research subjects react to us as extensions of academic power and not as regular people. Moreover, we often work to uplift our cultures in some manner, so this process is a strange, out-of-body experience where we act as community members on behalf of the community but feel like foreign intruders. In other words, ethnographers may believe that they are doing a decolonial project but feel like armchair scholars, gathering up our people's secrets to fill a foreign museum or library.

In fairness, one thing I appreciate about Malinowski is how he, in respect to his time, did a solid job of avoiding the extremes of the armchair and going-native scholar. I emphasize "in respect to his time" because he was, as evidenced by his notes, racist and sexist by today's standards.[3] He worked quite hard to understand the people he researched, primarily the Trobriand Islands of Papua New Guinea, or contemporary Melanesia. However, as he toiled to render details through years of on-the-ground research, he privately cursed indigenous informants who would not provide his needed insights and likely groped female informants. As an academic, he did act somewhat like an armchair scholar when published his research to comment on academic theories, like he does in this chapter's quotation. Like the going-native scholar, he did act with expertise, but did not claim to know everything about his research subjects. In later commentaries on Malinowski's work, Trobriand informants and scholars of Trobriand culture affirmed that the facts were largely accurate but he did not understand the meaning and did not develop solid inward understanding.[4]

Regarding the chapter's quotation, Malinowski is using his ethnographic research to contradict the armchair tendencies of sociologists. The specific points made in the quotation are synopses of previous arguments, which I will not lay out here. Malinowski brings the points together into a common critique of the sociological school's vision of religion, which is that it is circular or tautological. According to this critical reading, the sociological theory posits that when people gather together into the social (the object of sociologists' study), people come to a larger sense of themselves, and by extension the sense of something greater morphs into transcendence. The internal contradiction comes from a simultaneous assertion that the sense of something greater sacralizes society and the moral rules that govern it. The resulting tautology is that the social creates the sacred and the sacred creates society. Additionally, from Malinowski's research, the magical and religious (concepts treated separately by Malinowski) do not rely upon the social to function, and the inextricability of the social and sacred does not concur with other phenomena such as sacred rule-breaking, sacred introspective solitude, and non-sacred yet transcendent-feeling social occasions. That is, based on on-the-ground research, the sociological theory does not describe what is happening and it is not logically sound.

Instead, Malinowski asserts that people use magic and religion to push what is uncertain and full of anxiety to something predictable and reassuring. His argument is somewhat psychological, because magic and religion provide certitude and security. It is also somewhat Marxist, where calling to the transcendent is a response to real-world needs. More holistically, in my view, his theory is part of the evolutionary theory of religion, where at stages of human evolution different aspects of life are controllable through science while the magical and religious provide control over the remainder, or the uncontrollable. For example, his work on gardens elaborates practical steps that his research subjects take to grow crops, and this is the "scientific" part that is controllable for their stage of humanity. To control the uncontrollable, like rainfall rates, his subjects use magic. When humans can control more phenomena through practical, learned methods and technology, then a different set of aspects of life are the domain of the magical and religious. In sum, the sociological school's focus on the social blinds them to the role of the individual in magic and religion, including the sacred power of individual magicians and priests.

Ethnographers, for their part, become focused on their individual subjects and sometimes do not see the larger structures of society and patterns

116   **FIELDNOTES IN THE CRITICAL STUDY OF RELIGION**

across societies. For example, if one's research subjects divide the sacred and profane in one way, it does not mean that others in their society, let alone other societies on the same level of civilization, maintain the same divisions. Also, ethnographers may not see larger social patterns influencing regional perspectives, such as the benefit of adopting a Christian perspective when Christian imperialists influence the economy of the overarching area, or the social cohesion of embracing local indigenous traditions in protest of the larger cultural influence of Christian imperialists.

Contemporary sociologists and ethnographers generally acknowledge the weaknesses of their methods and the respective fields have adopted ways of compensating. For my research, both the methods of sociology and ethnography are valuable for analyzing different sets of data—if society, then sociology, if on-the-ground, then ethnography. I can see the way that the social provides a sense of the transcendent to mundane aspects of life, and how the transcendent confirms the sense that morality is essential to individuals and not contextual. On the ground, I see how certain things deemed sacred or profane by one culture are not seen that way for research subjects. It is my job as an ethnographer not to impose my view or presumptions of the divide between religious and nonreligious, but to observe subjects acting in accordance with their own views. Moreover, by understanding the history of each school's blind spots, I actively consider alternate perspectives to come to my best reading of the larger social and on-the-ground realities. I may be wrong in my scholarly determinations, but that is the role of the academic to provide the best reading in their learned view, and other scholars are free to rebut. I do my best to balance perspectives in my work, but, based on my psychic pain, the conflict of my academic ancestors, Malinowski and Durkheim, seems to remain an internal tension.

The problems for the field of religious studies do not emanate from my own internal conflicts and anxieties of interdisciplinarity, or from Malinowski's or Durkheim's individual shortcomings, or from an overreliance on the sociological or the ethnographic school, but from its larger project. The larger project can be felt in Malinowski's language describing his research subjects, and I have alluded to this discussion with terms like "civilization." Just a few pages before this chapter's quotation, he writes, "I have seen and felt savages shrink from an illicit action with the same horror and disgust with which the religious Christian will shrink from the committing of what he considers sin."[5] My point is not about his specific argument, which is that his research subjects react emotionally to immoral acts as powerfully as any modern Christian. The problematic words are "savage" and "Christian," which are meant to be categorically different, both in religious practice and in civilizational status. In other words, Malinowski and the sociological school considers their research subjects to be on a similar, low plane of civilization, where Christians are significantly higher. This basic outline of strata of peoples of the world underlies evolutionary theories of religion, where society is supposed to progress from savage to religious to scientific, as they advance in civilization. Colonial domination confirms the stratification of the peoples of the world, where non-Christians are depicted as categorically inferior.

Personally, this language hurts me as a person of Asian descent. I am not Melanesian, but similar language has been applied to Japanese people and Japanese Americans. In part, my ethnography of Japanese Americans counters narratives of uncivilized savagery of Japanese Americans, who throughout Japanese American history were depicted as vicious rapists, inscrutable spies, and emotionless robots.[6] The theme of savage Asians is part of the discourse called Orientalism, as coined by Edward Said, which reduces any group east of Western Europe in similar fashion.[7] To summarize this argument, the colonial project includes the reduction of explored and exploited peoples. Orientalist scholars use the reduction to create scientific theories of human civilization, such as the theory that civilization progresses from magic, to religion, to science. This means that to do religious studies as a person of Asian descent often requires learning theories built upon the reduction of Asians. The process is complicated, but scholars from historically oppressed backgrounds learn to use the theories for the value that they provide and try to avoid the racist and chauvinistic parts. Like I mentioned earlier, the sociological and ethnographic perspectives shape two sides of my academic lens, and I find value in the perspectives. These methods even empower me to do research that unravels bigoted views of Asian Americans and in other ways uplifts Asian Americans. Those benefits do not erase the racism and chauvinism, and I suggest we should not only find ways to spot the underlying bigotry but also envision ways to excise our scholarship from the whole Era.

To reach this goal, one may object that the most important task to take on first is the decolonial project, which is a term to describe the complicated ways of spotting the structures of colonialism and the results of colonialism while also searching for ways to remove these colonial structures and vestiges. The task of decolonizing our lives, minds, and scholarship is gargantuan, multifaceted, and multigenerational, and in no way am I implying that we can skip this nuanced mountain of work. However, this fight between academic humans can more fully insert us within anthropocentrism and obfuscate larger issues of our Era; we would be focusing on the struggle between Morpheus and Smith, instead of the larger Matrix.

I think we can derive practical steps from the previous evaluation of sociology and ethnography of religion and then apply the process to the question of where to take religious studies next. The above process can be outlined as follows: (1) evaluate each argument; (2) evaluate the arguments against the

118   **FIELDNOTES IN THE CRITICAL STUDY OF RELIGION**

other; (3) find blind spots in each; (4) coalesce the blind spots into aspects of the larger era. Let us briefly do these steps to evaluate arguments about the future direction of the field and to reveal the underlying anthropocentrism.

1. Arguments (One voice is marked in regular font; the other voice is italicized)
Maintain our scholarly path because it builds toward truth.

We have the intellect and means to produce knowledge about upcoming issues. Knowledge provides power to control our environments and to stabilize society. Scholarship is about a conversation or debate of knowledge, leading to better knowledge and stability, and we can continue this into the next era.

First, decolonize our academic lens.

The goal of accumulating knowledge is a vestige of the colonial mindset and its corollary scientific positivism. While expanding, colonial powers sought to impose control and to legitimize it. All the while, they competed against each other with countering claims of legitimation, including moral uprightness and scientific expertise. The academic study of religion is an extension of colonial dominance and competition among colonial powers for legitimation. We cannot continue this pattern and address the needs of people worldwide.

2. Evaluate Counter Arguments
Better knowledge means refining methods and conclusions, including those based in bigoted and condescending thought. New fields of academia are being produced to do this very thing, so if sociology and ethnography are irredeemable, then new fields can be created to counter their colonial mindset.

New fields mean the insertion of existing power, like that of the university, science lab, military, and business, into scholarship. Therefore, any field—even those created for decolonization—bear the mark of existing power, which has foundations in colonialism. Hence, decolonized scholarship cannot be in academic fields as they are currently conceived.

3. Blind Spots in Each Argument
Academia tends to be utopic in its belief that it will continue to meet future challenges. In its self-confidence, it can overlook the ongoing harm done by its methods.

Decolonization tends to be utopic in its image of a world not undergirded by colonialism, along with its hope for scholarly methods wiped clean of the history of domination, exploitation, and reduction.

4. Coalescing Blind Spots (Voices come together)
Our era presumes that humans can find a way out the problems of the next era, which may already be upon us. We believe that through knowledge, science, and technology, and new revolutionary ways of doing so, we can control our

environments and societies. Science, as currently conceived or successfully decolonized, will assuage our anxieties, and the domain for magic and religion will shrink considerably and accordingly. Alternatively, we have faith that a transcendent power (that comes from our social cohesion) will solve the riddles of our era. We know of this power through the magic of medicine, the dazzles of technology, the moral strength of our traditions, and the effluence of love that unites the common people. The renewed, radically transformed world will appear all the more magical and religious, thanks to the way that humans will overcome their weaknesses and tensions, and consequently the new rules of society will have moral power.

There are considerable blind spots that underlie both arguments. For one, the problems are presumed similar to past challenges that we already overcame. Global warming is just more extreme weather, pandemics are just more potent diseases, technological warfare is just more lethal, and so on. Humanity needs to ramp up its global cooperation to meet the expanded problems, sometimes with radical social interventions. The solutions may involve some kind of semi-divine intervention of technology, like a breakthrough in medicine or computer science, but this is still human ingenuity. In this way, we approach future issues with hubris, unwarranted confidence in technological advancement, or trust in humanity's fundamental empathy.

At the same time as we place too much faith in humanity, or perhaps cannot envision a different way to exist, we do not consider the power of the nonhuman. Diseases are not only things that prey upon us, they have a will to live that may outdo ours. Extreme weather is not merely inconvenient, it literally terraforms the planet, on a scale that humans do not have the power to counter immediately. AI does not only solve practical problems, it can function on orders of magnitude beyond human conception. Agent Smith is a fictional AI law enforcement officer who battles mental projections of humans, but imagine an AI machine that can easily outsmart, out-predict, out-gun, and out-maneuver humans. That would not be a good movie for us. Additionally, it is not hard to see that humans likely will not be able to control technology that can meet superhuman challenges of the nonhuman.

Now that we have gone through steps one through four and revealed problems of our era, we can begin to consider steps that religious studies can take to meet future challenges. The first that I suggest is to recognize that the conceptions of religion correspond to our era's concerns and blind spots. The arguments about future directions of the field are one-part too centered on humans and one-part too reliant upon a consistent world. In class, I often provide a generic definition of religion: the connection of the transcendent with the mundane, where humans perform this essential connection. Yes, the definition gives power to the transcendent and mundane, but our anthropocentrism literally puts humans at the center of the universe, wielding our power for glory or doom. Accordingly, the sociological theory illustrates how societies use a sense of something greater to control individuals with sacred morals and duties (i.e., social power), and the evolutionary theory illustrates how magic and religion provide a sense that we can regulate the universe (i.e., magical thinking). But what happens to those theories when humans cannot regulate the universe with social power and magical thinking? Humans will not have the power to connect the transcendent and the mundane because they will be dominated by both. Consequently, orders of magic, religion, and society crumble. Based on this analysis, I suggest that we scholars of religion must reconceive the concept of religion for the next era, when humans will not have centralized power and control.

Fortunately, we scholars do not have to invent these conceptions; one can find humble religions all around the world and throughout history. In fact, this is a key role of decolonization in the post-Anthropocene: learn how colonized people conceived religion when they accepted their powerlessness in the face of the divine and mundane. Decolonization is also key to reenvisioning religion because one can feel the presence of the colonial mindset in many of our era's definitions. Religion is often framed as a task by the transcendent to control and to explore the world—new life and new civilizations—and to connect all the mundane world to Universal Truth. Excise this vestige of colonialism and embrace erased and reduced cultures, and maybe humanity's religions have a chance in the post-Anthropocene.

Finally, I want to emphasize that this push for decolonization and de-anthropocentrism cannot only be a human one—that would be anthropocentric and perhaps neocolonial. Instead, Others will be on the same level as us, requiring us to find ways to be in communion, and Others will be higher, determining the strata of beings, rules of society, and pace of life that humans must follow.

I did not say that this would be easy, but the larger framing puts the turmoil of religious studies in context. As we work through the details of academic arguments about religion—including its primary foundation, whether it be society or control of the uncontrollable—we can consider them within the scope of our era's blind spots. Malinowski and Durkheim are analyzing peoples considered less civilized, so their theories are situated within the colonial mindset and Anthropocene. If we maintain the same framing, then we at least must be conscious of our conception of civilization. If we contest the colonial framing, then we can actively undo the image of savagery, yet we should also be conscious of how we otherwise reinforce colonial structures and how we ignore the role of Others in our anthropocentrism. If we contest the anthropocentrism, then we can uplift the presence of Others, like the weather and crops in Malinowski's analysis of gardens, or perhaps investigate other Melanesian religions that place humans humbly below the mundane and transcendent. *And*, recognize that this is just our human work, which does not supersede or replace the work of Others.

If this analysis has provided nothing else, it should be humility in the face of academic strife. If even the towers of Malinowski and Durkheim fall victim to the blind spots of their era, so too we suffer from the same or analogous ones. We can be Morpheus and Smith, struggling in ignorance, or we can take a step back and realize that we are stuck together in the Matrix and that solutions will not come from our wills alone.

12

Mircea Eliade

Joseph Winters

*The world (that is, our world) is a universe within which the sacred
has already manifested itself, in which, consequently, the breakthrough from plane to plane has become possible and repeatable.
It is not difficult to see why the religious moment implies the
cosmogonic moment The sacred reveals absolute reality and at
the same time makes orientation possible; hence it founds the*
world *in the sense that it fixes the limits and establishes the order
of the world.*[1]

Mircea Eliade (1907–1986), the twentieth-century Romanian philosopher
and historian of religion, developed a conception of the sacred that
has recently been placed under suspicion. For some commentators, Eliade's
approach to religious phenomena, his tendency to focus on patterns and
similarities across religious experience, is ahistorical and insufficiently attentive
to context, the material world, and the relationships of power that condition and
organize experience. Similarly, his commitment to religion as an autonomous
realm with a unique essence that cannot be explained by non-religious factors
becomes, for some of Eliade's detractors, a protective strategy. This sui generis
understanding of religion is a way for scholars to mark territory and determine
who can make valid inquiries within the study of religion.[2] In addition to these
concerns, critics have underscored Eliade's brief affiliation with fascist, anti-
Semitic movements and his hope that these movements might bring about
spiritual renewal in an increasingly secularized world.[3] Consequently, it would

seem that revisiting Eliade's corpus would be only useful as an opportunity to learn and demonstrate how not to study religiosity and practices of the sacred.

In what follows, I am not concerned with denouncing or defending Eliade's general theory of religion, his commitment to phenomenology, his fixation with essences, and so forth.[4] I am more interested in pursuing the generative tensions and frictions that pervade his writings on the sacred and profane, tensions exemplified in the quote above. On the one hand, the sacred for Eliade is a kind of breaking-through of a transcendent reality, a break patterned after the original rupture of divine creation. And yet this irruptive manifestation of another reality "founds the world" and facilitates the ordering of things. This interplay between the destabilizing and world-ordering senses of the sacred extends into another tension in Eliade's thought—while he describes the contrast between sacred and profane existence as a qualitative one, he also demonstrates that the manifestation of the divine necessarily happens through the profane, a process that connects these two different planes. In fact, the passage between the sacred and the profane maps onto Eliade's insistence that even nonreligious people are committed to something like sacrality, or practices, experiences, and spaces that orient them to the world in a certain manner. In this essay, I simply track these series of tensions and ambiguities in Eliade's thought, showing their enduring significance for religious studies and related fields such as decolonial thought and Black studies.

Sacrality, Thresholds, and the Making of Worlds

To begin to understand Eliade's formulation of religious experience, it is helpful to consider his tribute or "shout out" to Rudolph Otto's work, particularly the latter's description of the holy as *mysterium tremendum* (a terrifying and awe-inspiring power).[5] Even though Eliade claims to have different aims than Otto's inquiry into the irrational and non-conceptual aspects of the sacred, he accepts the Otto-inspired claim that "the sacred always manifests itself as a reality of a wholly different order from 'natural' realities."[6] Consequently, "man becomes aware of the sacred because it manifests itself, shows itself, as something wholly different from the profane."[7] The language of the wholly other, of absolute alterity, underscores the vertical and qualitative difference between the sacred and the profane, a quasi-ontological difference that is manifested through various hierophanies.[8] The appearance of the divine exhibits to human subjects a profound power that also reveals the insignificance of man and the natural world, apart from the powers that created that world. And yet Eliade insists that in order for a hierophany to show itself, and to be experienced by man, this appearance must occur through the ordinary world, through trees, symbols, rituals, myths, heroic figures, and so forth. As Eliade puts it, "We are confronted by [a] mysterious act—the manifestation of something of a wholly different order, a reality that does not belong to our world, in objects that are an integral part of our natural 'profane' world."[9] Therefore, when Eliade speaks of the division of the sacred and profane as an "abyss," we should be reminded that religious experience constitutes a bridge over and within that abyss. In other words, his tendency to describe these "two modalities of experience" as completely different is in tension with an assumption of an a priori communicability between the two experiences, or planes, in question. Thus, Eliade can sum up toward the end of his book, "Whatever the historical context in which he is placed, homo religious always believes there is an absolute reality, the sacred, which *transcends this world but manifests itself in this world*, thereby sanctifying it and making it real."[10]

While the transcendent can only be actualized through the immanent, Eliade maintains that without the appearance of the Other, humans would not even be able to distinguish between the religious and nonreligious. To put it differently, the irruption of the hierophany makes the sacred/profane demarcation possible in the first place; it enables humans to set apart certain spaces or objects as more significant than others. Consequently, for the religious person in touch with the sacred, "space is not homogenous; he experiences interruptions, breaks in it, some parts of space are qualitatively different from others."[11] According to Eliade, religious people affirm a fundamental non-homogeneity regarding space, being, and experience. They live according to a constitutive opposition between space that is meaningful and coherent and parts of the world that are amorphous and without form. The preservation of space that is meaningful and that participates in the "really real" wards off the chaos associated with homogenous space, with profane existence, or with life that does not involve stabilizing interruptions and separations. This is because religious demarcations between the structured and the chaotic repeat and participate in the original acts of creation that instituted the world. For Eliade, a world is made possible by establishing limits, fixed points, and central axes within and against "a formless expanse."[12] A world is what is carved out from an undifferentiated region, enabling religious people to mark and identify the separation between two disparate kinds of spaces and modes of being. Consequently, to build a home, to construct a city, or to settle territory is analogous to "founding a world" as these endeavors establish a paradigm for orientation. These activities enable humans to communicate with the gods and imitate the work of divine creation.

Here we should pause and think through recurring frictions and ambiguities in Eliade's formulation of the sacred. On the one hand, Eliade continues to make strong contrasts when juxtaposing sacred and profane existence, particularly regarding the kinds of qualities, dispositions, and capacities that each modality affords. For religious persons, the sacred provides access to "the real, at once power, efficacity, the source of life and fecundity," whereas profane life is kind of stuck in illusion and threatened by irrelevance.[13] Reenacting the work of the gods enables humans to dwell in the world as home, as a stable abode. To the contrary, for the irreligious person, "there is no longer any world, there are only fragments of a shattered universe."[14] Without perpetual contact with divine creation, or the powers of world production, one barely lives and cannot quench the "ontological thirst" to fully participate in being.[15] And yet this complete separation between sacred and profane existence never really holds for Eliade. He reminds the reader that "profane existence is never found in the pure state."[16] Therefore, "even the most desacralized existence still preserves traces of a religious valorization of the world."[17] For instance, nonreligious people might treat certain places (birthplace) as unique and exceptional; they may distinguish certain experiences as being different in kind than the typical interactions that comprise ordinary life. Citizen-subjects within a particular nation-state are often educated to think of certain places, events, legal documents, and foundational figures as if they are sacred, as if they represent quasi-transcendent phenomena around which social life is organized and solidified.[18] Eliade is invested in delineating these "crypto-religious" examples to show that even in a disenchanted world, vestiges of religious man will always remain, in part because religiosity is woven into the fabric of human life.[19] But we might simply read Eliade's insistence that profane life never exists in a pure state as an acknowledgment of fluidity, overlap, and continuity between the religious and the secular, or sacred and profane experience. Or perhaps we might read Eliade in a direction closer to Émile Durkheim, an author for whom sacrality does not always involve the presence of, and commitment to, gods and supernatural beings. But this might be going too far.

In the same way that Eliade refuses the possibility of a purely profane space, and by implication a purely sacred space, he broaches the language of the threshold to describe the passage from one realm to another. Using the example of a door located between the street and the inside of a church or temple, Eliade writes, "The threshold that separates the two spaces also indicates the distance between two modes of being, the profane and the religious. The threshold is the limit, the boundary, the frontier that distinguishes and opposes two worlds—and at the same time the paradoxical place where the worlds communicate, where passage from the profane to the sacred world becomes possible."[20] The threshold, which is an "object of great importance," is simultaneously the interval at which the differences between two things are the most amplified and when a kind of crossing and boundary-blurring occurs. To put it differently, the threshold is a limit that brings into focus both contrast and intimacy; it acts as a border that separates "entirely different spaces" while allowing for movement and transition between these spaces. Without the threshold, this border and opening, communication between the gods and humans would be impossible. Even though Eliade prioritizes the appearance of the divine as the foundation for religiosity and world-making, one could say that the threshold is the condition of possibility for religious experience. It enables the irruption of the sacred to be manifested, actualized, and experienced within the profane world. It is the occasion for contact, touch, relation, interaction, and passage. And while the threshold often retains its function as a border between two different realms, we should keep in mind the paradoxical nature of this in-between position.

One way to flesh out the implications of the threshold and concomitant concepts (separation and contact) is to think through Eliade's brief allusion to the religious underpinnings of colonial encounters, or his description of how the world-instituting sacred has been implicated in settler colonial projects. Recall that for Eliade, a world is defined against formless space, or space that is undifferentiated and without stable borders and limits. The religious person inhabits a well-defined world that is part of a broader cosmos; anything that is on the other side of that established world is indeterminate, unknown, and foreign. And yet a kind of transformation can happen when inhabitants of an ordered world cross over and consecrate the "unknown space that extends beyond its frontiers."[21] Possession of land, accompanied by performing rituals and building altars, is equivalent to converting chaos into form and extending the order-instituting work of divine creation. As Eliade puts it, "An unknown, foreign, and unoccupied territory (which often means, 'unoccupied by our people') still shares in the fluid and larval modality of chaos. By occupying it and, above all, by settling in it, man symbolically transforms it into a cosmos through a ritual repetition of [divine creation]."[22] Settling unknown territory entails a certain imagination of that territory as devoid of form and stability and in need of an external imposition of structure and organization. The pursuit of settlement also assumes that the threshold between our world and their world is fluid and permeable even as that fluidity can become the occasion for dispossession in the name of a rigid contrast between world and wilderness, or sacred and profane. Exemplified by the Spanish and Portuguese conquest of the Americas, taking possession of foreign territory is, for the colonizer, a form of renewal and the giving of new life to regions and peoples considered not quite alive.

One might consider this connection between the consecration of space and the colonial occupation of land as a dynamic that is no longer prevalent in a modern, secularized world. In a world organized by nation-state sovereignty, militarism, and the operations of capitalism, it might seem that Eliade's religious lexicon is outdated. This suspicion is compounded when Eliade makes distinctions between traditional and modern societies, designating to the former myths that involve gods slaying the monsters and dragons of the underworld prior to creation. The renewal of the world, for traditional religious societies, required the repetition of "the victory of the gods over the forces of darkness, death, and chaos."[23] Religious people in premodern worlds communicated with the gods by removing or overcoming forces associated with darkness and disorder. Yet Eliade reminds the reader that modern subjects are very much committed to constructing boundaries to hold at bay beings, populations, and dangers that threaten to bring about "ruin, disintegration, death." He contends that a religious conception of the world remains in collective anxieties about "the civilized world" being inundated with chaotic forces from within and elsewhere. (Here we might think of the kinds of discourses that mark migrants from Haiti and Central America as a peril to US safety and border maintenance.) For Eliade, the enduring opposition between a coherent world and disorder indicates trepidation at the prospect of "the abolition of an order, a cosmos, an organic structure, and reimmersion in the state of fluidity, of formlessness—in short, of chaos."[24] For Eliade, religiosity persists in humanity's need for order, the desire to inhabit a world that provides structure and orientation. Those qualities that might violate or profane this attachment to order—darkness, formlessness—must be contained, eliminated, or incorporated into a well-ordered cosmos.

Eliadean Implications for Religious Studies and Related Fields

Eliade is often accused of treating religion as a separate sphere with its own unique qualities and features. And yet he also provides resources for students of religion to reject a rigid religious/secular opposition through his description of sacrality as a kind of world-making. Since religiosity primarily involves remaking and inhabiting a world that provides humans with their bearings, something like sacrality accompanies the human search for meaning and the desire to fully exist against the "terror of nothingness."[25] In addition, even though Eliade does not focus on the power relationships and discourses that determine what gets set apart as sacred, he describes a genre of the sacred that is intimately bound up with land occupation and settler colonial histories. Furthermore, his description of religious experience suggests that humans are closest to the gods when they are transforming figures of darkness and disorder into a world that is organized by "structure, forms, and norms."[26] This motif of space that is devoid of structure and legibility prior to an external imposition brings to mind legacies of racial, gender, and sexual domination, legacies that include systemic attempts to regulate and suppress bodies and regions considered ungovernable.

One author who has both developed and modified Eliade's ideas about religion is the late Charles Long. While Eliade offers brief examples of colonial dispossession, Long foregrounds European conquest and colonial encounters as primary zones of religious meaning-making in the modern world. Similar to Eliade, Long defines religion as a general orientation toward the world, "orientation in the ultimate sense, that is, how one comes to terms with the ultimate significance of one's place in the world."[27] And yet Long invites us to consider what this religious orientation looks like for people, especially Black and indigenous subjects in the Americas, who reside on the underside of colonial modernity. To put it differently, Long draws attention to those peoples and regions that the conquistador/European settler treated as unintelligible, wild, and in need of redemption and new life. He shifts attention to the practices and modes of survival that reside in spaces that Eliade's conception of "world" is defined against. Along these lines, Long introduces the language of the "opaque" to describe the Black and Native experiences of terror, struggle, and creativity under duress. The term "opaque" can refer to that which is unclear and that which resists transparency. Opacity similarly alludes to muddiness or those qualities that threaten Euro-centric attachments to purity. These related meanings are pertinent to the colonial situation since coloniality was propelled and justified by symbolic systems that associated nonwhiteness with evil, contamination, and pollution.[28] In addition, colonial projects were informed by Enlightenment-inspired hopes that human reason could make the world a transparent (and controllable) object of knowledge. This will to transparency must either exclude or violently assimilate those beings and phenomena that appear obscure, that do not fit within neat categories, and that blur lines of demarcation. In response to this predicament, Long's emphasis on the opaque indicates a moment of overlap between religious and secular paradigms, especially those frameworks that would consign opaque populations to meaninglessness, a designation that anticipates the imposition of form from an outside power (church or state). In response to the imperial handling of the opaque, Long insists that "these bodies of opacity, these loci of meaninglessness ... were paradoxically loci of a surplus of meaning,"[29] meanings constructed through the creation of gods, rituals, folklore, literature, and music. Consequently, for Long, coloniality is a predicament defined by both terror and creative refusal by the oppressed.

The juxtaposition of Eliade and Long, and the attention to the colonial underside of world-making, invites further study into the links between religion and colonialism, undertaken by authors like David Chidester and Richard King.[30] We might say that attention to boundary-making, orientation, and the various contrasts between world and chaos, enables us to examine settler colonialism (and related arrangements) as a religious project, and inversely religious studies as a product of colonial encounters and relationships of domination. One advantage of this approach is that it encourages students of religion to read and explore authors in fields such as Black and decolonial studies who are not often affiliated with religious studies or theories of religion. I am thinking of figures, like W. E. B Du Bois and Sylvia Wynter, who have examined the religious and theological underpinnings of racial and colonial formations.

Consider the work of Du Bois, a philosopher, sociologist, and activist, whose ideas continue to influence multiple fields. In Du Bois's 1920 essay, "The Souls of White Folk," he describes whiteness as a religion. Rejecting the notion that whiteness is reducible to pigmentation, Du Bois describes it as a belief system, one that includes the presumed superiority of white peoples over non-white peoples and a devotion to "ownership of the earth forever and ever, Amen."[31] Here Du Bois implicitly refuses any durable distinction between belief and practice; in fact belief in whiteness is directly connected to property, ownership, and the operations of expansive capitalism. Whiteness is a belief system that propels and legitimates the conversion of opaque regions and populations into the property of European and American imperial endeavors. Within this "religion of whiteness," the agents of Euro-American civilization can treat themselves as "supermen" and "world-mastering demi-gods."[32] Or in Eliade's language, they can imitate the gods by occupying, settling, and governing foreign territories. Du Bois's interpretation of Western imperialism in religious terms nullifies linear secular narratives that would describe modernity as a progressive shift away from the significance of religion. For Du Bois, the religion of whiteness is the "nation's life"; it holds and binds the nation together even as this life is predicated on death-producing rituals. Consequently, the study of religion enables us to examine the practices, rituals, and beliefs that sustain colonial and imperial agendas.

The Jamaican philosopher and critic Sylvia Wynter continues these lines of thought in her description of Western Man, or the dominant representation of humanity unduly defined by whiteness, masculinity, and property ownership. According to Wynter, Western Man has been constructed over and against non-Europeans, Native Americans, and Black people. What is crucial for her is that this bifurcation between Western Man and its racial others is an extension and reexpression of previous theological demarcations.[33] Racial and colonial hierarchies are updated versions of the kinds of invidious distinctions made between the redeemed and the unredeemed, the Christian and the infidel, inhabitable and uninhabitable land, and spirit and flesh. In each of these binaries, or ways of carving up the earth, the first term in the binary represents symbolic life while the opposing term signifies death. These divisions are rearticulated, for instance, in Darwin's notion of natural selection, where some species and groups are fit for preserving life and others are selected for erasure. Although Wynter tends to accept a rather conventional understanding of secularization, where modern scientific frameworks replace theocentric paradigms, she contends that what remains across this transition is a sense of planetary nonhomogeneity.[34] If Eliade claims that spatial nonhomogeneity is the hallmark of religious experience and the making of sacred space, then we might say that Western Man, according to Wynter's analysis, is a religious figure. Consequently, any criticism of Man and the imperial agendas attached to this prevailing conception of the ideal human must include a critical engagement with religiosity and grammars of the sacred.

Conclusion

In this essay, I have tried to stay away from debates about the validity of Eliade's approach to religious experience, which some have criticized as being ahistorical and simplifying. While there is merit to these criticisms, this essay concentrated on the generative tensions in Eliade's work that the student of religion inherits—the interplay between immanence and transcendence, the double quality of the sacred as irruptive and world-ordering, the importance of the threshold as an indicator of both separation and passage, and the sacrality of world-making as a motif that crosses the secular/religious divide. Because Eliade describes the sacred, or a certain genre of the sacred, in terms of re-creating order against the threat of chaos, a process exemplified in settler colonial projects, I demonstrated how his ideas are pertinent to Black religious thought, Black studies, and decolonial thought. My hope is not to convince readers that Eliade's arguments and descriptions are right. My hope is that readers will find in Eliade's work frictions, paradoxes, and dilemmas that spark new paths and inquiries for thinking about religion and its entanglements.

13

Max Weber

Andrew Tobolowsky

The external courses of religious behavior are so diverse that an understanding of this behavior can only be achieved from the viewpoint of the subjective experiences, ideas, and purposes of the individuals concerned—in short, from the viewpoint of the religious behavior's "meaning."[1]

Max Weber (1864–1920) was a tremendously influential German scholar, well-known for contributions to a number of different fields. He was primarily what we would call a sociologist, someone who studies societies and human behavior to better understand the world. His work often explored the relationship between economics and social realities, most famously in *The Protestant Ethic and the Spirit of Capitalism*, published in 1905, which made the argument that Protestant views on the importance of hard work were instrumental in the adoption and evolution of capitalist economic practices in northern Europe.[2] This work displays his characteristic sense of the relationship between religion and other social phenomena—while others reflect the breadth of his interests, including his studies of Hinduism, Buddhism, Confucianism, Taoism, and "Ancient Judaism."[3]

The quote above comes from *The Sociology of Religion*, which was originally part of a mammoth collection called *Wirtschaft und Gesellschaft*, or in English, "Economy and Society." This larger collection was first published in 1921–2, by his widow Marianne, after Weber's death from complications related to the "Spanish Flu" in 1920, and *Sociology of Religion* is not the only monograph to have been published separately from within it.[4] Obviously, the combination of Weber's interest in sociological explanations with his studies of so many different traditions produced the quote above—a kind of prescription for religious studies.

The assignment inspiring this collection of essays is to revisit some of the more influential ideas of immensely influential figures in order to assess their value for the contemporary student or scholar of religion, and to recontextualize them in light of current trends. Obviously, no nineteenth- or early twentieth-century ideas are untouched by the passage of time—all of them are based on at least some assumptions that are no longer valid, and all of them were produced through methodologies that would not, today, meet all of the standards for careful and rigorous scholarship. In Weber's case, for example, one scholarly tool that most would consider essential to the study of different religious traditions today is mastery of the languages of those you are studying—which, Weber did not always have.[5]

Nevertheless, Weber is of course right that the global practice of religion is possessed of an extraordinary variety—so much so that we can certainly wonder whether the category "religion" is doing us any good. On the one hand, it has the great advantage of being comprehensible—if you were to say "religion" to your friends, family, coworkers, or enemies, they would presumably feel like they knew what you meant. If you went to a bookstore, you might head toward, or avoid, the "religion" section, and you might do the same with a museum's collection of "religious" art and artifact. And at some point, or another, most people will probably hear someone blame "religion" for some of the world's ills—or someone else suggest that we don't have enough of it around. Meanwhile, on college campuses, there are departments, minors, majors, PhD students, and academic journals of religion.

At the same time, we can certainly ask whether it would be obvious to, say, a space alien visiting Earth, that a Buddhist monk and a Catholic priest were engaged in the same form of activity, even after a considerable study. Even living on this planet, it's worth acknowledging that someone who attends a Jewish, Buddhist, Hindu, Christian, or Muslim place of worship may do at least a few things that are entirely different from those that occur at any other, and the same is true of anyone who attempts to live a particularly Jewish, Buddhist, Hindu, Christian, or Muslim life. One person may keep kosher, considering it a religious practice, another might meditate, burn incense, go to mass, or fast. One may think of divine beings as all-knowing, all-powerful, and basically kind, another as running the gamut from mighty and benevolent to petty and mischievous. For that matter, one may believe in many divine beings, one, or none—or in a heaven or hell, in reincarnation, or in nothing at all. And, of course, we have to remember that far from all of those who consider themselves Jewish, Buddhist, Hindu, Christian, Muslim, or anything else keep strict observances—or would even necessarily agree on what that would mean.

For the contemporary scholar of religion, likely more so than Weber, the question is less *whether* it is possible to identify so many diverse practices and belief systems as religion as it is what happens when we do. In other words, we have to recognize that when we call Christianity and, say, Hinduism, religions alike, there is a danger of treating them as more alike than they actually are. And indeed, there is rather a long history of Western scholars especially importing notions of how modern, Western religions typically work to non-Western and ancient traditions, and sometimes dramatically mischaracterizing them in the process. We might think, for example, that terms like "god" or "prayer" have universal meanings—and we would think wrong.

Meanwhile, on college campuses, another aspect of the problem of using "religion" as a catchall term emerges: what counts as religion? Do I, primarily a scholar of the history of ancient Israel, belong in a religious studies department, simply because the Hebrew Bible was written there, or should I be in a history department unless I can come up with particular insights about ancient Israelite *religion*? In this case, the choice of what to count as a "religion" is not at all objective but reflects social constructions. The idea that anything having to do with ancient Israel is religious—even, say, a study of the Israelite economy—is entirely a reflection of the role ancient Israel plays in the contemporary imagination, *via* the Bible, rather than anything inherent to Israel, which was one ancient nation among many. Similarly, you will rarely find someone who studies Roman or Greek religion in a religious studies department, as opposed to a classics department, because the discipline of classics has a particular academic history that makes it so—but where should someone who studies Christianity in the Roman Empire go?

At any rate, Weber's "prescription" really applies only to the study of religious practices, after their identity as religious practices has already been asserted. Yet it does have relevance for the larger problems I just mentioned because there are, of course, many ways to study religious practices, and some assume the essential similarity between these in different contexts more than others. In Weber's day, for example, some scholars were most interested in the possibility that many contemporary religions had emerged from the same, more ancient set of religious beliefs—an ancient, uniform Indo-European or Semitic religion, reflected now in many different variants spread around the globe. Others believed that all religions, and indeed societies, progressed through a series of stages from the most primitive to the most sophisticated.[6] Both of these models encouraged scholars to think in terms of similarities—what different descendants of the same "proto" religion shared with each other, or different religions allegedly at the same stage of development. Both, naturally, also tended toward making different practices seem far more similar than they actually are, in the hunt for universal explanations. And the same, for the record, is true of some contemporary framings—"Judeo-Christian" religions, or "Abrahamic" religions, which suggests the existence of essential similarities between two, or three, really quite distinct systems of belief and practice.

This is the way in which Weber's suggestion is a good one—studying religion from the outside, so to speak, is a great way to get it wrong. And today, we have other problems in that direction. Ours is an era in love with supposedly objective analyses, and data that tends toward the mathematical. These can be useful, especially when they are used to answer the right questions. But they have limits that are not always acknowledged, and especially with respect to valuing the testimony of subjective experiences. More than that, metrical analyses of all sorts, which, in addition to their role elsewhere, are given ever more power over what universities, scholars, and teachers are supposed to do, are often not very good at assessing precisely the complexity that makes analysis useful in the first place.

By making practitioners the ultimate authority on what their practice "means," however, Weber sidesteps many issues of analysis. One is the assumption of universality I sketched above. If we recognize the need to ask practitioners themselves why they are, say, praying or fasting, we will no longer be stuck merely applying our knowledge of what those terms mean in more familiar contexts where they might not belong. In one religious tradition, a person may pray to receive things in this life, while in another that might be considered blasphemous. One may fast to attain a more spiritual state, to be expiated from sin, or both. Prayer, for one, may be informal speech to a divine being anywhere, the other an embodied performance at a particular holy site. And so on.

Yet meaning goes beyond definition—it concerns how people understand the things they do, and what they hope to achieve through them. And it is easy to see how an attempt to understand religious activity without talking to insiders on this subject can go awry. We can imagine, for example, a database aimed at codifying and so understanding, the practice of animal sacrifice in contemporary and ancient contexts. Notwithstanding whatever good such a database might do—and I don't presume to know the scope of that good—it is easy to see where it might run afoul. Say that such a database, for example, included information on who was allowed to sacrifice—just priests? Heads of households? All private citizens? Men and women both? Say that it included where sacrifices can happen: only at holy sites, only at home, or anywhere at all. It might include whether sacrifice is a daily or weekly practice, or only on specific holy days. It might include what kind of animals are typically sacrificed: chickens, cows, sheep, and so on and so forth. It might even include rather more minute details, like whether the blood of the sacrificed animal was considered polluting, or what happens to the slaughtered animal—whether, for example, it is disposed of or eaten.

The problem is that even such a database as this would produce a situation in which two cultures where only male priests can sacrifice, they sacrifice mainly cows and sheep, and only on special holy days, will inevitably look similar. Once we start asking questions about what sacrifices are *for*, however, this might turn out to be entirely an illusion. In one culture, sacrifices might be regarded as a necessary performance simply because the gods or other divine and semi-divine beings might starve without them. In the other, they might be how you convince the gods to hear your prayers—and the likelihood of their hearing might be thought to depend on the richness of the sacrifice. In one context, sacrifices might be intended to procure blessings, and in another, to ward off ills. If we did not ask insiders for their own perspective, we would not learn that the grand similar ties that emerge from an outsider's analysis were essentially a coincidence.

Today, the value of privileging insider accounts is felt more keenly and in more ways than Weber himself could have imagined—and in part because of the legacy of thinkers like Weber himself. In short, there has long been a tendency, in the discipline, to privilege the views of Western, post-Enlightenment thinkers over non-Western peoples historically regarded as primitive, or otherwise deficient, because of the pro-Western frame of those performing the analyses. Beyond that, when dealing with practices that no longer exist, there is and has been a strong tendency to take surviving accounts by outsiders at something like face value—even when we know those outsiders were in fact inimical to the practices they described. We might think, for example, of the accounts of Aztec religious practices made by their Spanish conquerors, or by early North American settlers of various Native American groups. We might think of medieval Christian accounts of the Crusades, or of encounters with North African groups.

In fact, even in the ancient world we face problems of this sort. As a biblical scholar, for example, I can say that it is still typical today to regard the Canaanites as "pagans," primitive and strange in comparison to the Israelites. This, of course, is the Israelite view of the matter, but it is unlikely to be the one the Canaanites themselves embraced. In fact, it can be somewhat difficult, outside of the Bible, to know for sure whether there are Canaanites at all. There were, certainly, Semitic peoples and Semitic civilizations in the region prior to the rise of Israel, including the Phoenicians. What is less clear is the extent to which the people of different Semitic settlements regarded each other as the same people. We might also say that it is still common for people to claim that the "Old Testament" god is angrier, and vengeful, than the New Testament god, and common enough for some to believe that the Hebrew Bible was created with some consciousness of the coming of Christianity in mind. In both cases, this is the Christian view of the matter. Hebrew Bible scholars typically point out the complexity of the text's presentation of God, who can be both vengeful and merciful in different contexts, and of course, the Hebrew Bible as a whole was completed centuries before anyone had even heard of Christianity. Indeed, even the framing "Old Testament" is Christian, since the term implies the "New," which did not exist when it was first written, or for some time to come.

As we reassess the damage done by an overreliance on these Western accounts, one obvious solution is to do what we can to restore the viewpoints of insiders to their proper place. Wherever contemporaneous accounts of religious practices by practitioners survive, we can perform acts of recovery, re-centering the histories and perspectives of the people who actually experienced the acts in question, and sidelining outsider viewpoints that have been unfairly elevated, sometimes for quite a long time. In other cases, especially in more distant historical periods, this is not possible—outsider accounts may be all we have. Here, however, we can still recognize that outsiders, especially outsiders with agendas, are not always reliable narrators. We can remember that the norms of historical and anthropological description, which today at least aspire to objectivity, have not existed very long. If most of what we have to work with is indeed a conquistador's account of Aztec religion, we can hardly neglect it, but can recognize some of the ways in which someone who viewed the Aztecs as primitives to be exterminated or converted is likely to lead us astray in describing those practices as they really were, and the meanings they really had. Western scholars especially can also learn how contemporary approaches are shaped by the history of Western thought itself and be open to the possibility that other intellectual histories would produce other conclusions.

Yet even as many now engage more seriously with the effort to allow religious practitioners to speak for themselves than ever was done in Weber's time, two new issues loom on the horizon. The first is that even as oral traditions are increasingly, and correctly seen as a neglected source of insider knowledge—neglected, often enough, because of a Western prejudice against indigenous accounts—studies of memory continue to show that oral histories are often unreliable. This does not mean they are worthless, or unable to reflect genuine historical experiences, but that they cannot simply substitute for the rigorous kind of inquiry we can perform on contemporary practices. We cannot, in other words, solve the problem of biased outsider accounts simply by replacing them with oral histories, however necessary it is to include these. As a result, future inquires will have to walk a middle path, restoring to insider narratives the respect they have too often been denied, while acknowledging the substantial ambiguities that will remain wherever oral traditions are all we have to go on.

MAX WEBER

Second, as Weber knew well, meaning is a complex business. While we learn much from insider accounts, the surface-level meaning, and the official meaning of a practice is not its only meaning. Once we know everything about what a sacrifice is supposed to accomplish in a given context, for example, a little more investigation may also reveal that the setting of the sacrifice provides a necessary social context for all kinds of interactions—business deals, marriage arrangements, or simply a highlight of the year's social events. This, too, is something we will learn primarily from insiders, but often from an analysis that goes beyond what is literally said about an event's meaning. Thus, again, the challenge is to give insider accounts the respect they deserve—and avoid discriminatory framings of what insiders can know in comparison to more perceptive outsiders—while still engaging at a level of analysis that goes beyond the most explicit levels of discourse, or in Weber's phrasing, the viewpoint of the individuals concerned.

Ultimately then, Weber's observation, in its original context, is of course a product of its own time and aspects of the larger arguments it is a part of could not be made today. At the same time, it does gesture to something important, and something newly reflective of scholarly approaches to the study of religious practices, especially by European and American scholars engaged in the study of traditions from other regions and more distant eras. What I have tried to show in this essay is not only how Weber's basic insight reflects contemporary reassessments of how we study religious traditions, but also something of the new challenges that have arisen as these reassessments continue.

Afterword: *Revisiting Classics* and Plotting Futures for the *Field* of Religious Studies

Richard Newton

In most academic settings, scholarly pursuits are segmented into discrete subject matters. A course of study is presented as a journey through classes such as math, science, history, and language arts. Taken together, an education in these subjects contributes to the lofty goal of training students to comprehend the world more fully. Perhaps you recognize this from the general curriculum undertaken on the way to earning some degree.

However, what may be less familiar is the arbitrary or superficial nature of these institutional classifications. As much as we think about school in terms of these discrete subject matters, we often associate learnedness with the ability to integrate skills and content-knowledge from across a course of study. Consider the thrill a student receives when they can apply that algorithm they learned in math to an experiment in physics that replicates a historic discovery famously depicted in art that they read about in literature class. The exclamation "Eureka!" is a legendary example of just this kind of synergy.

According to myth, a local ruler grew suspicious that a gold crown he had commissioned was in fact gilded silver. The ruler knew the exact amount of gold he had allocated for the job. And the crown indeed weighed as much as the gold provided, but the ruler was unsure how to figure out the purity of the gold crown without damaging it—which was out of the question. So he tasked the ancient Greek scholar, Archimedes of Syracuse, to find a way.[1]

The answer would come to Archimedes in the bathtub of all places. When he submerged himself, he noticed that the water rose. This led him to hypothesize that the difference between the volume of the risen water level and the volume prior to his entry was equal to the volume of the submerged portion of his body.[2] Furthermore, if two objects of the same size were submerged, then the water would rise more for the denser object. Thus a gilded silver crown would be more voluminous than an equal mass of pure gold since more silver would be needed to approximate the mass of gold. In the Roman architect Vitruvius's (first century CE) telling of this tale, Archimedes shouted the Greek word, "Eureka!," "I found it!," after discovering this eloquent solution.[3] And the exclamation persists in modern English to this day.

We may not all be genius enough to have such moments in the bathtub, but we do hope to find such occasions of learning in higher education. When one registers for a class, one expects to find out things about a specific subject. But if we take subject classifications too seriously, might we be undermining those eureka moments for which we were searching in the first place? Eureka moments occur where we least expect them, the last place we look, and the sites we thought we knew all too well.

Toward this end, imagine if a school's curriculum was organized around broader problems rather than specific subjects. Instead of math or physics or literature, one attended classes to interrogate the very concept of measurement, power, representation—or any other term we presume to understand but that bear revisiting. Were those before us never wise enough to have looked back, our world may still be flat and or the center of the universe.

Thus, I find it instructive to recall that "Eureka!"—"I found it!"—comes from the same root as the word "heuristic," a term used in school to discuss *how* we learn something. Archimedes's discovery is as much a product of him being a good student or disciple of certain subject matters as it is mischievous wandering in a field of questions. The two need not be mutually exclusive. Today's heuristics are yesterday's eureka moments. And were we not to question today's heuristics, the eureka moments—that is, the pursuit and production of knowledge—would end. The one helps us appreciate the other.

So too is the case for the academic study of religion. It has been a *discipline* or subject matter in which students are tutored, as well as a *field* or space in which scholars explore the human condition.[4] Many have been tempted to equate the enterprise with a definitive history of it, but I think this misses the point. The academic study of religion has neither a single creation story nor a Big Bang. It is a curiosity sparked time and time again. There are a variety of arguments that have ignited debate. And there is no shortage of issues that scholars have explored (and have yet to explore) regarding religion. Thus the academic study of religion can be understood as the discourse betwixt and between these many eureka moments.

As the essays in this volume demonstrate, scholars working out of anthropology, sociology, psychology, history, philosophy, and other disciplines have brought to bear their methods on the issues pertaining to religion. The data for this research spans timelines, maps, and the speculative imagination. And though universities have institutionalized the development of religio-centric

AFTERWORD

endeavors like religious studies or comparative religion, those endeavors—and the guilds that further them—are a subset rather than a synonym of the academic study of religion. The discourse is too expansive to be constrained to a class of subjects or scholars.

The historian of religions Charles H. Long (1926–2020) framed the field this way, "But if the discipline of history of religions did finally emerge as an academic discipline, it too had to face the problem of every modern discipline in the human sciences. Religion could no longer be defined in its traditional manner. The mode of analysis became almost identical with the definition of the datum."[5] Thus our expertise is *less* in the mastery of examples of religion (e.g., Buddhism, Islam, Christianity, etc.) or even keywords that have been used to elaborate on religion (e.g., myth, truth-claims, scriptures, ethics, violence, ritual) and *more* in the navigation of the many potential eureka moments that have emerged around both.

One lesson to take from such an approach is that to be an expert in our field is to commit to accounting for how these eureka moments—taken together—clarify and problematize our conception of religion and what it represents in the human condition. The scholar resolves to frame the synergies and ruptures that occur when we question the findings of those similarly interested in the academic study of religion.

The contributors to this volume recognize that the rejection of no-longer helpful arguments indeed happens, but that outright dismissals have ramifications for the field and those working in it. We are products of the generations before us, taking for granted their gains, striving to avoid their missteps, and all the while burdened to distinguish ourselves in the place and moments we find ourselves. Critical scholarship holds these proclivities in tension. And as such, the critical study of religion requires a level of humility. Scholars are forever sophomores, a term derived from the Greek words for "wisdom" and "foolishness." Thus it is imperative that we dedicate ourselves to presenting the best possible understanding while knowing full-well that our colleagues and students will exceed our advances.

That said, we would be remiss were we to think that we are all that different from the sophomores of ages past who had their own chips on their shoulder about how they would study religion differently. One might consider Friedrich Max Müller's once-famous intervention into the nineteenth-century field he called scientific study of religion in *Chips from a German Workshop* (1871),[6] alongside the twentieth-century scholar Jonathan Z. Smith's self-reflexive bio-bibliographic essay, "When the Chips Are Down," where among other things, he discusses his critical engagement with his University of Chicago colleague, Mircea Eliade, and the development of his own work on comparison, redescription, translation, and generalization, which emerged out of such critique.[7] The order of theorizing represented by this juxtaposition is not a sign of aloof navel-gazing but, as Smith put it, a field's "liveliness."[8] Reflexive engagement can be generative.

Hence when I imagine the field and its future, I remember the comment a former student made years ago in the first college-level Introduction to Religious Studies course that I taught. We were using our college as a thought experiment on social formation, and the student pointed out how every four years, our campus reinvents itself with an entirely new student body that claims to go to the same exact school as the student body that existed before but is no longer there. So too is the academic study of religion. We who participate in it today lay hold to a heritage of people who lived in radically different worlds—a world without social media, the internet, personal computers, and televisions. And yet we continue to explore a field on terms that we must negotiate with each supposed new discovery.

So then what do we make of the appeals to canons of older, one-time foundational thinkers for orienting the work we carry out as scholars today? Sometimes we approach the past as an archive of academic cautionary tales; other times, as a library of relevant thought-provoking prompts deserving of continued consideration. This volume encourages a more transgressive approach. You are invited to continue to seek out the potential eureka moments made visible when we revisit the classics critically.

What lessons are there to be learned in the fieldwork of those before us? And what possibilities lie ahead in your own fieldwork? Each contributor has experimented with engaging a classical scholar's work within the productive tension Vaia Touna prefaced at the beginning of the volume. And at this juncture, we might similarly consider what is to be learned about the study of religion when we consider these experiments together. Where might we notice our fieldwork heading?

For instance, all the contributors placed a premium on historicizing the classical scholars they engaged, but what stood out to me was how they move beyond biography and toward contextualization of broader socio-material conditions. As Aaron W. Hughes and Russell T. McCutcheon make clear in the introduction, "if we are to understand more fully the various approaches to religion in the nineteenth century, let alone how they have shaped our present moment, then we must connect it to concepts such as secularization and burgeoning industrialization and nationalism on the one hand, but also, on the other, to imperialism and colonialism." These powerful dynamics inform the culture and institution of the studies as classic.

In guiding us through the work of Friedrich Max Müller, Brent Nongbri challenges us to reflect on the perennial Shakespearean question, "What's in a name?" As previously mentioned, the field that I have been referring to here as the academic study of religion—often spoken of today as religious studies, comparative religions, and the history of religions—was understood by Müller as a "science." And his contribution to this initiative benefited from the amassing of Sanskrit texts as part of the British East India Company's exploits in Asia just as it was inspired by the classificatory efforts of contemporary natural sciences like those behind the novel establishment of the Periodic Table of Elements. For Müller, the building blocks of the physical universe had an analog in the building blocks of human culture—which he understood as represented in language. The culmination of its construction was not language, but humanity's "true and sacred character."

By his own admission, the science of religion had utility for missions and presented a scenario of encounter in which the knowledgeable scholar can be more equipped to interpret a text and a people than those who identify with either, making for a science that neither value-free or nor objective. But before we dismiss Müller's comparative philology for some more sophisticated schema for organizing humanity, Nongbri cautions us to watch out for the terms on which they will have us notice—and fail to notice—the world around us.

In her reading of William James, Emily Suzanne Clark documents how scholars past and present have mused about interiority as a more fitting site of investigation. To James's chagrin, "science" had enough cultural capital by the nineteenth century to have become synonymous with erudition. But Clark does not let us overlook North Americans' growing fascination with the metaphysics of the private domain. James sought not far off peoples but the tantalizing prospect that was the innermost reaches of those around him. James's survey of experiences puts stock in personal accounts as the best raw data for the academic study of religion.

That said, one should not see James as eschewing the public for the private space. Clark notes how seventeenth-century Mesmerism, which had posited a relationship between cosmology and the psychology of human behavior, became a tempting lever for increasing the productivity of "enslaved laborers in the Caribbean" and "mill and textile workers" in the northeastern United States. James, Clark argues, is better understood as an advocate for attending to an internal dimension of human experience too often overlooked by scholars. More recent literature in affect theory, the cognitive science of religion, and the new materialism have sought to ground the idea of experience. One haunting question from James's work is the extent to which we as interested observers are creating the things we are looking for, the "it" that serendipitously will have us shout, "Eureka!"

Mitsutoshi Horii reminds us that this order of reflexivity is not necessarily a belated postmodern disposition in the field. E. B. Tylor's take on the "explosion of data" that emanated from colonial enterprises was a gauntlet thrown back to the Western academy. Yes, Tylor's diction and charting of social evolutionary stages were rooted in what most twenty-first-century readers would disapprovingly recognize as racist presuppositions. But Tylor's pioneering work in social anthropology situated the religions of colonized peoples (i.e., "savage" peoples) within a taxonomy that included "colonizing" peoples (i.e., "civilized" peoples). "Religion" was a category elastic enough to encompass a broader and diverse humanity than our contemporary aversion to all things racist may allow us to readily admit.

And that is to our detriment when we fail to notice how the blanket inclusivist projection of "religion" on peoples is as chauvinistic an impulse as the measurement of civilization. These peoples for whom "religion" is a foreign concept were doing just fine without it. So what work is it doing for them when applied? And what work is it doing for scholars of religion? The problem is that rather than actually serving as an analytical category, the term is usually applied in relation to groups that have more or less made peace—or better said, have been pacified—by Western modern political projects. Thus, beyond retrospective studies of this history, "religion" is a vocabulary word that offers no descriptive utility to contemporary scholars.

Horii's strong pronouncement does not mean that the academic study of religion is somehow meaningless. On the contrary, I take it as making clear the need for greater focus on what we intend to analyze. Christopher M. Jones comes to this recommendation through his own wrestling with the work of Joseph Kitagawa. A less revered member of the "Chicago School" that shaped the history of religions in the United States, Kitagawa's dual role as scholar and Dean of the University of Chicago Divinity School exudes a pragmatic approach to the field. Scholars are experts in select data domains of knowledge but are also equipped to draw upon that expertise to offer insight into data domains outside of it to the extent to which they are prepared. As Jones describes, the esteemed Japanologist exemplified this with his study of Maoism (which Kitagawa called a "quasi-religion") as much as he empowered others to do this, such as the Indologist Mircea Elide's and the African Americanist Charles H. Long's contributions to Chicago's enduring comparativist tradition.

The scholar's ability to do this relies on an understanding of the field as comprised of sociopolitical formations related to the history of "religion" (e.g., religion as traditions) as well as patterns of meaning (e.g., religion as myths, rituals, scriptures, beliefs, etc.) that we have come to recognize in our study of that history. Though contemporary critical approaches reject sui generis appeals, Kitagawa shows no reservation in finding something "religious" as being the litmus test of significance. But rather than holding this against Kitagawa, Jones has us instead ask to what essentialist notions are we beholden to as evidenced in our scholarly interests.

This recommendation helps me all the more appreciate Krista Dalton's reading of James Frazer and twenty-first-century scholarship. The folklorist and anthropologist Frazer advocated a shift away from the classic texts of antiquity (a la Müller) to the living traditions of the peasantry. The conceit was that the latter offered a better frame of reference for European self-understanding. Yet more than a methodological debate on origins, the preference for one over the other, Dalton explains, was part of broader nineteenth-century conversations on racial descent and cultural engineering. If the vestiges of primitivity could be found in contemporary impulses, then people could better determine what ideas, practices, and people were obsolete and which ones were worth preserving.

And as repugnant as we may find this application of social Darwinism, we can still manage to appreciate the irony that Frazer's attention to oral tradition and the histories of the non-elite was relatively progressive, paving the way for today's fieldwork on lived religion, materiality, and popular culture. As long as scholars see themselves as being in possession of authentic essences, forms, testaments, and understandings of people, then scholars will be tempted to reduce the people they study to a level of simplicity that would be otherwise abhorrent.

This is all the more reason for us not to conflate the hierarchical ordering of humans with the management, organization, and analysis of data. And a driving question of our fieldwork becomes how we as scholars attend to phenomena that one time or another have been classified in relation to religion in a manner that recognizes them as patterned and socially constructed features (often called culture) while honoring people's complexity?

Not all attempts at meeting this charge have been convincing. Islamicist Wilfred Cantwell Smith proposed a model of comparison that championed intelligibility in the description of an object of study. Scholarly accounts should not only be comprehensible to academic readers, but also to a more global community that includes the very people being studied. Edith Szanto explains that while this ethos may make sense for community-building, it establishes a slippery slope that erodes the scholarly distance from which critical fieldwork can be done. This is not to say ethnography and encounter are counterposed to critical approaches. The issue is when scholarly accounts become subject to a practitioner's or the observed's discretionary approval.

Additionally, Szanto questions the assumption of W. C. Smith's vision of scholarship as colloquy or meal-table. Mutuality does not necessarily bring about the altruistic ends that its champions purport. Here Szanto underscores how diplomacy presumes exclusionary social boundaries, conditional violence, and indifferent to others that enable political formations like the United Nations, whose missional integrity simultaneously calls for global welcome while barring members who disagree with its priorities, protocols, and presuppositions. If surveying has a role in scholarship, it is in the tracing of fissures, fusions, and limits of our social formations. And a lack of empathy is not necessarily callous. It is perhaps methodologically necessary if we are to continue the curious work of inquiry.

In reviewing Sigmund Freud's legacy in the field, Robyn Faith Walsh foregrounds another fundamental element of critical scholarship: namely that we need to understand the limits of analytical shorthands, especially those that have become commonplace. Freudian psychology pervades the very language Westerners use to make sense of the world. Among all the classic scholars discussed in this book, perhaps none of them enjoy the popular legacy or prominence associated with Freud.

How ironic then that we must work as hard at deconstructing the idea of the unconscious at least as much as Freud tried to establish the influential hidden realm of cognition that exists outside of rationality but must be understood to comprehend how people operate. Freud is famous for providing a language for expounding upon the motivations of those we study, and in some ways paved a way to think interdisciplinarily in our redescriptions. The contribution worth maintaining, for Walsh, is that we are to think about people as a complex of gendered, sexed, and nationalist (among other) considerations often buried underneath more pronounced concerns. But Freud is also a chief example of a scholar with some findings that are better left as a relic than a resource.

For Tenzan Eaghll, Gerard van der Leeuw is a classic scholar whose work still has much for us to discover anew. Van der Leeuw exemplifies an intellectual shift away from outlining objective reality (e.g., the search for the real) and toward the investigation of perception, that is, the mechanics of subjective reality. In our own day, this shift is characterized in the field as a distinction between the studies of experience, such as lived religion, material religion, and phenomenology and studies of social construction. But Eaghll's philosophical genealogy offers a different understanding of this important tension. The excerpt from Van der Leeuw represents a eureka moment in which a scholar asks how and why experience became an important unit of understanding.

Prior to the critical turn, experience was generally presumed to be important because it was true—a reflection of the world as it must be. Van der Leeuw saw experience as important because it was complex, the result of human creativity—a creativity so layered that it renders meaningless the line between fact and fiction. The philosopher of religion was not unlike Kant, Nietzsche, Hegel, and Derrida in questioning humans' capacity for rationality. But van der Leeuw was more like another philosopher of religion discussed in this volume, Rudolf Otto, in seeing the denaturalization of reality as necessitating a more robust phenomenology of God than an utter rejection of it.

Eaghll's critical reading renders van der Leeuw as a kind of comparative cipher that contemporary scholars can use to evaluate today's theories in the field. For example, cognitive scientists and a material religionist may differ methodologically, but their search for a more measured and complete

AFTERWORD

phenomenology operates from a similar theoretical presupposition about reality—namely, that it is out there. Similarly, scholars working in feminist, postcolonialist, ethnic studies may join constructivists in maintaining the social construction of reality, but when the former's methods claim to privilege the experiences of women, subalterns, or marginalized peoples as somehow authentic representations of religion, then they have for more in common with scholars in the cognitive science of religion and materialists than constructivists.

Still, for all of their debates, the constructivists and cognitive scientists of religion share a preference for empiricism that is less of a concern for materialists and those aiming to somehow archive or recover personal experience. Even though van der Leeuw's work is of an older vintage, it marks an intellectual position emblematic and even useful for thinking through our fieldwork.

Martha Smith Roberts models this in her thinking with Rudolf Otto. Otto is most frequently remembered for his expounding on *The Idea of the Holy.* The phenomena of interest for him was what he called the *numinous*, a Latin term used in philosophy and theology to name the very essence of reality. Bound with this was humanity's experience of it, as simultaneously awful and awesome, *mysterium tremendum et fascinans.* Like Eaghll, Roberts identifies the relevance of Otto for today in its location of scholarly inquiry. Setting aside the essentialist claims and ranking of religiosity therein, Otto does advance a thesis that questions the trustworthiness of rationality.

Contemporary scholars in the United States have followed suit in four ways. The first is to challenge the Eurocentric assumptions of human meaning-making. Here Roberts highlights the study of Black religion as a subfield that offered a corrective. The second is the lived religion approach that we have already discussed as we have the third, that is the interest in the cognitive science of religion, or the mental processes responsible for the phenomenon of religion. And finally there is affect theory, which is interested in the exploration of religion as located in the realms of embodiment like emotion, sense, and feeling that can be stimulated in ways that circumvent and even precede cognition. Among Roberts's insights is how all of these explanations postulate an understanding of the human that is no more self-evident than that posed by Otto, and all of them present renderings of the human that are subject to social power dynamics, suggesting that this is a crucial element of the academic study of religion at least as it is practiced today.

Lauren Horn Griffin argues that sociopolitical contexts shape all the forms we study and that this sets forth a clarifying challenge for the critical scholar of religion: the need to compare case studies in a manner that surfaces similarities without insisting on unwarranted harmonization and highlights distinctions without unnecessary exoticization. And though we might point to Carl Jung as having failed at this on account of his still-influential ideas of archetypes and personality types, Griffin contends that Jung's fieldwork is worth a second look. A student of psychology and mythology, Jung is well aware that while the behaviors that scholars observe may coincide with explanatory models of our own design, the behaviors we describe are also conditional upon factors for which we may not have controlled. The skepticism we apply to dream interpretations should be applied to scholarly interpretations until evidence can dispel reservations. Thus, comparativists need to be ready to distinguish between causation, correlation, and the confirmation bias of their own classifications. Working in a period flush with myths, texts, and artifacts, the Jung reflected in the quotation pushes back against the scholarship-as-museum collection where these finds are stripped from their respective contexts.

But his alternative is also problematic. The idealized presentation of psychological forms, even when attached to clever dioramas of specific human experiences, can be as contrived as the assuming labels derived from personality quizzes, standardized tests, and stereotypical worldview presentations. Griffin has us add essentialist framings of world religions to this. However, like Jung, she does not have us smash the glass encasing scholars constructed dioramas. Rather, she encourages us not to miss the reflection in the glass, the work done to carefully (or not so carefully) stage their findings, even and especially when that work seems seamless. That too is potentially telling.

And it is also potentially unsettling when we think of the ramifications of reflexivity and reassess claims to ethical progress in today's critical approaches. In some caricature of academic fieldwork, the past represents a moment where scholars were blithe in their treatment of their ethnographic subjects, indifferent to the concerns of the observed. The quotation from anthropologist Bronislaw Malinowski complicates this portrait. A silver-age champion of the method known as participant observation, Malinowski was not so callous as to think he had indigenous people of the South Pacific figured out. On the contrary, his investment in going there to understand them pushed back against those who believed armchair studies of Western universities were sufficient facilities for research. Nevertheless, as Brett Esaki teases out, Malinowski's take on ethnography was predicated on the hubris that he and his kind were qualitatively different than those being studied.

And as we grapple with determining how to sharpen our research methods while shedding the colonialist sensibilities that gave the occasion for use of these tools, we cannot afford to rest on the laurels of relative sophistication or modern liberal (as in the democratic tradition of John Locke) morality. Esaki explains that the fine print of our social contracts have long been replete with clauses that tip the balance of power toward the knowing scholar and away from the to-be-known subject. And should we not want to align ourselves with the regrettable aspects of Malinowski's example, we would do well to

AFTERWORD 151

follow him by having the intellectual humility to invite reasoned challenge to our best ideas. Our field notes must always be subject and open to review. That is—or at least, could be and maybe, should be—a statute of a critical approach in the academic study of religion today.

It is difficult to actively subject oneself to the level of review where one's "eureka moments" may be shown to be false positives. But I read the contributions in this volume as developing for me the capacity to do just that. They model a scholarly enterprise bent not on the next great discovery but on the articulation and investigation of generative questions. Yes, academics need to learn what they have not studied before. But they would also do well to retread the paths they think they have worn, for there are still lessons to find. The last places we look are the places we think we have already been.

I was reminded of this in Joseph Winters's reading of Mircea Eliade. Eliade is a fascinating figure in so far as he is arguably the most prolific scholar in the field of the twentieth century, at least in the United States' foray into the academic study of religion. Between his role in the prolific and previously mentioned "Chicago School" and his editing of the first edition of the sixteen-volume *Encyclopedia of Religion*, Eliade's is a prime example of a classical approach. It is also a bold opportunity to practice the historicizing, forethought, and humility that this volume has sought to develop.

Winters is well aware of Eliade's work history with a Romanian fascist group associated with an anti-Semitic political agenda as he is with the classic scholar's influential and yet heavily challenged arguments about the sacred's world-building power. But instead of granting either of these as grounds for throwing Eliade out of the canons of academic fieldwork, Winters examines Eliade as a case study in social cosmogony, how human beings found worlds through the manufacturing of cultural norms and political entanglements. We need not grant Eliade's arguments about the transcendent, but Winters, in studying Eliade, presents how appeals to the transcendent can be violently compelling and stillingly mystifying.

Our field investigates the histories, politics, material, media, discourses, psychologies, sociologies, and other constructions that humans have cultivated and that come into view through a study of phenomena people have variably associated with "religion." And those associations are also among the matters to investigate. The quotation from sociologist Max Weber abbreviates this as a study of meaning as practiced by the religious. Andrew Tobolowsky makes plain the difficulty such an approach poses for the scholar. Whose meaning properly constitutes the religious or the meaningful? What I gather from Tobolowsky's essay is that today's scholars have come to a place where objectivity is understood to be an illusion or better said a meticulously refined social construction. The question is now how does subjectivity matter. Weber is correct that there are meaningful insights to be found in the first-hand accounts of those we study, but also with those who have tried to interpret and explain them, a plethora of information that may leave us wondering who can we trust. The mode of the scholar is not trust but engagement. How is all of this data meaningful? What questions does it help us answer? And what questions does it prompt us to raise?

The relevance of these questions do not make for an intrinsically novel presentation of the field, but they do make for a noteworthy one, one that invites others to follow and trod paths toward insights yet to be had about the familiar and strange alike. It makes for a field comprised not of supposedly must-read canons or even the question, "to read or not to read" a given work, but of opportunities to narrate the relationship between our work. And it compels us to fathom the implications of what such critically collaborative theorizing can bring to bear on our understanding of the human condition.

As this volume makes clear, the field today is not that of Müller or Tiele. The niche symposia, lectures, and exchanges from its *naissance* have been supplanted by large-scale scholarly societies and associations. But even before the travel restrictions brought about in response to the Covid-19 pandemic, few of the scholars in this volume would have had occasion to intellectually engage with each other at conferences let alone would have seen themselves as mutually contributing to a field-oriented discourse. For more often than not, subfield specialization takes priority over the broader generalist discussions that were at least gestured to by those scholars in contention of being remembered as "classic" (though Marcel Gauchet's 1999 political history of religion is one among many extant exceptions).[9] And I think a return to the mode of fieldwide engagement is long overdue. That is one among other lessons that this volume acknowledges that we have to learn from our scholarly progenitors, just as we are confident, dear reader, that the future of the field resides in the discipline to revisit what you found and didn't find here—the eureka to come!

Notes

Preface: Taking Notes in the Field of Religious Studies: Critical Methods

1 Bruce Lincoln, *Theorizing Myth: Narrative, Ideology and Scholarship* (Chicago: University of Chicago Press), 216.

2 The quotation comes from the preface to the 1999 paperback edition of Jacques Waardenburg, *Classical Approaches to the Study of Religion: Aims, Methods, and Theories of Research. Introduction and Anthology*, 2nd ed. (Berlin: Walter de Gruyter, 2017), xiii.

3 Russell T. McCutcheon, "Foreword: *Plus ça change*," in Waardenburg, *Classical Approaches to the Study of Religion*, ix.

4 Hayden White, *Tropics of Discourse: Essays in Cultural Criticism* (Baltimore, MD: Johns Hopkins University Press), 125.

5 McCutcheon, "Foreword," v–vi.

6 Ibid., xii.

Introduction: Revisiting the Past ..., Again

1 Jonathan Z. Smith, "Religion, Religions, Religious," in *Critical Terms for Religious Studies*, ed. Mark C. Taylor (Chicago: University of Chicago Press, 1998), 275.

2 Huston Smith, *The Religions of Man* (New York: Mentor Books, 1958), 17.

3 Nelson Maldonado-Torres, "Religion, Modernity, and Coloniality," in *Religion, Theory, Critique: Classic and Contemporary Approaches and Methodologies*, ed. Richard King (New York: Columbia University Press, 2017), 547.

4 Edward Burnett Tylor, *Primitive Culture: Researches into the Development of Mythology, Philosophy, Religion, Art, and Custom* (London: John Murray), 1:184. Citations refer to the sixth edition of 1920.

5 James Cowles Prichard, *Researches into the Physical History of Man* (London: W. Phillips, 1813), 13.

1 Friedrich Max Müller

1 Friedrich Max Müller, *Chips from a German Workshop: Essays on the Science of Religion* (London: Longmans, Green, 1867), 1.xx.

2 See, for example, Walter H. Capps, *Religious Studies: The Making of a Discipline* (Minneapolis, MN: Fortress, 1995), 68: "[Müller] must be regarded as one of the chief founders—as well as one of the most prominent sustaining patrons—of the new science of the study of religion."

3 For a chronology of Müller's life and an overview of his career, see Lourens P. van den Bosch, *Friedrich Max Müller: A Life Devoted to the Humanities* (Leiden: Brill, 2002). For an alternative take on Müller's views on Christianity, see Tomoko Masuzawa, "Our Master's Voice: F. Max Müller after a Hundred Years of Solitude," *Method and Theory in the Study of Religion* 15 (2003): 305–28.

4 Friedrich Max Müller, *Introduction to the Science of Religion* (London: Longmans, Green, 1873), 15–16. Müller was here summarizing the viewpoint of Johann Wolfgang von Goethe (1749–1832), who demanded a comparative approach to language, claiming that "If you have no familiarity with foreign languages, then you don't really know your own language" ("Wer fremde Sprachen nicht kennt, weiß nichts von seiner eigenen"); see Johann Peter Eckermann and Friedrich Wilhelm Riemer (eds.), *Goethe's Werke: Vollständige Ausgabe letzter Hand*, vol. 49 (Stuttgart: J.G. Cotta'sche Buchhandlung, 1833), 44.

5 Eric J. Sharpe, *Comparative Religion: A History*, 2nd ed. (La Salle, IL: Open Court, [1975] 1986).

6 Müller, *Chips from a German Workshop*, 1.xxi.

7 For the quotations, see Cornelis P. Tiele, "Religions," in *Encyclopaedia Brtiannica*, 9th ed. (Edinburgh: Adam and Charles Black, 1886), 20.358–71, at 20.369. For his more extended arguments, see Cornelis P. Tiele, *Elements of the Science of Religion*, 2 vols. (Edinburgh: Blackwood, 1897–9).

8 Louis Henry Jordan, *Comparative Religion: Its Genesis and Growth* (Edinburgh: T&T Clark, 1905), 63 (emphasis added).

9 See Brent Nongbri, *Before Religion: A History of a Modern Concept* (New Haven, CT: Yale University Press, 2013). It is interesting to see a reflection, albeit a distorted one, of the specifically Christian character of the enterprise of comparative religion in Müller's own writings:

> It is Christianity alone, which, as the religion of humanity, as the religion of no caste, of no chosen people, has taught us to study the history of mankind, as our own, to discover the traces of a divine wisdom and love in the development of all the races of the world, and to recognise, if possible, even in the lowest and crudest forms of religious belief, not the work of the devil, but something that indicates a divine guidance. … In no religion was there a soil so well prepared for the cultivation of Comparative Theology as in our own. (Müller, *Introduction to the Science of Religion*, 38–9)

NOTES 155

10 Peter Harrison, *Religion and the Religions in the English Enlightenment* (Cambridge: Cambridge University Press, 1990), 174.

11 Müller's statements on this point are fairly unambiguous. For example: "No human beings have been found anywhere who do not possess something which to them is religion" (*Lectures on the Origin and Growth of Religion*, 2nd ed. (London: Longmans, Green, 1878), 79).

12 Müller's preferred term was "physical sciences" (as opposed to the "historical sciences"). He made extended arguments for the classification of the "Science of Language" as a physical science (see, for instance, Friedrich Max Müller, *Lectures on the Science of Language*, first series, 2nd rev. ed. (London: Longman, Green, Longman, and Roberts, 1862), 1–27). I am not aware of such explicit claims for the classification of the "Science of Religion," but contemporary reactions to Müller seem to have found this implication in his writings. Thus William D. Whitney wrote in 1881:

> The comparative study of the non-Christian religions has, as everyone knows, become in recent time a prominent subject of public attention, and is likely so to continue. It has even been ticketed with the name of a "science," in accordance with the fashion of the day—or, it may be said, with the intent of claiming for this department of investigation a breadth of basis, a strictness of method, and a certainty of attained results analogous with those of other departments commonly called by the same name. As to whether the claim is well founded opinions will, and with good reason, differ. (William D. Whitney, "On the So-called Science of Religion," *Princeton Review* 57 (1881): 429–52, at 429)

13 Müller was not fond of the terminology of "comparative religion," preferring "comparative theology," on analogy with naming conventions of other sciences: "The name of comparative religion should be avoided. We do not speak of comparative language but of comparative philology. No one would use comparative bones in the sense of comparative anatomy. If theology is the science of religion, comparative theology is the natural name for a comparative study of religions" (Friedrich Max Müller, "The Principles of the Science of Religion Or Comparative Theology," in *Universal Religion: A Course of Lessons, Historical and Scientific, on the Various Faiths of the World*, ed. Edmund Buckley (Chicago: University Association, 1897), 17–29, at 21).

14 Friedrich Max Müller, *Theosophy or Psychological Religion* (London: Longmans, Green, 1893), vi–vii.

15 Müller, *Introduction to the Science of Religion*, 123.

16 Jordan, *Comparative Religion*, 13–14. Italics in original.

17 See the essays collected in Andrew Pickering (ed.), *Science as Practice and Culture* (Chicago: University of Chicago Press, 1992).

18 For a recent example, see Donald Wiebe, "An Old *Methodenstreit* Made New: Rejecting a 'Science-Lite' Study of Religion," in *Evolution, Cognition, and the History of Religion: A New Synthesis, Festschrift in Honour of Armin W. Geertz*, ed. Anders Klostergaard Petersen, Ingvild Sælid Gilhus, Luther

H. Martin, Jeppe Sinding Jensen, and Jesper Sørensen (Leiden: Brill, 2019), 130–40.

19 An especially prominent example is the popular work of Stephen Prothero, *Religious Literacy: What Every American Needs to Know—And Doesn't* (San Francisco, CA: HarperCollins, 2007).

20 Jonathan Z. Smith, *Drudgery Divine: On the Comparison of Early Christianities and the Religions of Late Antiquity* (Chicago: University of Chicago Press, 1990), 52. Italics in original.

21 Friedrich Max Müller (ed.), *The Sacred Books of the East, Translated by Various Oriental Scholars*, vol. 1 (Oxford: Clarendon, 1879), xi–xii. For a contextualization of this project, see Arie L. Molendijk, *Friedrich Max Müller and the* Sacred Books of the East (Oxford: Oxford University Press, 2016).

22 Müller, "The Principles of the Science of Religion," 29. Italics in original.

23 Müller, *Chips from a German Workshop*, 1.170–1.

24 For examples of scholars attempting to dictate good and bad religious practice and a critique of this overall approach, see Aaron W. Hughes, *Islam and the Tyranny of Authenticity: An Inquiry into Disciplinary Apologetics and Self-Deception* (Sheffield: Equinox, 2015).

25 Here I have in mind evolutionary and cognitive science approaches to religion, which seem to me to be at risk of biologizing or medicalizing and thus naturalizing and universalizing a local and culturally specific taxon (religion). A more fruitful way of proceeding with cognitive science and evolutionary theory may be to turn to the larger cognitive phenomena of which religion is but one local, culturally specific example. See Maurice Bloch, "Why Religion Is Nothing Special but Is Central," *Philosophical Transactions of the Royal Society B: Biological Sciences* 363 (2008): 2055–61.

2 William James

1 William James, *The Varieties of Religious Experience: A Study in Human Nature* (New York: Modern Library, 1902), 490.

2 Ibid., 31.

3 Ibid., 489. Italics in original.

4 Birgit Meyer, "Medium," *Material Religion* 7.1 (2011): 58.

5 Catherine Albanese, *A Republic of Mind and Spirit: A Cultural History of American Metaphysical Religion* (New Haven, CT: Yale University Press, 2007), 6.

6 Emily Ogden, *Credulity: A Cultural History of US Mesmerism* (Chicago: University of Chicago Press, 2018), 71–5.

7 Andrew Jackson Davis, *The Magic Staff: An Autobiography of Andrew Jackson Davis* (New York: J. S. Brown, 1857), 218.

NOTES

8 Saidiya Hartman, *Wayward Lives, Beautiful Experiments: Intimate Histories of Riotous Black Girls, Troublesome Women, and Queer Radicals* (New York: W.W. Norton, 2019), xiv.

9 Affect theory originally developed in psychology and has become increasingly popular and further developed in many humanities fields. It considers how affects, or emotions, are not merely internal events or states but rather move through the social, cultural world. In its integration in the humanities, affect theory argues that emotions become linked to certain objects, ideas, and behaviors, which enables emotion to be a key component in the creation of social identities and assumptions.

10 Donovan Schaefer even characterized James's work as "politically detached" in *Religious Affects: Animality, Evolution, and Power* (Durham, NC: Duke University Press, 2015), 8.

11 Jenna Supp-Montgomerie, "Affect and the Study of Religion," *Religion Compass* 9.10 (2015): 335.

12 Schaefer, *Religious Affects*, 23.

13 Sara Ahmed, "Affective Economies," *Social Text* 22.2 (Summer 2004): 117. Italics in original.

14 James, *Varieties*, 31.

15 Gananth Obeyesekere, *Medusa's Hair: An Essay on Personal Symbols and Religious Experience* (Chicago: University of Chicago Press, 1981), 1.

16 Ibid., 169.

17 Ibid., 179.

18 See Paul Christopher Johnson, "An Atlantic Genealogy of 'Spirit Possession,'" *Comparative Studies in Society and History* 53.2 (2011): 393–425.

19 Katherine Dunham, *Island Possessed* (Chicago: University of Chicago Press, 1994), 63.

20 Sui generis (Latin for "of its own kind") studies of religion argue that religion should be taken at its word in terms of what it accomplishes or means, rendering it irreducible to other modes of analysis. Often, in the study of religion, this includes assuming a level of authenticity or "realness" to the religious experience or idea presented.

21 Ann Taves argues this most effectively in Ann Taves, "William James Revisited: Rereading *The Varieties of Religious Experience* in Transatlantic Perspective," *Zygon: Journal of Religion and Science* 40.2 (2009): 415–32.

22 James, *Varieties*, 490.

23 Ibid., 489.

24 Ibid.

25 William James, "The Confidences of a Psychical Researcher," *American Magazine* 68 (October 1909): 587.

26 Krister Dylan Knapp, *William James: Psychical Research and the Challenge of Modernity* (Chapel Hill: University of North Carolina Press, 2017), 7.

27 James, "The Confidences of a Psychical Researcher," 587.

28 James's unease was recounted in a letter sent to a friend. See Deborah Blum, *Ghost Hunters: William James and the Search for Scientific Proof of Life after Death* (New York: Penguin, 2006), 100.

29 To put it more clearly, actor-networking theory developed initially in anthropology and sociology and argues that all entities in the physical and social world operate together in a dynamic series of relationships. The nature of these relationships can change over time. Additionally, the theory calls for scholars to pay attention to both living and non-living components of the social and physical world, as non-living objects and entities also contribute to the creation of the social, cultural world.

30 Bruno Latour, *Reassembling the Social: An Introduction to Actor-Network Theory* (New York: Oxford University Press, 2005), 259.

31 James, "The Confidences of a Psychical Researcher," 580.

32 Ibid., 587.

3 Edward B. Tylor

1 E. B. Tylor, "On the Limits of Savage Religion," *Journal of the Anthropological Institute of Great Britain and Ireland* 21 (1892): 298–9.

2 P. Tremlett, L. T. Sutherland, and G. Harvey, "Introduction: Why Tylor, Why Now?," in *Edward Burnett Tylor, Religion and Culture*, Kindle edition, ed. P. Tremlett, L. T. Sutherland, and G. Harvey (London: Bloomsbury, 2017), Location 61.

3 M. Trouillot, *Global Transformations: Anthropology and the Modern World* (New York: Palgrave Macmillan, 2003), 7–28.

4 Ibid., 141.

5 Tremlett, Sutherland, and Harvey, "Introduction: Why Tylor, Why Now?," Location 92.

6 T. Ellingson, *The Myth of the Noble Savage* (Berkeley: University of California Press, 2001), xiii.

7 Ibid.

8 J. Z. Smith, "Religion, Religions, Religious," in *Critical Terms for Religious Studies*, ed. M. C. Taylor (Chicago: University of Chicago Press, 1998), 269.

9 See T. Fitzgerald, *Discourse on Civility and Barbarity: A Critical History of Religion and Related Categories* (Oxford: Oxford University Press, 2007) and "Encompassing Religion, Privatized Religions and the Invention of Modern Politics," in *Religion and the Secular: Historical and Colonial Formations*, ed. T. Fitzgerald (London: Routledge, 2007), 211–40.

10 C. Cotter and D. Robertson (eds.), *After World Religions: Reconstructing Religious Studies* (London: Routledge, 2016).

11 Fitzgerald, *Discourse on Civility and Barbary*.

12 T. Masuzawa, *The Invention of World Religions* (Chicago: University of Chicago Press, 2005).

NOTES

13 S. K. Sanderson, *Evolutionism and Its Critics: Deconstructing and Reconstructing an Evolutionary Interpretation of Human Society* (London: Paradigm Publishers. 2007), 15.

14 Ibid., 15.

15 Ibid., 16.

16 Tylor, "On the Limits of Savage Religion," 283.

17 J. Cox, "The Debate between E. B. Tylor and Andrew Lang over the Theory of Primitive Monotheism: Implications for Contemporary Studies of Indigenous Religions," in *Edward Burnett Tylor, Religion and Culture*, Kindle edition, ed. P. Tremlett, L. T. Sutherland, and G. Harvey (London: Bloomsbury, 2017), Locations 190–541.

18 Ibid., Location 196.

19 J. Cox, *The Invention of God in Indigenous Societies* (London: Routledge, 2014).

20 L. C. Wyman, "Navajo Ceremonial System," in *Handbook of North American Indians*, ed. A. Ortiz and W. C. Sturtevant (Washington, DC: Smithsonian Institution Press, 1985), 10: 536.

21 Ibid., 136.

22 T. Wenger, *We Have a Religion: The 1920s Pueblo Indian Dance Controversy and American Religious Freedom* (Chapel Hill: University of North Carolina Press. 2009), 1.

23 Ibid., 6.

24 B. Denison, *Ute Land Religion in the American West, 1879–2009* (Lincoln: University of Nebraska Press, 2017), 4.

25 Ibid., 19.

26 M. P. Guéno, "Native Americans, Law, and Religion in America," *Oxford Research Encyclopaedia of Religion*, 2017.

27 T. Wenger, "'A New Form of Government': Religious-Secular Distinctions in Pueblo Indian History," in *Religion as a Category of Governance and Sovereignty*, ed. S. Trevor, N. Goldenberg, and T. Fitzgerald (Leiden: Brill. 2015), 68–89.

28 Denison, *Ute Land*, 6.

29 Wenger, *We Have a Religion*, 5.

30 Ibid., 5–6.

31 Denison, *Ute Religion*, 19.

32 Wenger, *We Have a Religion*.

33 Wenger, "'A New Form of Government,'" 69.

34 Ibid., 70.

35 Ibid., 75.

36 Ibid., 77.

37 Denison, *Ute Religion*.

38 Ibid., 5.

39 Ibid., 7.

4 Joseph Kitagawa

1 J. Kitagawa, *The History of Religions: Understanding Human Experience*, AAR Studies in Religion 47 (Atlanta, GA: Scholars Press, 1987), 157.

2 N. A. Falk and H. B. Earhart, "Perfect in Dress and Address: Remembering Joseph Mitsuo Kitagawa 1915–1992," *Criterion* 32.1 (1993): 13–14.

3 Kitagawa, *The History of Religions*, 14 and L. van den Bosch, "Friedrich Max Müller and the Science of Religion," in *Religion, Theory, Critique: Classic and Contemporary Approaches and Methodologies*, ed. Richard King (New York: Columbia University Press, 2017), 69–74.

4 J. Turner, *Philology: The Forgotten Origins of the Modern Humanities* (Princeton, NJ: Princeton University Press. 2014), 244–8.

5 Kitagawa, *The History of Religions*, 16.

6 Ibid., 157.

7 Ibid., 19.

8 J. Smith, "Preface," in *Imagining Religion: From Babylon to Jonestown* (Chicago: University of Chicago Press, 1982), xi.

9 Kitagawa, *The History of Religions*, 17–18 and 151–2.

10 Ibid., 20.

11 Ibid., 21.

12 See J. Kitagawa, *The Quest for Human Unity: A Religious History* (Minneapolis, MN: Fortress, 1990), 1–2, R. McCutcheon. *Critics Not Caretakers: Redescribing the Public Study of Religion*, Issues in the Study of Religion (Albany, NY: SUNY Press, 2001), 6–14 and T. Asad. "The Construction of Religion as an Anthropological Category," in *Genealogies of Religion: Discipline and Reasons of Power in Christianity and Islam* (Baltimore, MD: Johns Hopkins University Press, 1993), 27–53. On a "polythetic" definition of religion, see J. Smith. "Fences and Neighbors: Some Contours of Early Judaism," in *Imagining Religion: From Babylon to Jonestown* (Chicago: University of Chicago Press, 1982), 1–18.

13 Kitagawa, *The History of Religions*, 30–1.

14 Kitagawa, *The Quest for Human Unity*, 16–18.

15 J. Kitagawa, "One of the Many Faces of China: Maoism as a Quasi-Religion," *Japanese Journal of Religious Studies* 1 (1974): 135–6.

16 The quintessential expressions of this perspective, still very much in use in scholarship today, are C. Geertz, "Religion as a Cultural System," in *The Interpretation of Cultures* (New York: Basic Books, 1973), 87–125 and Eliade, *The Quest* (Chicago: University of Chicago Press, 1969).

17 McCutcheon, *Critics Not Caretakers*, 24–6.

18 W. Proudfoot, *Religious Experience* (Berkeley: University of California Press, 1985), 197.

19 See Proudfoot, *Religious Experience*, 194–5 and A. Taves, *Religious Experience Reconsidered: A Building-Block Approach to the Study of*

NOTES   **161**

Religion and Other Special Things (Princeton, NJ: Princeton University Press, 2009), 88–9.

20 J. Blum, "On the Restraint of Theory," in *Theory in a Time of Excess: Beyond Reflection and Explanation in Religious Studies Scholarship*, ed. Aaron W. Hughes (Sheffield: Equinox, 2017), 21–31.

21 Kitagawa, *The History of Religions*, 157.

22 Ibid., 152–3.

23 Ibid., 156.

24 Ibid., 146–50.

25 McCutcheon, *Critics Not Caretaker*, 3–20.

26 I. Strenski, *Thinking about Religion: An Historical Introduction to Theories of Religion* (Malden, MA: Blackwell, 2006), 309–11.

27 Falk and Earhart, "Perfect in Dress and Address," 13–14.

28 Ibid., 13.

29 Ibid., 10.

5 James G. Frazer

1 James Frazer, *The Golden Bough: A Study in Comparative Religion* (London: Macmillan, 1890), viii.

2 I want to thank Joy Brennan for her insightful comments and conversation about this piece. I also want to thank David Maldonado Rivera and Daniel Picus for their suggestions and for their pre-modernist camaraderie.

3 James Frazer, *The Golden Bough* (Project Gutenberg, 2003), 1,004. Ebook #3623.

4 Jason A. Josephson-Storm, *The Myth of Disenchantment* (Chicago: University of Chicago Press, 2017), 129.

5 Though as Sheldon Pollock notes, linguistic relationships between Persian and Sanskrit were already being detected by Indic philology. "Future Philology? The Fate of a Soft Science in a Hard World," *Critical Inquiry* 35.4 (2009): 939.

6 James Frazer, "'The Golden Bough' and the Study of Religion: Preface to the First Edition, March 1890," in *Classical Approaches to the Study of Religion*, ed. Jacques Waardenburg, 2nd ed. (Berlin: De Gruyter, 2017), 240. See Robert Ackerman, "Frazer on Myth and Ritual," *Journal of the History of Ideas* 36.1 (1975): 115–34.

7 Frazer, "'The Golden Bough,'" 240.

8 *The Golden Bough* was initially published as a two-volume work in 1890, expanded to three volumes in 1900, and expanded again into twelve volumes between 1906 and 1915.

9 James Frazer, "Taboo," *Encyclopedia Britannica*, 9th ed. 23 (1888): 15–18.

10 Godfrey Lienhardt, "Frazer's Anthropology: Science and Sensibility," *Journal of the Anthropological Society of Oxford* 24.1 (1993): 1–12.

11 Josephson-Storm, *Myth of Disenchantment*, 132.

12 "Frazer wanted his reader to think of Christian faith or at least Christian praxis as superstitious and atavistic." Josephson-Storm, *Myth of Disenchantment*, 133.

13 This thinking draws upon the theories of Michel de Certeau, *The Practice of Everyday Life* (Berkeley: University of California Press, 2011).

14 David Hall, "Introduction," in *Lived Religion in America: Toward a History of Practice*, ed. David Hall and Robert Orsi (Princeton, NJ: Princeton University Press, 1997), vii.

15 Rodney Stark, "Secularization, Rip," *Sociology of Religion* 60.3 (1999): 249–73.

16 Rachel Gross, *Beyond the Synagogue: Jewish Nostalgia as Religious Practice* (New York: New York University Press, 2021).

17 Anthony Petro, "Bob Flanagan's Crip Catholicism, Transgression, and Form in Lived Religion," *American Religion* 1.2 (2020): 1–26.

18 Monographs emblematic of this turn include Meredith B. McGuire, *Lived Religion: Faith and Practice in Everyday Life* (Oxford: Oxford University Press, 2008); Robert A. Orsi, *The Madonna of 115th Street: Faith and Community in Italian Harlem, 1880–1950* (New Haven, CT: Yale University Press, 2010); Courtney Bender, *Heaven's Kitchen* (Chicago: University of Chicago Press, 2011); and Nancy Ammerman, *Sacred Stories, Spiritual Tribes: Finding Religion in Everyday Life* (Oxford: Oxford University Press, 2013).

19 David Hall, "Introduction," ix.

20 Nancy Ammerman, "Lived Religion as an Emerging Field: An Assessment of its Contours and Frontiers," *Nordic Journal of Religión and Society* 29.2 (2016): 88.

21 Robert Orsi, "Is the Study of Lived Religion Irrelevant to the World We Live in? Special Presidential Plenary Address, Society for the Scientific Study of Religion, Salt Lake City, November 2, 2002," *Journal for the Scientific Study of Religion* 42.2 (2003): 172.

22 Christian Smith, *Religion: What It Is, How It Works, and Why It Matters* (Princeton, NJ: Princeton University Press, 2017), 21. Italics in original.

23 David Chidester, *Religion: Material Dynamics* (Berkeley: University of California Press, 2018), 14.

24 Annette Yoshiko Reed, "Christian Origins and Religious Studies," *Studies in Religion/Sciences Religieuses* 44.3 (2015): 307–19. Many studies deconstructing the Christian framing of religion exist, including J. Z. Smith, "Religion, Religions, Religious," in *Critical Terms for Religious Studies*, ed. Mark Taylor (Chicago: University of Chicago Press, 1998), 269–84; Talal Asad, *Genealogies of Religion* (Baltimore, MD: Johns Hopkins University Press, 1993); Brent Nongbri, *Before Religion* (New Haven, CT: Yale University Press, 2013).

25 In fact, if the author is no longer perceived as the ultimate owner of the text, then the traces by which a certain text is constituted, transmitted,

NOTES

and reformed suggest more about its broader communities of people than the author. Roland Barthes, "The Death of the Author," *Contributions in Philosophy* 83 (2001): 3–8.

26 See, for example, Jörg Rüpke's *On Roman Religion: Lived Religion and the Individual in Ancient Rome* (Ithaca, NY: Cornell University Press, 2016); Valentino Gasparini, Maik Patzelt, and Rubina Raja, *Lived Religion in the Ancient Mediterranean World* (Berlin: De Gruyter, 2020); Nicola Denzey Lewis, "Ordinary Religion in the Late Roman Empire: Principles of a New Approach," *Studies in Late Antiquity* 5.1 (2021): 104–18.

27 Hannah Cotton, "The Rabbis and the Documents," in *Jews in a Graeco-Roman World*, ed. Martin Goodman (Oxford: Oxford University Press, 1998), 190.

28 Hugo Lundhaug and Liv Ingeborg Lied, "Studying Snapshots: On Manuscript Culture, Textual Fluidity, and New Philology," in *Snapshots of Evolving Traditions: Jewish and Christian Manuscript Culture, Textual Fluidity, and New Philology*, ed. H. Lundhaug and L. Lied (Berlin: De Gruyter, 2017), 6.

29 Chidester, *Religion: Material Dynamics*, 3.

30 Kathryn Rudy, "Kissing Images, Unfurling Rolls, Measuring Wounds, Sewing Badges and Carrying Talismans: Considering Some Harley Manuscripts through the Physical Rituals They Reveal," *e-British Library* 5 (2011): 1.

31 Ibid., 21.

32 Ibid., 30.

33 See, for example, Brad Hostetler, "The Visual Structure of Epigrams and the Experience of Byzantine Space: A Case Study on Reliquary Enkolpia of St. Demetrios," in *From the Human Body to the Universe: Spatialities of Byzantine Culture*, ed. Ingela Nilsson and Myrto Veikou (Leiden: Brill, forthcoming).

34 See, for example, Avigail Manekin Bamberger, "Jewish Legal Formulae in the Aramaic Incantation Bowls," *Aramaic Studies* 13.1 (2015): 69–81.

35 See, for example, John Ma, *Statues and Cities: Honorific Portraits and Civic Identity in the Hellenistic World* (Oxford: Oxford University Press, 2013).

36 See, for example, Philip Esler, *Babatha's Orchard: The Yadin Papyri and an Ancient Jewish Family Tale Retold* (Oxford: Oxford University Press, 2017).

37 See, for example, Karen Stern, *Writing on the Wall: Graffiti and the Forgotten Jews of Antiquity* (Princeton, NJ: Princeton University Press, 2018).

38 Walter Benjamin, "The Translator's Task," in *The Translation Studies Reader*, ed. L. Venuti (Oxfordshire: Routledge, 1997), 75–83.

39 Pollock, "Future Philology?," 934.

40 C. Michael Chin, "Marvelous Things Heard: On Finding Historical Radiance," *Massachusetts Review* 58.3 (2017): 480.

41 Annette Yoshiko Reed, *Jewish-Christianity and the History of Judaism* (Heidelberg: Mohr Siebeck, 2018).

6 Wilfred Cantwell Smith

1 Wilfred Cantwell Smith, *The Meaning and End of Religion* (New York: Macmillan, [1962] 1991), 188–9.

2 S. McDonough, "Wilfred Cantwell Smith in Lahore 1940–1951," *The Legacy of Wilfred Cantwell Smith*, ed. E. Bradshaw Aitken and A. Sharma (Albany: State University of New York Press, 2017), 148.

3 Ibid., 149.

4 A. Hughes, "The Study of Islam before and after September 11: A Provocation," *Method and Theory in the Study of Religion* 24.4/5 (2012): 318.

5 Ibid.

6 Ibid.

7 T. Asad, "Reading a Modern Classic: W. C. Smith's 'The Meaning and End of Religion,'" *History of Religions* 40.3 (2001): 207.

8 Cf. S. Smith, "Wilfred Cantwell Smith: Love, Science, and the Study of Religion," *Journal of the American Academy of Religion* 81.3 (2013): 762–75.

9 W. C. Smith, *Towards a World Theology: Faith and the Comparative History of Religion* (New York: Macmillan, 1981), 193.

10 W. C. Smith, "Comparative Religion: Whither—and Why?," in *The History of Religions: Essays in Methodology*, ed. M. Eliade and J. Kitagawa (Chicago: University of Chicago Press, 1959), 35–7.

11 Asad, "Reading a Modern Classic," 191–3.

12 R. McCutcheon, *Critics not Caretakers: Redescribing the Public Study of Religion* (Albany: State University of New York Press, 2021).

13 E. Ali-Dib, "Inter-Religious Dialogue in Syria: Politics, Ethics and Miscommunication," *Political Theology* 9.1 (2008): 93–113.

14 A. Hussain, "Religious Studies Today: A Conversation with Amir Hussain," *New Books Network*, 2021, https://newbooksnetwork.com/islam-in-amer ica-an-conversation-with-amir-hussain?fbclid=IwAR23e3zd8BIETyFb0fksnySx Q4hZ4U55T5nYgrG1sHwsNyRcDyDIP4NtJOI.

15 A. Hussain, *Muslims and the Making of America* (Waco, TX: Baylor University Press, 2016).

16 "History of the United Nations," *United Nations*, n.d., https://www.un.org/en/ about-us/history-of-the-un.

17 Ibid.

18 G. Agamben, *Homo Sacer: Sovereign Power and Bare Life*, trans. D. Heller-Roazen (Stanford, CA: Stanford University Press, 1998), 39–48.

19 V. Malarek, *The Natashas: Inside the New Global Sex Trade* (New York: Arcade, 2003), 157–8.

20 United Nations Charter, "United Nations Charter" (full-text), *United Nations*, 1945, https://www.un.org/en/about-us/un-charter/full-text (accessed November 20, 2021).

NOTES

21 M. Foucault, *"Society Must Be Defended": Lectures at the Collège de France, 1975–1976*, trans. D. Macey (New York: Picador, 2003), 15.

22 "College of Arts Receives the UNESCO Chair for Genocide Prevention Studies in the Muslim World." *University of Baghdad*, 2020, https://en.uobaghdad.edu.iq/?p=23786.

23 "About Us," *UNESCO Chair for Inter-religious Dialogue Studies in the Islamic World*, n.d., http://chair.uokufa.edu.iq/about-us/.

24 Smith, *The Meaning and End of Religion*, 188–9.

7 Sigmund Freud

1 Sigmund Freud, *Totem and Taboo: Resemblances between the Psychic Lives of Savages and Neurotics* (New York: Moffat, Yard, [1913] 1918), 52; German from Sigmund Freud, *Totem und Tabu: einige Übereinstimmungen im Seelenleben der Wilden und der Neurotiker* (Internationaler psychoanalytischer Verlag, 1920), 42.

2 Of the numerous examples I could provide to demonstrate this point allow to me to offer the case of Margaret Wise Brown. She of *The Runaway Bunny* (1942), *Goodnight Moon* (1947), *The Big Red Barn* (1954), and *Home for a Bunny* (1956) fame was a member of the Bank Street Writers Lab in New York in the mid-twentieth century, an organization that sought new linguistic and pedagogical approaches to children's literature (the "Here and Now" movement). In pursuit of this goal, the organization provided instruction to its writers in Freudian theory. Coupling psychoanalytics with modernism, Brown's descriptions of her own processes and desired writing outcomes are imbued with Freudian language of the unconscious, free-association, dream interpretation, and projection. Her *The Dream Book* (1950) is arguably the most conspicuous instance of these efforts in print. Yet, here is an author through whom Freudian terms and concepts are established—and naturalized—among even the earliest readers. For more on Brown and her background, see Amy Gary, *In the Great Green Room: The Brilliant and Bold Life of Margaret Wise Brown* (New York: Flatiron Books, 2016).

3 Recent exceptions include certain books published in the Class 200: New Studies in Religion series with the University of Chicago Press, which at times lean heavily on Freud. William Parsons argues, by contrast, that the majority of "post-Freudian developments in the psychoanalytic theory of religion tend to gravitate closer to the positions advocated by [William] James and [Carl] Jung"; see William B. Parsons, *Freud and Religion: Advancing the Dialogue* (Cambridge: Cambridge University Press, 2009), 5.

4 Michel Foucault, "What Is an Author?," in *Aesthetics, Method, and Epistemology*, ed. James D. Faubion, trans. Robert Hurley, et al. (New Press, 1998), 205–22, cit. 209–10. For those with good reason to resist the theoretical framing of Foucault (or lack thereof), take the testimony of W. H. Auden in his eulogy of Freud: "[To] us he is no more a person | now, but a whole climate of opinion | under whom we conduct our different lives."

NOTES

Auden, "In Memory of Sigmund Freud," cited from Parsons, *Freud and Religion*, 1.

5   Some terminology associated strongly with Freud—for example, "narcissism"—can be traced to earlier nineteenth-century writers; however, the enormity of his popularity and influence often sustains the narrative of Freud as originator. One helpful volume on terminology, attribution, and scholarship is *Classical Myth and Psychoanalysis: Ancient and Modern Stories of the Self*, ed. Vanda Zajko and Ellen O'Gorman (New York: Oxford University Press, 2022).

6   On the so-called evolution of "primitive" religion to "magic" and then (civilized) religion and science, particularly in the influential work of James Frazer's *The Golden Bough* (1890), see Jason Ā. Josephson-Storm, *The Myth of Disenchantment: Magic, Modernity, and the Birth of the Human Sciences* (Chicago: University of Chicago Press, 2017), 140. Josephson-Storm also addresses Freud's interpretations of Tylor and Frazer on these subjects in *Totem and Taboo* on 193.

7   For a critique of this approach, see Tomoko Masuzawa, *The Invention of World Religions* (Chicago: University of Chicago Press, 2005).

8   Aaron W. Hughes and Russell T. McCutcheon, "Introduction: Revisiting the Past …, Again," in *Fieldnotes in the Study of Critical Religion,* ed. Richard Newton and Vaia Touna (London: Bloomsbury, 2023), 6.

9   One reason, among many, to consult the original languages in which Freud wrote.

10 George S. Williamson, *The Longing for Myth in Germany: Religion and Aesthetic Culture from Romanticism to Nietzsche* (Chicago: University of Chicago Press, 2004), 211.

11 See, for example, Braun, *Jesus and Addiction to Origins: Toward an Anthropocentric Study of Religion*, ed. Russell T. McCutcheon (Bristol, CT: Equinox, 2020).

12 See Williamson, *Longing for Myth in Germany*, 212; for a detailed account of the genealogies and methods of German Romantic thought and its implications for the study of religion, see Marchand, *German Orientalism in the Age of Empire: Religion, Race, and Scholarship* (Cambridge: Cambridge University Press, 2009).

13 Williamson, *Longing for Myth in Germany*, 219.

14 Both Steinthal and Lazarus were Jewish which is relevant primarily because of the anti-Semitic resistance they faced in the largely Protestant and Catholic dominated landscape of intellectual life (as did Freud). The study of psychology was also referred to in some circles as a "Jewish science," meaning a discipline that emerged from the research and work of primarily Jewish scholars. For more on this, see Williamson, *Longing for Myth in Germany*, 219–29.

15 Daniel Pals, "Religion and Personality: Sigmund Freud," in *Nine Theories of Religion*, 3rd ed. (New York: Oxford University Press, [1996] 2015), 51.

NOTES 167

16 Historian Allan Megill refers to this fallacy as "hermeneutic naïveté"; Allan Megill, *Historical Knowledge, Historical Error: A Contemporary Guide to Practice* (Chicago: University of Chicago Press, 2007), 86. On Freud perceived as a "scientific"-minded skeptic of "spirituality" and the occult, in part thanks to later characterizations by Jung and media, see Josephson-Storm, *The Myth of Disenchantment*, 191.

17 Marchand, *German Orientalism in the Age of Empire*, 255.

18 Hughes and McCutcheon, "Introduction," 6.

19 Freud, *Totem and Taboo*, 3.

20 Ibid., 19, emphasis original.

21 Pals, "Religion and Personality," 48–9.

22 For an excellent example and analysis of this phenomenon in Freud, see Seán Burke, *The Death and Return of the Author: Criticism and Subjectivity in Barthes, Foucault and Derrida* (Edinburgh: Edinburgh University Press, [1992] 2008), 181–3.

23 For example, see Scott Atran, *In Gods We Trust: The Evolutionary Landscape of Religion* (New York: Oxford University Press, [2002] 2005).

24 Ibid., 10.

25 Simone de Beauvoir, *The Second Sex*, trans. Constance Borde, et al. (New York: Vintage Books, [1949] 2011), 79.

26 See, for example, Reuben M. Rainey, *Freud as Student of Religion: Perspectives on the Background and Development of His Thought* (Missoula: Scholars Press, 1975).

27 See Pals, "Religion and Personality," 49–79, cit. 55.

28 See Ibid., 57; Parsons, *Freud and Religion*, 35.

29 See Freud's early papers on the effects of cocaine, for example: Sigmund Freud, "Beitrag zur Kenntniss der Cocawirkung," *Separatabdruck aus Dr. Wittelshöfer's, "Wiener Med. Wochenschrift"* (Nr. 5, 1885).

30 Too often, Andreas-Salomé's contributions to scholarship and fields like psychoanalysis are reduced to her male relationships, including her early close association with Nietzsche. Terms like "muse," "mythical goddess," "vestal virgin," "she-Narcissus," "girl-philosopher," and "femme fatale" are commonplace; see, Julia Vickers, *Lou von Salomé: A Biography of the Woman Who Inspired Freud, Nietzsche and Rilke* (Jefferson, NC: McFarland, 2008), 170.

31 Freud's family and ferocious entourage of mentees—both favored and estranged—did a great deal to promote his legacy. Vickers offers one mythologizing perspective: "Carl Jung, years after he had broken off from his mentor, Sigmund Freud, wrote that Freud was an historical necessity. Freud was an important safety valve for Victorian era, an era beset with intense sexual repression, resulting in deep-rooted neurosis. However, Jung believed that Freud overextended his theory by reducing *all* psychic products, such as art, philosophy and religion, to nothing more than expressions of repressed sexual instinct. With the benefit of Jung and others who refined many of

168 NOTES

Freud's seminal ideas, we now see many of Freud's theories as partially preserved antiques"; Vickers, *Lou von Salomé*, 161.

32 See Parsons, *Freud and Religion*, 10. On the use of Freud and psychoanalytic theory among feminist scholars of the 1970s–1990s in particular, see *Modern Christian Thought, Volume II: The Twentieth Century*, ed. James C. Livingston, et al. (Hoboken, NJ: Prentice-Hall, 2000), "Feminist Theology," 417–42, esp. 419.

33 Here I do not mean in the field of religious studies alone, but in the domains of domestic violence (e.g., his theories on masochism used as a justification for violence against women) and even his theories on infant sexuality as a defense for child abuse. The medical literature on these critiques is vast.

34 See Parsons, *Freud and Religion*, 1–2 for more discussion.

35 Rogers Brubaker, *Ethnicity without Groups* (Cambridge, MA: Harvard University Press, 2004), 10.

36 Pals, "Religion and Personality," 59n12. For comprehensive reviews of Sigmund Freud's life and the trajectory of his work, see Pals, "Religion and Personality: Sigmund Freud," 49–79. Also see Gay's somewhat paradoxically titled "Freud: A Brief Life," in *Totem and Taboo: Some Points of Agreement between the Mental Lives of Savages and* Neurotics, trans. and ed. James Strachey, intr. Peter Gay (New York: W. W. Norton, 1989), ix–xxiii. On Freud's upbringing and relationship to Judaism, as well as his struggles with anti-Semitism in Catholic Vienna, see Parsons, *Freud and Religion*, 32–5. Parsons also notes that Freud often "[identified] with biblical figures, of which Moses and Joseph were particularly prominent" (34).

8 Gerardus van der Leeuw

1 Gerardus van der Leeuw, *Religion in Essence and Manifestation* (Princeton, NJ: Princeton University Press, [1933] 1986), 671.

2 Friedrich Nietzsche, "The Madman," in *The Gay Science* (New York: Vintage Books, [1962] 1974), 181.

3 Immanuel Kant, *Critique of Pure Reason*, trans. Norman Kemp Smith (London: Palgrave Macmillan, 1918), 32.

4 G. W. F. Hegel, *Elements of the Philosophy of Right*, ed. Alan W. Wood, trans. H. B. Nisbet (Cambridge: Cambridge University Press, 1991), 23.

5 Jacques Derrida, *Writing and Difference*, trans. Alan Bass (New York: Routledge, 1981), 192.

6 Tenzan Eaghll, "Learning about Religion Leads to Tolerance," in *Stereotyping Religion: Critiquing Clichés*, ed. Craig Martin and Brad Stoddard (New York: Bloomsbury Press, 2017).

7 van der Leeuw, *Religion in Essence and Manifestation*, 671.

8 See Kevin Hill, *Nietzsche's Critiques: The Kantian Foundations of His Thought* (Oxford: Oxford University Press, 2003) and Paul Slama, "Nietzsche's

Engagement with Kant and the Kantian Legacy," *Nietzsche-Studien* 49.1 (2020): 353–67.

9 Kant, *Critique of Pure Reason*, 8.

10 Ibid., 9.

11 Friedrich Nietzsche, *Basic Writings*, ed. Walter Kaufmann et al. (New York: Modern Library, 2000), 770.

12 Nietzsche, *The Gay Science*, 181.

13 Friedrich Nietzsche, *Dawn: Thoughts on the Presumptions of Morality*, trans. Brittain Smith et al. (Stanford, CA: Stanford University Press, 2011), 67.

14 Li Guiyan, "Nietzsche's Nihilism," *Frontiers of Philosophy in China* 11. 2 (2016): 298–319.

15 Nietzsche, *Dawn*, 170.

16 Michel Foucault, "Nietzsche, Genealogy, History," in *Language, Counter-Memory, Practice: Selected Essays and Interviews*, ed. D. F. Bouchard (Ithaca, NY: Cornell University Press. 1977), 142.

17 Richard King, *Religion, Theory, Critique: Classic and Contemporary Approaches* (New York: Columbia University Press, 2017), 2.

18 William Arnal, "Critical Responses to Phenomenological Theories of Religion: What Kind of Category is 'Religion'?," in *Religion, Theory, Critique: Classic and Contemporary Approaches and Methodologies*, ed. Richard King (New York: Columbia University Press, 2017), 421.

9 Rudolf Otto

1 Rudolf Otto, *The Idea of the Holy: An Inquiry into the Non-Rational Factor in the Idea of the Divine and Its Relation to the Rational* (New York: Oxford University Press, 1958), 118.

2 Walter H. Capps, *Religious Studies: The Making of a Discipline* (Minneapolis, MN: Fortress Press, 1995), 20.

3 Russell T. McCutcheon, *Studying Religion: An Introduction*, 2nd ed. (New York: Routledge, 2019), 229.

4 Ivan Strenski, *Thinking about Religion: An Historical Introduction to Theories of Religion* (Oxford: Blackwell, 2006), 121.

5 Daniel L. Pals, *Introducing Religion: Readings from the Classic Theorists* (Oxford: Oxford University Press, 2009), 206.

6 Otto, *The Idea of the Holy*, 63.

7 Ibid., 65.

8 John Lyden, *Enduring Issues in Religion* (San Diego, CA: Greenhaven Press, 1995), 33.

9 Gary E. Kessler, *Studying Religion: An Introduction through Cases*, 3rd ed. (New York: McGraw-Hill, 2008), 141.

10 Craig Martin, *A Critical Introduction to the Study of Religion*, 2nd ed. (New York: Routledge, 2017), 9.

11 Ibid.

12 Ibid.

13 Gregory D. Alles, "Toward a Genealogy of the Holy: Rudolf Otto and the Apologetics of Religion," *Journal of the American Academy of Religion* 69.2 (2001): 323.

14 Ibid., 333.

15 Ibid., 334.

16 Otto, *The Idea of the Holy*, 114.

17 Ibid., 112.

18 Ibid., 113. Italics in original.

19 Ibid.

20 Ibid., 8.

21 Ibid., 1.

22 M. Andersen, U. Schjoedt, K. L. Nielbo, and J. Sorensen, "Mystical Experience in the Lab," *Method & Theory in the Study of Religion* 26.3 (2014): 226.

23 Ibid., 238.

24 Otto, *The Idea of the Holy*, xxi.

25 Donovan O. Schaefer, *The Evolution of Affect Theory: The Humanities, the Sciences, and the Study of Power* (Cambridge: Cambridge University Press, 2019), 2.

26 Ibid., 1.

27 Donovan O. Schaefer, *Religious Affects: Animality, Evolution, and Power* (Durham, NC: Duke University Press, 2015), 6–7.

10 Carl Jung

1 Carl Jung, "The Psychological Aspects of the Kore," in *The Archetypes of the Collective Unconscious*, 2nd ed., trans. R. F. C. Hull, ed. M. Fordham and H. Read (Princeton, NJ: Princeton University Press, [1954] 1959), 182.

2 Tyler Gunther, (@greedypeasant), "I Hope He Doesn't Recognize My Voice," #confession #catholic #medievaltiktok #fyp #foryou #foryoupage" TikTok video, June 7, 2021, https://www.tiktok.com/foryou?lang=en&amp%3Bis_c opy_url=1&amp%3Bis_from_webapp=v1&is_copy_url=1&is_from_web app=v1&item_id=6959560258318535938#/@greedypeasant/video/69595602 58318535938. Italics added.

3 Donald Lopez, "Belief," in *Critical Terms for Religious Studies*, ed. Mark C. Taylor (Chicago: University of Chicago Press, 1998), 34.

4 Campbell still used in film studies/screenwriting courses and his hero's journey has been popularized further since being discussed by YouTube

NOTES

personality and author Jordan Peterson. See Sarah Bond and Joel Christensen, "The Man behind the Myth: Should We Question the Hero's Journey?" *Los Angeles Review of Books*, August 12, 2021, https://lareview ofbooks.org/article/the-man-behind-the-myth-should-we-question-the-heros-journey/?fbclid=IwAR3_Ild95Jp15Oc2FvJ14elCjPS6EzDD7PGv8WXpfTgiUc HCQ08Om-IxAas.

5 Carl J. Jung and Carl Kerényi, eds., *Essays on a Science of Mythology* (Princeton, NJ: Princeton University Press, [1949] 1969).

6 Ibid., 182.

7 Ibid., 183.

8 For example, see Tomoko Masuzawa, *The Invention of World Religions: Or, How European Universalism Was Preserved in the Language of Pluralism* (Chicago: University of Chicago Press, 2005).

9 Jung, "The Psychological Aspects of the Kore," 182.

10 Ibid., 183 (emphasis in original).

11 Ibid., 182.

12 Ibid., 183.

13 Ibid.

14 Ninian Smart, *World Philosophies* (London: Routledge, 1999), 1.

15 Daniel Pals, *Nine Theories of Religion*, 3rd ed. (New York: Oxford University Press , 2015), 319.

16 Clifford Geertz, *The Interpretation of Cultures* (New York: Basic Books, 1993).

17 Jung, "The Psychological Aspects of the Kore," 182.

18 Aaron W. Hughes and Russell T. McCutcheon, "Introduction: Revisiting the Past …, Again," in *Fieldnotes in the Study of Critical Religion,* ed. Richard Newton and Vaia Touna (London: Bloomsbury, 2023), 3.

19 Smart, *World Philosophies*. Smart also warned against explanation and did not see what he was doing as providing a definition nor essence. In fact, Smart criticized Mircea Eliade and R. C. Zaehner for not being descriptive enough in "Retrospect and Prospect: The History of Religions," in *The Notion of Religion in Comparative Research: Selected Proceedings of the XVIth Congress of the International Association for the History of Religions*, ed. Ugo Bianchi (Rome: "L'Erma" di Bretschneider, 1994), 901.

20 T. Asad, "Anthropological Conceptions of Religion: Reflections on Geertz," *Man* 18.2 (1983): 252.

21 See, for example, M. Emre, *The Personality Brokers: The Strange History of Myers-Briggs and the Birth of Personality Testing* (New York: Knopf Doubleday, 2018).

22 For example, N. W. Hudson and R. C. Fraley, "Volitional Personality Trait Change: Can People Choose to Change Their Personality Traits?," *Journal of Personality and Social Psychology* 109.3 (2015): 490–507.

23 Jennifer V. Fayard, "When Personality Test Results Are Wrong, but Feel So Right." *PsychologyToday*, September 29, 2019. https://www.psychologyto

172 NOTES

day.com/us/blog/people-are-strange/201909/when-personality-test-results-are-wrong-feel-so-right.

24 Asad, "Anthropological Conceptions of Religion," 35.

11 Bronislaw Malinowski

1 Bronislaw Malinowski, *Magic, Science and Religion and Other Essays*, ed. Robert Redfield (Boston, MA: Beacon Press, [1925] 1948), 41.

2 Lilly Wachowski and Lana Wachowski (dirs.), *The Matrix* (Burbank, CA: Warner Home Video, 1999).

3 For a brief collection of the controversies and evaluation, see Gavin Weston and Natalie Djohari, *Anthropological Controversies* (New York: Taylor & Francis Group, 2020), 41–64.

4 Bronislaw Malinowski and Michael W. Young, *The Ethnography of Malinowski: The Trobriand Islands 1915–18* (Boston, MA: Routledge & Kegan Paul, 1979), 14–16.

5 Bronislaw Malinowski, *Magic, Science and Religion and Other Essays*, 38.

6 Brett J. Esaki, *Enfolding Silence: The Transformation of Japanese American Religion and Art under Oppression* (New York: Oxford University Press, 2016).

7 Edward W. Said, *Orientalism* (New York: Vintage Books, 1994).

12 Mircea Eliade

1 Mircea Eliade, *The Sacred and the Profane* (New York: Harcourt Brace, 1957), 30.

2 See, for instance, Russell McCutcheon's powerful critique of Eliade in *Manufacturing Religion: The Discourse on Sui Generis Religion and the Politics of Nostalgia* (New York: Oxford University Press, 1997). The term sui generis means unique or "of its own kind." A sui generis approach to religion treats religious life as a domain that has its own unique essence and identity.

3 For a helpful discussion about Eliade's involvement with the fascist group, the Iron Guard, in the 1930s, see https://lareviewofbooks.org/article/mircea-eliade-and-antisemitism-an-exchange/.

4 Phenomenology is a strand of philosophy that concentrates on the experience of consciousness and its encounter with objects.

5 See Otto's *The Idea of the Holy*, trans. John Harvey (New York: Oxford University Press, 1958).

6 Eliade, *The Sacred and the Profane*, 10.

7 Ibid., 11.

8 Ontology refers to the study of being, nature, or what is fundamental to existence. A hierophany is the manifestation of the divine or sacred.

NOTES

9 Eliade, *The Sacred and the Profane*, 11.

10 Ibid., 202 (emphasis added).

11 Ibid., 20.

12 Ibid.

13 Ibid., 28.

14 Ibid., 24.

15 Ibid., 64.

16 Ibid., 23.

17 Ibid.

18 This is articulated in someone like Robert Bellah's writings on civil religion. See, for instance, Bellah. "Civil Religion in America," *Daedalus* 134.4 (Fall 2005): 40–55.

19 Crypto-religious refers to practices and rituals that may appear profane and secular but secretly harbor religious sensibilities. The term "disenchantment" describes a world in which scientific reasoning has undermined the credibility of certain religious claims.

20 Eliade, *The Sacred and the Profane*, 25.

21 Ibid., 29.

22 Ibid., 31.

23 Ibid., 49.

24 Ibid., 49–50.

25 Ibid., 64.

26 Ibid., 31.

27 Charles Long, *Significations: Signs, Symbols, and Images in the Interpretation of Religion* (Aurora, GA: Davies Group, 1999), 7.

28 See Long, 199–204.

29 Ibid., 211.

30 See, for instance, Chidester, *Savage Systems: Colonialism and Comparative Religion in Southern Africa* (Charlottesville: University of Virginia Press, 1996). Also see Richard King, *Orientalism and Religion: Post-Colonial Theory, India, and the Mystic East* (New York: Routledge, 1999).

31 Du Bois, *Darkwater: Voices from within the Veil* (Mineola, NY: Dover, 1999), 18.

32 Ibid., 20.

33 See, for instance, Wynter, "Unsettling the Coloniality of Being /Power/ Truth/Freedom: Towards the Human, after Man, Its Overrepresentation—An Argument," *New Centennial Review* 3.3 (Fall 2003): 257–337.

34 The term is used over twenty times in "Unsettling the Coloniality of Being/ Power/Truth/Freedom."

13 Max Weber

1 Max Weber, *The Sociology of Religion*, trans. Talcott Parsons. 2nd ed. (Boston: Beacon Press, [1922; 1963] 1993), 1.

2 A good summary of his interests and program can be found in Talcott Parsons, "Introduction," in *The Sociology of Religion*, by Max Weber, 4th ed. (Boston, MA: Beacon Press, 1993), xxix–lxxvii.

3 Originally published as *Konfusizanismus und Taoismus* (1915), *Hinduismus und Buddhismus* (1916), and *Das antike Judentum* (1917–19).

4 M. Rainer Lepsius, " 'Wirtschaft Und Gesellschaft'—The Legacy of Max Weber in the Light of the Max Weber-Gesamtausgabe," *Max Weber Studies* 12.1 (2012): 13–23.

5 Parsons, "Introduction," xxxvi. Parsons also observes, on this page, that "many of his detailed facts and interpretations cannot be accepted today as reliable, in part because of the very scope of his inquiries and in part because of rapid progress in the sociology of religion since Weber's time. Many of his empirical generalizations ... are clearly dated." However, he believes that Weber's overall framework "is less likely to be dated by the contributions of the intervening half-century than is the case with many matters of specific fact, and of middle-level generalization," which may be so, Parsons, xxxvii.

6 Weber himself was not immune to the appeal of either "evolutionary" approach. Parsons, "Introduction," xxxvii–xxxviii.

Afterword: *Revisiting Classics* and Plotting Futures for the *Field* of Religious Studies

1 David Biello, "Fact or Fiction?: Archimedes Coined the Term 'Eureka!' in the Bath," *Scientific American*, December 8, 2006, https://www.scientificameri can.com/article/fact-or-fiction-archimede/ (accessed May 20, 2022).

2 Joe Schwarcz, "Is It True That Archimedes Formulated His Famous Principle Based on an Observation He Made as He Immersed Himself in a Bath?," *McGill University: Office for Science and Society*, March 4, 2022, https:// www.mcgill.ca/oss/article/history/it-true-archimedes-formulated-his-famous-principle-based-observation-he-made-he-immersed-himself (May 20, 2022).

3 Morris Hicky Morgan, *Vitruvius: The Ten Books on Architecture* (Cambridge, MA: Harvard University Press, 1914), 253–4.

4 On the debate regarding how to conceptualize the academic study of religion, see Matthew C. Bagger, "The Study of Religion, Bricolage, and Brandom," in *Theory in a Time of Excess: Beyond Reflection and Explanation in Religious Studies Scholarship*, ed. Aaron W. Hughes (Sheffield, UK: Equinox, 2017), 139–49 and Bruce Lincoln, "The (Un)discipline of Religious Studies," in *Gods and Demons, Priests and Scholars: Critical Explorations in the History of Religions* (Chicago: University of Chicago Press, 2012), 131–6.

NOTES

5 Charles H. Long, "The Study of Religion: Its Nature and Its Discourse," in *Significations: Signs, Symbols and Images in the Interpretation of Religion* (Aurora, CO: Davies Group, [1986] 1995), 24.

6 Friedich Max Müller, *Chips from a German Workshop* (New York: Charles Scribner, 1871).

7 Jonathan Z. Smith, "When the Chips are Down," in *Relating Religion: Essays in the Study of Religion* (Chicago: University of Chicago Press, 2004), 1–60.

8 Ibid., 32.

9 Gauchet, Marcel, *The Disenchantment of the World: A Political History of Religion*, 2nd ed., trans. Oscar Burge (Princeton, NJ: Princeton University Press, 1999).

Bibliography

Preface

Lincoln, Bruce. *Theorizing Myth: Narrative, Ideology and Scholarship*. Chicago: University of Chicago Press, 1999.

McCutcheon, Russell T. "Foreword: *Plus ça change*." In *Classical Approaches to the Study of Religion: Aims, Methods, and Theories of Research. Introduction and Anthology*, ed. Jacques Waardenburg, 2nd ed., v–xii. Berlin: Walter de Gruyter, 2017.

Waardenburg, Jacques. *Classical Approaches to the Study of Religion: Aims, Methods, and Theories of Research. Introduction and Anthology*, 2nd ed. Berlin: Walter de Gruyter, 2017.

White, Hayden. *Tropics of Discourse: Essays in Cultural Criticism*. Baltimore, MD: Johns Hopkins University Press, 1986.

Introduction: Revisiting the Past …, Again

Capps, Walter. *Religious Studies: The Making of a Discipline*. Minneapolis, MN: Fortress Press, 1995.

Coward, Harold. *Fifty Years of Religious Studies in Canada: A Personal Retrospective*. Waterloo, ON: Wilfrid Laurier University Press, 2014.

Hume, David. *A Natural History of Religion*. Stanford, CA: Stanford University Press, [1757] 1957.

Hume, David. *Dialogues Concerning Natural Religion*. New York: Hafner, [1779] 1969.

Jastrow, Morris. *The Study of Religion*. London: Walter Scott, 1902.

King, Richard (ed.). *Religion, Theory, Critique: Classic and Contemporary Approaches and Methodologies*. New York: Columbia University Press, 2017.

Lowenthal, David. *The Past Is a Foreign Country*. Cambridge: Cambridge University Press. 1985.

Malinowski, Bronislaw. *Argonauts of the Western Pacific: An Account of Native Enterprise and Adventure in the Archipelagoes of Melanesian New Guinea*. London: George Routledge & Sons, 1922.

Maldonado-Torres, Nelson. "Religion, Modernity, and Coloniality." In *Religion, Theory, Critique: Classic and Contemporary Approaches and Methodologies*, ed. Richard King, 547–54. New York: Columbia University Press, 2017.

Preus, J. Samuel. *Explaining Religion: Criticism and Theory from Bodin to Freud*. New Haven, CT: Yale University Press, 1987.

BIBLIOGRAPHY

Prichard, James Cowles. *Researches into the Physical History of Man.* London: W. Phillips, 1813.

Schleiermacher, Friedrich. *Der Christliche Glaube*, 2 vols. Berlin: Georg Reimer, 1830–1.

Schleiermacher, Friedrich. *Uber die Religion: Reden an die Gebildeten unter ihren Verächtern.* Berlin: Johann Friedrich Unger, 1799.

Sharpe, Eric J. *Comparative Religion: A History.* London: Gerald Duckworth, 1975.

Smith, Huston. *The Religions of Man.* New York: Mentor Books, 1958.

Smith, Jonathan Z. "Religion, Religions, Religious." In *Critical Terms for Religious Studies*, ed. Mark C. Taylor, 269–84. Chicago: University of Chicago Press, 1998.

Trouillot, Michel-Rolph. *Silences the Past: Power and the Production of History.* Boston: Beacon Press. 1995.

Tylor, Edward Burnett. *Primitive Culture: Researches into the Development of Mythology, Philosophy, Religion, Art, and Custom.* London: John Murray, 1871. Page references are to the sixth edition of 1920.

Waardenburg, Jacques. *Classical Approaches to the Study of Religion: Aims, Methods and Theories of Research.* Berlin: Walter de Gruyter, 1973.

Waitz, Theodor. *Die Anthropologie der Naturvölker*, 6 vols. Leipzig: Friedrich Fleischer, 1859–72.

Chapter 1 Friedrich Max Müller

Bloch, Maurice. "Why Religion Is Nothing Special but Is Central," *Philosophical Transactions of the Royal Society B: Biological Sciences* 363 (2008): 2055–61.

Capps, Walter H. *Religious Studies: The Making of a Discipline.* Minneapolis, MN: Fortress Press, 1995.

Eckermann, Johann Peter, and Friedrich Wilhelm Riemer (eds.). *Goethe's Werke: Vollständige Ausgabe letzter Hand*, volume 49. Stuttgart: J. G. Cotta'sche Buchhandlung, 1833.

Harrison, Peter. *Religion and the Religions in the English Enlightenment.* Cambridge: Cambridge University Press, 1990.

Hughes, Aaron W. *Islam and the Tyranny of Authenticity: An Inquiry into Disciplinary Apologetics and Self-Deception.* Sheffield: Equinox, 2015.

Jordan, Louis Henry. *Comparative Religion: Its Genesis and Growth.* Edinburgh: T&T Clark, 1905.

Masuzawa, Tomoko. "Our Master's Voice: F. Max Müller after a Hundred Years of Solitude." *Method and Theory in the Study of Religion* 15 (2003): 305–28.

Molendijk, Arie L. *Friedrich Max Müller and the Sacred Books of the East.* Oxford: Oxford University Press, 2016.

Müller, Friedrich Max. *Chips from a German Workshop: Essays on the Science of Religion.* London: Longmans, Greens, 1867.

Müller, i Friedrich Max. *Introduction to the Science of Religion.* London: Longmans, Green, 1873.

Müller, Friedrich Max. *Lectures on the Science of Language*, first series, 2nd rev. ed. London: Longman, Green, Longman, and Roberts, 1862.

BIBLIOGRAPHY

Müller, Friedrich Max. *Lectures on the Origin and Growth of Religion*, 2nd ed. London: Longmans, Green, 1878.

Müller, Friedrich Max. "The Principles of the Science of Religion or Comparative Theology," in *Universal Religion: A Course of Lessons, Historical and Scientific, on the Various Faiths of the World*, ed. Edmund Buckley, 17–29. Chicago: University Association, 1897.

Müller, Friedrich Max (ed.). *The Sacred Books of the East, Translated by Various Oriental Scholars*, volume 1. Oxford: Clarendon, 1879.

Müller, Friedrich Max. *Theosophy or Psychological Religion*. London: Longmans, Green, 1893.

Nongbri, Brent. *Before Religion: A History of a Modern Concept*. New Haven, CT: Yale University Press, 2013.

Pickering, Andrew (ed.). *Science as Practice and Culture*. Chicago: University of Chicago Press, 1992.

Prothero, Stephen. *Religious Literacy: What Every American Needs to Know—And Doesn't*. San Francisco: HarperCollins, 2007.

Sharpe, Eric J. *Comparative Religion: A History*, 2nd ed. La Salle, IL: Open Court, [1975] 1986.

Smith, Jonathan Z. *Drudgery Divine: On the Comparison of Early Christianities and the Religions of Late Antiquity*. Chicago: University of Chicago Press,1990.

Tiele, Cornelis P. *Elements of the Science of Religion*, 2 vols. Edinburgh: William Blackwood, 1897–9.

Tiele, Cornelis P. "Religions." In *Encyclopaedia Brtiannica*, 9th ed., 20.358–71. Edinburgh: Adam and Charles Black, 1886.

van den Bosch, Lourens P. *Friedrich Max Müller: A Life Devoted to the Humanities*. Leiden: Brill, 2002.

Whitney, William D. "On the So-called Science of Religion." *Princeton Review* 57 (1881): 429–52.

Wiebe, Donald. "An Old *Methodenstreit* Made New: Rejecting a 'Science-Lite' Study of Religion." In *Evolution, Cognition, and the History of Religion: A New Synthesis, Festschrift in Honour of Armin W. Geertz*, ed. Anders Klostergaard Petersen, Ingvild Sælid Gilhus, Luther H. Martin, Jeppe Sinding Jensen, and Jesper Sørensen, 130–40 Leiden: Brill, 2019.

Chapter 2 William James

Ahmed, Sara. "Affective Economies." *Social Text* 22.2 (Summer 2004): 117–39. Project MUSE.

Albanese, Catherine. *A Republic of Mind and Spirit: A Cultural History of American Metaphysical Religion*. New Haven, CT: Yale University Press, 2007.

Blum, Deborah. *Ghost Hunters: William James and the Search for Scientific Proof of Life after Death*. New York: Penguin, 2006.

Davis, Andrew Jackson. *The Magic Staff: An Autobiography of Andrew Jackson Davis*. New York: J. S. Brown, 1857.

Dunham, Katherine. *Island Possessed*. Chicago: University of Chicago Press, 1994.

BIBLIOGRAPHY

Hartman, Saidiya. *Wayward Lives, Beautiful Experiments: Intimate Histories of Riotous Black Girls, Troublesome Women, and Queer Radicals*. New York: W.W. Norton, 2019.

James, William. "The Confidences of a Psychical Researcher." *American Magazine* 68 (October 1909): 580–9.

James, William. *The Varieties of Religious Experience: A Study in Human Nature*. New York: Modern Library, 1902.

Johnson, Paul Christopher. "An Atlantic Genealogy of 'Spirit Possession.' " *Comparative Studies in Society and History* 53.2 (2011): 393–425.

Knapp, Krister Dylan. *William James: Psychical Research and the Challenge of Modernity*. Chapel Hill: University of North Carolina Press, 2017.

Latour, Bruno. *Reassembling the Social: An Introduction to Actor-Network Theory*. New York: Oxford University Press, 2005.

Meyer, Birgit. "Medium." *Material Religion* 7.1 (2011): 58–65. https://doi.org/10.2752/175183411X12968355482015.

Obeyesekere, Gananth. *Medusa's Hair: An Essay on Personal Symbols and Religious Experience*. Chicago: University of Chicago Press, 1981.

Ogden, Emily. *Credulity: A Cultural History of US Mesmerism*. Chicago: University of Chicago Press, 2018.

Schaefer, Donovan. *Religious Affects: Animality, Evolution, and Power*. Durham, NC: Duke University Press, 2015.

Supp-Montgomerie, Jenna. "Affect and the Study of Religion." *Religion Compass* 9.10 (October 2015): 335–45. https://doi.org/10.1111/rec3.12166.

Taves, Ann. "William James Revisited: Rereading *The Varieties of Religious Experience* in Transatlantic Perspective." *Zygon: Journal of Religion and Science* 40.2 (2009): 415–32.

Chapter 3 Edward B. Tylor

Cotter, C. R., and D. G. Robertson (eds.). *After World Religions: Reconstructing Religious Studies*. London: Routledge, 2016.

Cox, J. "The Debate between E. B. Tylor and Andrew Lang over the Theory of Primitive Monotheism: Implications for Contemporary Studies of Indigenous Religions." In *Edward Burnett Tylor, Religion and Culture*, Kindle edition, ed. P. Tremlett, L. T. Sutherland, and G. Harvey, Locations 190–541. London: Bloomsbury, 2017.

Cox, J. *The Invention of God in Indigenous Societies*. London: Routledge, 2014.

Denison, B. *Ute Land Religion in the American West, 1879–2009*. Lincoln: University of Nebraska Press, 2017.

Ellingson, T. *The Myth of the Noble Savage*. Berkeley: University of California Press, 2001.

Fitzgerald, T. *Discourse on Civility and Barbarity: A Critical History of Religion and Related Categories*. Oxford: Oxford University Press, 2007.

Fitzgerald, T. "Encompassing Religion, Privatized Religions and the Invention of Modern Politics." In *Religion and the Secular: Historical and Colonial Formations*, ed. T. Fitzgerald, 211–40. London: Routledge, 2007.

BIBLIOGRAPHY

Guéno, M. P. "Native Americans, Law, and Religion in America." In *Oxford Research Encyclopaedia of Religion*. 2017. Available at: https://oxfordre.com/religion/religion/view/10.1093/acrefore/9780199340378.001.0001/acrefore-9780199340378-e-140 (accessed July 2, 2021).

Masuzawa, T. *The Invention of World Religions*. Chicago: University of Chicago Press, 2005.

Sanderson, S. K. *Evolutionism and Its Critics: Deconstructing and Reconstructing an Evolutionary Interpretation of Human Society*. London: Paradigm, 2007.

Smith, J. Z. "Religion, Religions, Religious." In *Critical Terms for Religious Studies*, ed. M. C. Taylor, 269–84. Chicago: University of Chicago Press, 1998.

Tremlett, P., L. T. Sutherland, and G. Harvey. "Introduction: Why Tylor, Why Now?" In *Edward Burnett Tylor, Religion and Culture*, Kindle edition, ed. P. Tremlett, L. T. Sutherland, and G. Harvey, Locations 55–184. London: Bloomsbury, 2017.

Trouillot, M. *Global Transformations: Anthropology and the Modern World*. New York: Palgrave Macmillan, 2003.

Tylor, E. B. "On the Limits of Savage Religion." *Journal of the Anthropological Institute of Great Britain and Ireland* 21 (1892): 283–301.

Wenger, T. "A New Form of Government': Religious-Secular Distinctions in Pueblo Indian History." In *Religion as a Category of Governance and Sovereignty*, ed. S. Trevor, N. Goldenberg, and T. Fitzgerald, 68–89. Leiden: Brill, 2015.

Wenger, T. *We Have a Religion: The 1920s Pueblo Indian Dance Controversy and American Religious Freedom*. Chapel Hill: University of North Carolina Press, 2009.

Wyman, L. C. "Navajo Ceremonial System." In *Handbook of North American Indians*, ed. A. Ortiz and W. C. Sturtevant, 10: 536–57, Washington, DC: Smithsonian Institution Press, 1985.

Chapter 4 Joseph Kitagawa

Asad, T. "The Construction of Religion as an Anthropological Category." In *Genealogies of Religion: Discipline and Reasons of Power in Christianity and Islam*, 27–53. Baltimore, MD: Johns Hopkins University Press, 1993.

Blum, J. "On the Restraint of Theory," In *Theory in a Time of Excess: Beyond Reflection and Explanation in Religious Studies Scholarship*, ed. Aaron W. Hughes, 21–31. Sheffield: Equinox, 2017.

van den Bosch, L. "Friedrich Max Müller and the Science of Religion." In *Religion, Theory, Critique: Classic and Contemporary Approaches and Methodologies*, ed. Richard King, 69–74. New York: Columbia University Press, 2017.

Eliade, M. *The Quest*. Chicago: University of Chicago Press, 1969.

Falk, N. A., and H. B. Earhart. "Perfect in Dress and Address: Remembering Joseph Mitsuo Kitagawa 1915–1992." *Criterion* 32.1 (1993): 10–16.

Geertz, C. "Religion as a Cultural System." In *The Interpretation of Cultures*, 87–125. New York: Basic Books, 1973.

Kitagawa, J. *The History of Religions: Understanding Human Experience*, AAR Studies in Religion 47. Atlanta, GA: Scholars, 1987.

Kitagawa, J. "One of the Many Faces of China: Maoism as a Quasi-Religion." *Japanese Journal of Religious Studies* 1 (1974): 125–41.

BIBLIOGRAPHY

Kitagawa, J. *The Quest for Human Unity: A Religious History*. Minneapolis, MN: Fortress Press, 1990.

McCutcheon, R. *Critics Not Caretakers: Redescribing the Public Study of Religion*, Issues in the Study of Religion. Albany, NY: SUNY Press, 2001.

Proudfoot, W. *Religious Experience*. Berkeley: University of California Press, 1985.

Smith, J. "Fences and Neighbors: Some Contours of Early Judaism." In *Imagining Religion: From Babylon to Jonestown*, 1–18. Chicago: University of Chicago Press, 1982.

Smith, J. "Preface." In *Imagining Religion: From Babylon to Jonestown*, i–xiii. Chicago: University of Chicago Press, 1982.

Strenski, I. *Thinking about Religion: An Historical Introduction to Theories of Religion*. Malden, MA: Blackwell, 2006.

Taves, A. *Religious Experience Reconsidered: A Building-Block Approach to the Study of Religion and Other Special Things*. Princeton, NJ: Princeton University Press, 2009.

Turner, J. *Philology: The Forgotten Origins of the Modern Humanities*. Princeton, NJ: Princeton University Press, 2014.

Chapter 5 James G. Frazer

Ackerman, R. "Frazer on Myth and Ritual." *Journal of the History of Ideas* 36.1 (1975): 115–34.

Ammerman, N. "Lived Religion as an Emerging Field: An Assessment of Its Contours and Frontiers." *Nordic Journal of Religión and Society* 29.2 (2016): 83–99.

Ammerman, N. *Sacred Stories, Spiritual Tribes: Finding Religion in Everyday Life*. Oxford: Oxford University Press, 2013.

Asad, T. *Genealogies of Religion*. Baltimore, MD: Johns Hopkins University Press, 1993.

Bamberger, A. M. "Jewish Legal Formulae in the Aramaic Incantation Bowls." *Aramaic Studies* 13.1: 69–81.

Barthes, R. "The Death of the Author." *Contributions in Philosophy* 83 (2001): 3–8.

Bender, C. *Heaven's Kitchen*. Chicago: University of Chicago Press, 2011.

Benjamin, W. "The Translator's Task," in *The Translation Studies Reader*, ed. L. Venuti, 75–83. Oxfordshire: Routledge, 1997.

Chidester, D. *Religion: Material Dynamics*. Berkeley: University of California Press, 2018.

De Certeau, M. *The Practice of Everyday Life*. Berkeley: University of California Press, 2011.

Chin, C. M. "Marvelous Things Heard: On Finding Historical Radiance," *The Massachusetts Review* 58.3 (2017): 478–91.

Cotton, H. "The Rabbis and the Documents." In *Jews in a Graeco-Roman World*, ed. Martin Goodman, 167–79. Oxford: Oxford University Press, 1998.

Denzey Lewis, N. "Ordinary Religion in the Late Roman Empire: Principles of a New Approach." *Studies in Late Antiquity* 5.1 (2021): 104–18.

BIBLIOGRAPHY

Esler, P. *Babatha's Orchard: The Yadin Papyri and an Ancient Jewish Family Tale Retold*. Oxford: Oxford University Press, 2017.

Frazer, J. *The Golden Bough: A Study in Comparative Religion*. London: Macmillan, 1890.

Frazer, J. "'The Golden Bough' and the Study of Religion: Preface to the First Edition, March 1890." In *Classical Approaches to the Study of Religion*, ed. J. Waardenburg, 181–92. Berlin: De Gruyter, 2017.

Frazer, J. "Taboo." In *Encyclopedia Britannica*, 9th ed., 23.15–18. Edinburgh: Adam and Charles Black, 1899.

Gasparini, V., M. Patzelt, and R. Raja. *Lived Religion in the Ancient Mediterranean World*. Berlin: De Gruyter, 2020.

Gross, R. *Beyond the Synagogue: Jewish Nostalgia as Religious Practice*. New York: New York University Press, 2021.

Hall, D. "Introduction." In *Lived Religion in America: Toward a History of Practice*, ed. D. Hall and R. Orsi, vii–xiii. Princeton, NJ: Princeton University Press, 1997.

Hostetler, B. "The Visual Structure of Epigrams and the Experience of Byzantine Space: A Case Study on Reliquary Enkolpia of St. Demetrios." In *From the Human Body to the Universe: Spatialities of Byzantine Culture*, ed. I. Nilsson and M. Veikou. Leiden: Brill, 2022.

Josephson-Storm, J. *The Myth of Disenchantment*. Chicago: University of Chicago Press, 2017.

Lienhardt, G. "Frazer's Anthropology: Science and Sensibility." *Journal of the Anthropological Society of Oxford* 24.1 (1993): 1–12.

Lundhaug, H., and L. Lied. "Studying Snapshots: On Manuscript Culture, Textual Fluidity, and New Philology." In *Snapshots of Evolving Traditions: Jewish and Christian Manuscript Culture, Textual Fluidity, and New Philology*, ed. H. Lundhaug and L. Lied, 1–19. Berlin, De Gruyter, 2017.

Ma, J. *Statues and Cities: Honorific Portraits and Civic Identity in the Hellenistic World*. Oxford: Oxford University Press, 2013.

McGuire, M. *Lived Religion: Faith and Practice in Everyday Life*. Oxford: Oxford University Press, 2008.

Nongbri, B. *Before Religion*. New Haven, CT: Yale University Press, 2013.

Orsi, R. "Is the Study of Lived Religion Irrelevant to the World We Live in? Special Presidential Plenary Address, Society for the Scientific Study of Religion, Salt Lake City, November 2, 2002." *Journal for the Scientific Study of Religion* 42.2 (2003): 169–74.

Orsi, R. *The Madonna of 115th Street: Faith and Community in Italian Harlem, 1880–1950*. New Haven, CT: Yale University Press, 2010.

Petro, A. "Bob Flanagan's Cr p Catholicism, Transgression, and Form in Lived Religion." *American Religion* 1.2 (2020): 1–26.

Pollock, S. "Future Philology? The Fate of a Soft Science in a Hard World." *Critical Inquiry* 35.4 (2009): 931–61.

Reed, A. Y. "Christian Origins and Religious Studies." *Studies in Religion/Sciences Religieuses* 44.3 (2015): 307–19.

Reed, A. Y. *Jewish-Christianity and the History of Judaism*. Heidelberg: Mohr Siebeck, 2018.

Rudy, K. "Kissing Images, Unfurling Rolls, Measuring Wounds, Sewing Badges and Carrying Talismans: Considering Some Harley Manuscripts through the Physical Rituals They Reveal." *e-British Library* 5 (2011).

Rüpke, J. *On Roman Religion: Lived Religion and the Individual in Ancient Rome*, Ithaca, NY: Cornell University Press, 2016.
Smith, C. *Religion: What It Is, How It Works, and Why It Matters*. Princeton, NJ: Princeton University Press, 2017.
Smith, J. Z. "Religion, Religions, Religious." In *Critical Terms for Religious Studies*, ed. Mark Taylor, 269–84. Chicago: University of Chicago Press, 1998.
Stark, R. "Secularization, Rip." *Sociology of Religion* 60.3 (1999): 249–73.
Stern, K. *Writing on the Wall: Graffiti and the Forgotten Jews of Antiquity*. Princeton, NJ: Princeton University Press, 2018.

Chapter 6 Wilfred Cantwell Smith

"About Us." *UNESCO Chair for Inter-religious Dialogue Studies in the Islamic World*. n.d. Available online: http://chair.uokufa.edu.iq/about-us/ (accessed November 29, 2021).
Ali-Dib, E. "Inter-Religious Dialogue in Syria: Politics, Ethics and Miscommunication." *Political Theology* 9.1 (2008): 93–113.
Agamben, G. *Homo Sacer: Sovereign Power and Bare Life*, trans. D. Heller-Roazen. Stanford, CA: Stanford University Press, 1998.
Asad, T. "Reading a Modern Classic: W. C. Smith's 'The Meaning and End of Religion.' " *History of Religions* 40.3 (2001): 205–22.
"College of Arts Receives the UNESCO Chair for Genocide Prevention Studies in the Muslim World." *University of Baghdad*. 2020. Available online: https://en.uobaghdad.edu.iq/?p=23786 (accessed November 29, 2021).
Foucault, M. *"Society Must Be Defended": Lectures at the Collège de France, 1975–1976*, trans. D. Macey. New York: Picador, 2003.
"History of the United Nations." *United Nations*. n.d. Available online: https://www.un.org/en/about-us/history-of-the-un (accessed November 29, 2021).
Hughes, A. "The Study of Islam Before and after September 11: A Provocation." *Method and Theory in the Study of Religion* 24.4/5 (2012): 314–36.
Hussain, A. *Muslims and the Making of America*. Waco, TX: Baylor University Press, 2016.
Hussain, A. "Religious Studies Today: A Conversation with Amir Hussain." New Books Network. 2021. Available online: https://newbooksnetwork.com/islam-in-america-an-conversation-with-amir-hussain?fbclid=IwAR23e3zd8BIET yFb0fksnySxQ4hZ4U55T5nYgrG1sHwsNyRcDyDIP4NtJOI (accessed October 1, 2021).
Hussain, A. "Towards a Hermeneutic of Humanity: Wilfred Cantwell Smith and the Study of Muslims." In *The Legacy of Wilfred Cantwell Smith*, ed. E. Bradshaw Aitken and A. Sharma, 135–46. Albany: State University of New York Press, 2017.
Mahmood, S. *Politics of Piety: The Islamic Revival and the Feminist Subject*. Princeton, NJ: Princeton University Press, 2005.
Malarek, V. *The Natashas: Inside the New Global Sex Trade*. New York: Arcade, 2004.
McCutcheon, R. *Critics Not Caretakers: Redescribing the Public Study of Religion*. Albany: State University of New York Press, 2001.

BIBLIOGRAPHY

McDonough, S. "Wilfred Cantwell Smith in Lahore 1940-1951." In *The Legacy of Wilfred Cantwell Smith* ed. E. Bradshaw Aitken and A. Sharma, 147–72. Albany: State University of New York Press, 2017.

Renan, E. "What Is a Nation? (Qu'est-ce qu'une nation?, 1882)." In *What Is a Nation? and Other Political Writings*, ed. and trans. M. F. N. Giglioli, 247–63. New York: Columbia University Press, 2018.

Smith, S. "Wilfred Cantwell Smith: Love, Science, and the Study of Religion." *Journal of the American Academy of Religion* 81 (2013): 757–90.

Smith, W. C. "Comparative Religion: Whither – and Why?" In *The History of Religions: Essays in Methodology*, ed. M. Eliade and J. Kitagawa, 13–58. Chicago: University of Chicago Press, 1959.

Smith, W. C. *Faith and Belief. The Difference between Them*. Oxford: One World, [1979] 1998.

Smith, W. C. *Islam in the Modern World*. Princeton, NJ: Princeton University Press, 1957.

Smith, W. C. *The Meaning and End of Religion*. New York: Macmillan, 1962.

Smith, W. C. *Towards a World Theology: Faith and the Comparative History of Religion*. New York: Macmillan, 1981.

"United Nations Charter (full-text)." United Nations. 1945. Available online: https://www.un.org/en/about-us/un-charter/full-text (accessed November 20, 2021).

Chapter 7 Sigmund Freud

Atran, Scott. *In Gods We Trust: The Evolutionary Landscape of Religion*. New York: Oxford University Press, [2002] 2005.

Braun, Willi. *Jesus and Addiction to Origins: Toward an Anthropocentric Study of Religion*, ed. Russell T. McCutcheon. Bristol, CT: Equinox, 2020.

Brubaker, Rogers. *Ethnicity without Groups*. Cambridge, MA: Harvard University Press, 2004.

Burke, Seán. *The Death and Return of the Author: Criticism and Subjectivity in Barthes, Foucault and Derrida*. Edinburgh: Edinburgh University Press, [1992] 2008.

de Beauvoir, Simone. *The Second Sex*, trans. Constance Borde, Sheila Malovany-Chevallier. New York: Vintage Books, [1949] 2011.

Foucault, Michel. "What Is an Author?" In *Aesthetics, Method, and Epistemology*, ed. James D. Faunion, trans. Robert Hurley et al., 205–22. New York: New Press, 1998.

Freud, Sigmund. "Beitrag zur Kenntniss der Cocawirkung," *Separatabdruck aus Dr. Wittelshöfer's, "Wiener Med. Wochenschrift"* 35.5 (1885): 1–8.

Freud, Sigmund. *Totem und Tabu: einige Übereinstimmungen im Seelenleben der Wilden und der Neurotiker*. Leipzig: Internationaler psychoanalytischer Verlag, 1920.

Freud, Sigmund. *Totem and Taboo: Resemblances between the Psychic Lives of Savages and Neurotics*. New York: Moffat, Yard, [1913] 1918.

Freud, Sigmund. *Totem and Taboo: Some Points of Agreement between the Mental Lives of Savages and* Neurotics, trans. and ed. James Strachey. With an introduction by Peter Gay. New York: W. W. Norton, 1989.

186 BIBLIOGRAPHY

Gary, Amy. *In the Great Green Room: The Brilliant and Bold Life of Margaret Wise Brown*. New York: Flatiron Books, 2016.

Hughes, Aaron W. and Russell T. McCutcheon, "Introduction: Revisiting the Past ..., Again." In *Fieldnotes in the Critical Study Religion: Revisiting Classical Theorists,* eds. Richard Newton and Vaia Touna, 1–9. London: Bloomsbury, 2023.

Josephson-Storm, Jason Ānanda. *The Myth of Disenchantment: Magic, Modernity, and the Birth of the Human Sciences*. Chicago: University of Chicago Press, 2017.

James C. Livingston, Francis Schüssler, with Sarah Coakley and James H. Evans Jr. (eds.). *Modern Christian Thought: Volume II. The Twentieth Century*. New Jersey: Prentice-Hall, 2000.

Masuzawa, Tomoko. *The Invention of World Religions*. Chicago: University of Chicago Press, 2005.

Marchand, Suzanne L. *German Orientalism in the Age of Empire: Religion, Race, and Scholarship*. Cambridge: Cambridge University Press, 2009.

Megill, Allan. *Historical Knowledge, Historical Error: A Contemporary Guide to Practice*. Chicago: University of Chicago Press, 2007.

Pals, Daniel L. *Nine Theories of Religion*, 3rd ed. New York: Oxford University Press, [1996] 2015.

Parsons, William B. *Freud and Religion: Advancing the Dialogue*. Cambridge: Cambridge University Press, 2009.

Rainey, Reuben M. *Freud as Student of Religion: Perspectives on the Background and Development of His Thought*. Missoula, MT: Scholars Press, 1975.

Ricoeur, Paul. *Freud and Philosophy*. New Haven, CT: Yale University Press, 1970.

Vickers, Julia. *Lou von Salomé: A Biography of the Woman Who Inspired Freud, Nietzsche and Rilke*. Jefferson, NC: McFarland, 2008.

Williamson, George S. *The Longing for Myth in Germany: Religion and Aesthetic Culture from Romanticism to Nietzsche*. Chicago: University of Chicago Press, 2004.

Zajko, Vanda, and Ellen O'Gorman (eds.). *Classical Myth and Psychoanalysis: Ancient and Modern Stories of the Self*. New York: Oxford University Press, 2022.

Chapter 8 Gerardus van der Leeuw

Arnal, William. "Critical Responses to Phenomenological Theories of Religion: What Kind of Category is 'Religion'?" In *Religion, Theory, Critique: Classic and Contemporary Approaches and Methodologies*, ed. Richard King, 421–34. New York: Columbia University Press, 2017.

Derrida, Jacques. *Writing and Difference*, trans. Alan Bass. New York: Routledge, 1981.

Eaghll, Tenzan. "Learning about Religion Leads to Tolerance." In *Stereotyping Religion: Critiquing Clichés*, ed. Craig Martin and Brad Stoddard. New York: Bloomsbury Press, 2017.

BIBLIOGRAPHY

Foucault, Michel. "Nietzche, Genealogy, History." In *Language, Counter-Memory, Practice: Selected Essays and Interviews*, ed. D. F. Bouchard, 139–64. Ithaca, NY: Cornell University Press, 1977.

Guiyan, Li. "Nietzsche's Nihilism." *Frontiers of Philosophy in China* 11.2 (2016): 298–319. https://dci.org/10.3868/s030-005-016-0022-5.

Hegel, G. W. F. *Elements of the Philosophy of Right*, ed. Alan W. Wood, trans. H. B. Nisbet. Cambridge: Cambridge University Press, 1991.

Hill, Kevin. *Nietzsche's Critiques: The Kantian Foundations of His Thought*. Oxford: Oxford University Press, 2003.

Kant, Immanuel. *Critique of Pure Reason*, trans. Norman Kemp Smith. London: Palgrave Macmillan, 1918.

Leeuw, Gerardus V. *Religion in Essence and Manifestation*, trans. J. E. Turner, Princeton, NJ: Princeton University Press, [1933] 1986.

Nietzsche, Friedrich. *Dawn: Thoughts on the Presumptions of Morality*, trans. Brittain Smith, afterword Keith Ansell-Pearson. Stanford, CA: Stanford University Press, 2011.

Nietzsche, Friedrich. *Anti-Christ, Ecce Homo, Twilight of the Idols*, ed. Aaron Ridley and Judith Norman. Cambridge: Cambridge University Press, 2005.

Nietzsche, Friedrich. *Basic Writings*, ed. Walter Kaufmann. New York: Modern Library, 2000.

Nietzsche, Friedrich. *The Gay Science*, ed. Walter Kaufman. New York: Vintage Books, 1974.

Rockmore, Tom. *Kant and Phenomenology*. Chicago: University of Chicago Press, 2011.

Slama, Paul. "Nietzsche's Engagement with Kant and the Kantian Legacy." *Nietzsche-Studien* 49.1 (2020): 353–67. https://doi.org/10.1515/nietz stu-2020-0025.

Smith, Jonathan Z. *Imagining Religion: From Babylon to Jonestown*. Chicago: University of Chicago Press, 1982.

Smith, Jonathan Z. "Religion, Religions, Religious." In *Critical Terms for Religious Studies*, ed. M. C. Taylor, 269–84. Chicago: University of Chicago Press, 1998.

Chapter 9 Rudolf Otto

Alles, Gregory D. "Toward a Genealogy of the Holy: Rudolf Otto and the Apologetics of Religion." *Journal of the American Academy of Religion* 69.2 (2001): 323–41. http://www.jstor.org/stable/1465785.

Andersen, M., U. Schjoedt, K. L. Nielbo, and J. Sorensen. "Mystical Experience in the Lab." *Method & Theory in the Study of Religion* 26.3 (2014): 217–45.

Capps, Walter H. *Religious Studies: The Making of a Discipline*. Minneapolis, MN: Fortress Press, 1995.

Gregg, Melissa, and Gregory J. Seigworth. *The Affect Theory Reader*. Durham, NC: Duke University Press, 2011.

Herling, Bradley L. *A Beginner's Guide to the Study of Religion*, 2nd ed. London: Bloomsbury Academic, 2016.

Kessler, Gary E. *Studying Religion: An Introduction Through Cases*, 3rd ed. New York: McGraw-Hill, 2008.

Long, Charles H. "Perspectives for a Study of Afro-American Religion in the United States." *History of Religions* 11.1 (1971): 54–66.

Long, Charles H. *Significations: Signs, Symbols, and Images in the Interpretation of Religion*. Aurora, CO: Davies Group, 1995.

Lyden, John. *Enduring Issues in Religion*. San Diego, CA: Greenhaven Press, 1995.

Martin, Craig. *A Critical Introduction to the Study of Religion*, 2nd ed. New York: Routledge, 2017.

McCutcheon, Russell T. *Studying Religion: An Introduction*, 2nd ed. New York: Routledge, 2019.

Otto, Rudolf, and John W. Harvey. *The Idea of the Holy: An Inquiry into the Non-Rational Factor in the Idea of the Divine and Its Relation to the Rational*. New York: Oxford University Press, 1958.

Pals, Daniel L. *Introducing Religion: Readings from the Classic Theorists*. Oxford: Oxford University Press, 2009.

Raboteau, Albert J. *Slave Religion: The "Invisible Institution" in the Antebellum South*. Oxford: Oxford University Press, 2004.

Schaefer, Donovan O. *The Evolution of Affect Theory: The Humanities, the Sciences, and the Study of Power*. Cambridge: Cambridge University Press, 2019.

Schaefer, Donovan O. *Religious Affects: Animality, Evolution, and Power*. Durham, NC: Duke University Press, 2015.

Strenski, Ivan. *Thinking about Religion: An Historical Introduction to Theories of Religion*. Oxford: Blackwell, 2006.

Taves, Ann. *Religious Experience Reconsidered: A Building-Block Approach to the Study of Religion and Other Special Things*. Princeton, NJ: Princeton University Press, 2009.

Trein, Lorenz. "Islamophobia Reconsidered: Approaching Emotions, Affects, and Historical Layers of Orientalism in the Study of Religion." *Method & Theory in the Study of Religion* 29.3 (2017): 205–20.

Vásquez, Manuel A. *More Than Belief: A Materialist Theory of Religion*. Oxford: Oxford University Press, 2011.

Chapter 10 Carl Jung

Asad, T. "Anthropological Conceptions of Religion: Reflections on Geertz." *Man* 18.2 (1983): 237–59. https://doi.org/10.2307/2801433.

Bond, Sarah, and Joel Christensen. "The Man behind the Myth: Should We Question the Hero's Journey?" *Los Angeles Review of Books*, August 12, 2021. https://lareviewofbooks.org/article/the-man-beh ind-the-myth-should-we-question-the-heros-journey/?fbclid=IwAR3_ lId95Jp15Oc2FvJ14elCjPS6EzDD7PGv8WXpfTgiUcHCQ08Om-IxAas (accessed November 9, 2022).

Emre, M. *The Personality Brokers: The Strange History of Myers-Briggs and the Birth of Personality Testing*. New York: Doubleday, 2018.

BIBLIOGRAPHY

Fayard, Jennifer V. "When Personality Test Results Are Wrong, but Feel So Right." *Psychology Today*, September 29, 2019. https://www.psychologyto day.com/us/blog/people-are-strange/201909/when-personality-test-resu lts-are-wrong-feel-so-right (accessed November 9, 2022).

Geertz, Clifford. *Local Knowledge: Further Essays in Interpretive Anthropology*. New York: Basic Books, 1983.

Geertz, Clifford. *The Interpretation of Cultures*. New York: Basic Books, 1973.

Hudson, N. W., and R. C. Fraley. "Volitional Personality Trait Change: Can People Choose to Change Their Personality Traits?" *Journal of Personality and Social Psychology* 109.3 (2015): 490–507.

Hughes, Aaron W. and Russell T. McCutcheon, "Introduction: Revisiting the Past…, Again." In *Fieldnotes in the Critical Study Religion: Revisiting Classical Theorists,* eds. Richard Newton and Vaia Touna, 1–9. London: Bloomsbury, 2023.

Jung, Carl G. *Psychology of the Unconscious: A Study of the Transformations and Symbolisms of the Libido: a Contribution to the History of the Evolution of Thought*, trans. M. Beatrice Hinkle, 87–126. New York: Dodd, Mead, 1925.

Jung, Carl G. "The Psychological Aspects of the Kore." In *The Archetypes of the Collective Unconscious*, 2nd edn., ed. C. G. Jung, M. Fordham, H. Read, trans. R. F. C. Hull, 182–203. Princeton, NJ: Princeton University Press, 1968 (Originally Published in 1954, English 1959).

Jung, Carl G., and Carl Keréryi, *Essays on a Science of Mythology: The Myth of the Divine Child and the Mysteries of Eleusis*. Princeton, NJ: Princeton University Press, [1949] 1969.

Lopez, Donald. "Belief." In *Critical Terms for Religious Studies*, ed. Mark C. Taylor, 21–35. Chicago: University of Chicago Press, 1998.

Masuzawa, T. *The Invention of World Religions: Or, How European Universalism Was Preserved in the Language of Pluralism*. Chicago: University of Chicago Press, 2005.

Pals, Daniel. *Nine Theories of Religion*, 3rd ed. New York: Oxford, 2015.

Smart, Ninian. *The Religious Experience of Mankind*. London: Collins, 1971.

Smart, Ninian. "Retrospect and Prospect: The History of Religions." In *The Notion of Religion in Comparative Research: Selected Proceedings of the XVIth Congress of the International Association for the History of Religions*, ed. Ugo Bianchi, 901–3. Rome: "L'Erma" di Bretschneider, 1994.

Smart, Ninian. *World Philosophies*. London: Routledge, 1999.

Tuckett, J. "Prolegomena to a Philosophical Phenomenology of Religion." *Method & Theory in the Study of Religion* 30.2 (2018): 97–136. doi: https://doi. org/10.1163/15700682-12341420.

Van der Leeuw, G. *Religion in Essence and Manifestation: A Study in Phenomenology*. Princeton, NJ: Princeton University Press, 2014.

Chapter 11 Bronislaw Malinowski

Esaki, Brett J. *Enfolding Silence: The Transformation of Japanese American Religion and Art under Oppression*. New York: Oxford University Press, 2016.

Malinowski, Bronislaw. *Magic, Science and Religion and Other Essays*, ed. Robert Redfield. Boston, MA: Beacon Press, 1948.

Malinowski, Bronislaw, and Michael W. Young. *The Ethnography of Malinowski: The Trobriand Islands 1915-18*. Boston, MA: Routledge & Kegan Paul, 1979.

Said, Edward W. *Orientalism*. New York: Vintage Books, 1994.

Wachowski, Lilly, and Lana Wachowski, directors. 1999. *The Matrix*. Warner Home Video.

Chapter 12 Mircea Eliade

Du Bois, W. E. B. *Darkwater: Voices from the Veil*. Mineola, NY: Dover Publications, 1999.

Eliade, M. *The Sacred and the Profane*. New York: Harcourt Brace, 1957.

Long, C. *Significations: Signs, Symbols, and Images in the Interpretation of Religion*, Aurora, CO: Davies Group, Publishers, 1995.

Chapter 13 Max Weber

Lepsius, M. Rainer. "'Wirtschaft Und Gesellschaft'—The Legacy of Max Weber in the Light of the Max Weber-Gesamtausgabe." *Max Weber Studies* 12.1 (2012): 13–23.

Parsons, Talcott. "Introduction." In *The Sociology of Religion* by Max Weber, xxix–lxxvii, 4th ed. Boston, MA: Beacon Press, 1993.

Weber, Max. *The Sociology of Religion*, 4th ed. Boston, MA: Beacon Press, 1993.

Afterword: *Revisiting Classics* and Plotting Futures for the *Field* of Religious Studies

Bagger, Matthew C. "The Study of Religion, Bricolage, and Brandom." In *Theory in a Time of Excess: Beyond Reflection and Explanation in Religious Studies Scholarship*, ed. Aaron W. Hughes, 139–49. Sheffield: Equinox, 2017.

Biello, David. "Fact or Fiction?: Archimedes Coined the Term 'Eureka!' in the Bath." *Scientific American*, December 8, 2006. Available online: https://www.scientificamerican.com/article/fact-or-fiction-archimede/ (accessed May 20, 2022).

Gauchet, Marcel. *The Disenchantment of the World: A Political History of Religion*, 2nd ed., trans. Oscar Burge. Princeton, NJ: Princeton University Press, 1999.

Lincoln, Bruce. "The (Un)discipline of Religious Studies." In *Gods and Demons, Priests and Scholars: Critical Explorations in the History of Religions*, 131–6. Chicago: University of Chicago Press, 2012.

BIBLIOGRAPHY

Long, Charles H. "The Study of Religion: Its Nature and Its Discourse." In *Significations: Signs, Symbols and Images in the Interpretation of Religion*, 15–30. Aurora, CO: The Davies Group, [1986] 1995.

Morgan, Morris Hicky. *Vitruvius: The Ten Books on Architecture*, 253–4. Cambridge, MA: Harvard University Press, 1914.

Müller, Friedich Max. *Chips from a German Workshop*. New York: Charles Scribner, 1871.

Schwarcz, Joe. "Is It True That Archimedes Formulated His Famous Principle Based on an Observation He Made as He Immersed Himself in a Bath?" *McGill University Press: Office for Science and Society*, March 4, 2022. Available online: https://www.mcgill.ca/oss/article/history/it-true-archimedes-formulated-his-famous-principle-based-observation-he-made-he-immersed-himself (accessed May 20, 2022).

Smith, Jonathan Z. "When the Chips are Down." In *Relating Religion: Essays in the Study of Religion*, 1–60. Chicago: University of Chicago Press, 2004.

Index

affect theory xv–xvi, 22–3, 75, 93–6, 145, 149, 157 n.9
African diasporic religions 23–5
Agamben, Giorgio 64–5
Ahmed, Sara 23, 94
Alles, Gregory D. 90
Andersen, M., U. Schjoedt, K. L. Nielbo, and J. Sorensen 93
animism (*see also* primitivism; savage) 32–3, 50
Anthropocene 113, 120
anthropocentrism 113, 117–20
antiquity 54–5, 57–8, 75, 137–8, 147
anti-Semitism 123, 151, 166 n.14, 168 n.36
Aquinas, Thomas 82
archetype 98–102, 104, 106, 150
armchair scholarship 6, 61, 72, 75, 113–15, 150
Arnal, William E. 85
Aryans 49–51, 71
Asad, Talal 43, 62, 105, 108
atheism 76, 81–3
authenticity, constructions of 19–20, 24–5, 52, 57, 149, 157 n.20
Aztecs 137–8

belief 3, 20, 31–4, 40, 49, 52–8, 62, 72–3, 81–4, 90–1, 99, 103–4
  as belief systems 31–3, 50, 54, 99, 105–6, 109, 130, 135–6
  as monotheistic vs. polytheistic 33
  as personal or private 36
  vs. practice (*see also* lived religion) 51, 53, 55, 58, 130, 136
  vs. superstition (*see also* primitivism) 31–4, 57, 154 n.9
Black studies xvi, 124, 131

Brown, Katherine McCarthy 92
Brubaker, Rogers 75
Buddhism 107
  Sinhalese Buddhism 23

Campbell, Joseph 100
capitalism 127, 130, 133
  market capitalism 37
  neoliberal capitalism 113
Capps, Walter H. 2, 88
category (*see* classification)
Chicago School (University of Chicago Divinity School) 39, 46, 143, 146, 151
Chidester, David 43, 53, 55, 129
Chin, C. Michael 57
Christianity 11, 13–14, 17, 50–1, 53, 57, 75, 81–4, 89–90, 93
  Catholicism 32, 35, 51, 81, 92, 98, 108, 134
  hegemony of 2, 12, 23, 30–5, 41, 53, 61, 92, 95, 116–17, 130
  Protestantism 53, 60, 80, 83, 89, 92, 93, 95, 133
civilization (*see also* primitivism; savage) 6, 29–35, 40, 51, 70–3, 112–13, 116–17, 120, 128, 130, 137, 146
Clark, Emily Suzanne xv, 145
classification 12–14, 16, 21, 31, 36, 41, 44, 51, 54, 59, 75, 78, 84–5, 90, 100–1, 106, 117, 134–9, 141–2, 145, 147, 150
  as anachronistic 57, 138
  as boundary formation 6, 9, 29–37, 44, 47, 57, 70–2, 116–17, 120, 124–9, 128–31, 146–7
  and power (*see* hierarchy; power)

INDEX

cognitive science of religion (CSR) 15, 93, 103, 145, 149, 156 n.25
colloquy 60–2, 68, 147
colonialism 3–6, 13, 22, 31–6, 43, 47, 51, 60, 70, 72, 75, 84–5, 94–5, 99, 105, 113–14, 117–18, 120, 124, 127–31, 144–5, 149, 150
comparative religion 2, 4, 6, 11–13, 16–7, 40, 50, 59–62, 66–7, 70, 72, 100–1, 103, 105, 143–4, 146, 150, 154 n.9, 155 n.12–13
    Christian hegemongy of (*see* Christiantity, hegemony of)
    as comparative mythology 71
    vs. comparative religions 61
    and "world religions" 13, 70
comparison xiii, xv–xvi, 6, 12–15, 25, 57, 61, 71, 73, 98, 147
    as critical method 15–16, 101, 143, 148
constructivism 84–6, 149
cosmology 35, 145
Cotton, Hannah 55
Cox, James 33–4
critical analysis 2–9, 73, 75, 85, 104–6, 142, 146–7
critical study of religion 15–16, 44, 89, 101, 104–9, 118–21, 143, 146–8, 149, 151

Dalton, Krista N. xv, 146–7
Darwin, Charles 51, 130
data 4, 39–46, 71–6, 90, 93, 145
    as classificatory process 40
    as scholarly creation 15–16, 80, 146, 152
    scholarship as data xiv–xv, 4
de Beauvoir, Simone 73
de Trobriand, Jean François Sylvestre Denis 4
death of god 77, 81–4
decolonization xvi, 114, 117–20, 124, 130–1
Deleuze, Giles 94
Denison, Brandi 35–6
Derrida, Jacques 79, 148
description xiv, 2–3, 5, 44–5, 61, 70, 75, 88, 91, 101, 103, 105–6, 128, 138, 143, 146–8

difference xiii, 4–9, 13, 15–17, 43, 63, 80, 84, 89, 116, 135–6
    as ontological 124, 126–7
Du Bois, W. E. B. 130
Dunham, Katherine 24
Durkheim, Émile 98, 102, 111–12, 116, 120–1, 126

Eaghll, Tezan xvi, 148–9
Eliade, Mircea xvi, 39–40, 42–3, 46–7, 85, 123–31, 143, 151
Enlightenment (European) 1, 30, 43, 88, 137
    as colonial 129
emotion (*see also* affect theory) 8, 19–23, 92–5, 107, 116–17, 149
    as feelings 2, 19, 22–3, 25, 87–96, 115, 149
Esaki, Brett xvi, 150
essentialism 44, 62, 87–8, 90–1, 93, 95, 101–2, 146, 149–50
ethnography of religion xiv–xvi, 4, 8, 24, 31, 50–1, 71–3, 92, 111–18, 147, 150
    as superior portal to the past 50
Evans-Pritchard, E. E. 100, 104
evolution, theory of 51
    as evolutionary theory of religion (*see also* savage) 6, 9, 32–3, 37, 51, 72–3, 113, 115, 117, 120, 135

Foucault, Michel 66, 84, 165 n.4
Frazer, James G. xii, xv, 49–57, 146–7
Freud, Sigmund xvi, 69–76, 85, 98, 102, 148, 165 n.2
functionalism 2, 34–6, 70, 80, 95, 98, 101–4

Gauchet, Marcel 152
Geertz, Clifford 103–5
genealogy 14, 41, 81, 84, 148
governance 4, 31–2, 34–6, 67, 120, 129–30
Griffin, Lauren Horn xvi, 149–50
Gross, Rachel B. 51

Hall, David A. 52
Harrison, Peter 13
Hartman, Saidiya 22

INDEX

Hegel, G. W. F. 61, 79, 81–4, 148
Herling, Bradley 88
hierarchy (*see also* classification;
  power) 6, 9, 12, 70–1, 74, 90, 92,
  95, 130, 147
hierophany 124–5, 172 n.8
homo religiosus 125
Horii, Mitsutoshi xv, 145–6
Hughes, Aaron W. xv, 60, 70, 72, 99,
  104, 144
Hurston, Zora Neale 22
Hussain, Amir 62

identity construction 6, 9, 13. 65, 92,
  94, 113, 135
indigenous religions 30–6, 43, 72–3,
  92, 113–14, 116, 129, 133
individualism 36, 63–4, 100, 108,
  111–12, 115–16
  experience 16, 19–20, 23, 25, 88,
    91, 96, 103, 139
  as individual vs. community 63
insider/outsider 22, 40, 47, 62, 70, 88,
  91–2, 114, 136–9
intellectual history 1, 70
interfaith dialogue xvi, 60–2, 67
  and world peace 62–6
interpretation 44–5, 58, 71–2, 91, 150
Islam 62, 64–7

James, William xv, 19–27, 145, 165 n.3
Jones, Christopher M. xv, 146
Jordan, Louis Henry 13–15
Josephson-Storm, Jason Ā. 51
Judaism 53, 55, 57, 75–6
Jung, Carl 97–109

Kant, Immanuel 78–81, 84–6, 148
Kerényi, Carl 100
Kessler, Gary 89
King, Richard 85
Kitagawa, Joseph xv, 39–47, 61,
  85, 146
knowledge production 4, 15 29, 57, 67,
  78, 81–2, 85, 99, 104–5, 118, 142
Kuhn, Adalbert 71

Lied, Liv Ingeborg and Hugc
  Lundhaug 55

Lincoln, Bruce xi, 174 n.4
lived religion xv, 51–3, 58, 92, 147–9
Long, Charles H. 39, 92, 129, 143, 146
Lowenthal, David 6
Lyden, John 89

Malinowski, Bronislaw 4, 111–21, 150
Maoism 44, 146
Marchand, Suzanne 72
Marion, Jean-Luc 85
Martin, Craig 89–90
Marx, Karl 85
Marxism 3, 60
Massumi, Brian 94
Masuzawa, Tomoko 43, 86
materiality xv, 3–6, 20–6, 40, 53–8,
  96–9, 123, 144, 147–9
  material culture 3, 20, 40, 75, 90, 92,
    104, 109
  material turn 92
Matrix, The (film) 111–13, 121
McCutcheon, Russell T. xii–xiii, xv, xix,
  43, 45, 70, 72, 86, 88, 99, 104, 144
meaning-making 94, 103–4, 108, 139
Mesmer, Franz Anton 21
Mesmerism 21, 23, 145
Morgan, David 90
Müller, Friedrich Max 11–17, 42, 50, 71,
  144–5, 147, 152, 154 n.4, 154 n.9,
  155 nn.12–13
Myers-Briggs Type Indicator (MBTI) 97,
  106, 108
mysterium tremendum et facinans 87,
  89, 91, 95, 124, 149
myth 40–1, 49–1, 98–109, 25, 128,
  143, 150
  as comparative mythology 71
  as meaning-making 104, 146
  as monomyth 100
  as myth-making xi–xii
  as myth-ritualism 50

narrative construction 2, 5, 13, 58, 81–2,
  86, 92, 100, 117, 130, 138
Newton, Richard xiii–xiv
Nietzsche, Friedrich xvi, 72, 77–86,
  148, 167 n.30
Nongbri, Brent xv, 144–5
numinous 42, 87–90, 93, 95–6, 149

INDEX

Obeyesekere, Gananth 23
objectivity (*see also* subjectivity) 43,
78, 85, 138
as social construction 151
Orientalism 117
origins xii, xiv, 2, 44, 55–6, 71, 79, 82,
98, 102, 147
Orsi, Robert A. 90
Otto, Rudolf xvi, 42–3, 80, 85, 87–96,
124, 148–9

Pals, Daniel 73, 88, 104
Parsis 16
past, the xii–xvi, 1–9, 50, 56–7, 61, 70,
79, 144, 150
as modern construction 78
Petro, Anthony 51
phenomenology of religion 3, 70, 72,
74, 79–80, 85–6, 87–8, 94–5, 99,
101–3, 105, 108, 124, 148–9
philology 11, 42, 50, 54–6, 71, 145,
155 n.13
as new philology 55
as theory of textuality 56
philosophy 7, 11, 40, 56, 59, 94,
142, 149
Copernican turn 78–81, 85
Pollock, Sheldon 56
postcolonialism 22, 85, 94, 99, 149
poststructuralism 78, 85, 94
power 6, 23, 43, 74, 89, 92, 94–6,
98–9, 104, 108–9, 118–20, 128,
142, 149–51
as institutional structures 20,
51–5, 58, 70, 91–2, 96, 98, 105,
141, 144
Preus, J. Samuel 2
Prichard, James Cowles 8
primitivism (*see also* civilization;
savage) 6–8, 33, 43, 49–51, 70–2,
75, 135, 137–8, 147
private vs. public 19–26
profane (*see also* sacred) 116, 124–7
psychical research 21, 25–7
psychoanalysis 23, 70–2
psychology 70–2, 75, 99–100, 105–6,
145, 148
and collective unconscious 98–102,
106, 108

as folk psychology
(*völkerpsychologie*) 71
and individual psyche 99–100, 103
Pueblo 35–6

Raboteau, Albert J. 92
racism xiii, 8, 30, 47, 51, 72, 114, 117,
129–30, 146
religion 21, 53–4, 103, 119
as discursive category 30, 37, 41, 59,
84–5, 146
as Euro- and Christian-centric 41, 61
interiority of 19–20, 22, 24, 102
institution (*see* institution)
as lived experience (*see* lived
religion)
as religious interiority 19, 21, 53
as *sui generis* xv, 9, 24, 40–5, 80,
85, 88, 95, 123, 146
as universal (*see also* comparative
religion) 12, 32, 40–4, 85,
113, 136,
as "wholly other" (*see also* profane;
sacred) 85, 87, 89, 124–5
religion, as academic discipline xi–xvi,
2–9, 41, 128–31, 135, 142–52
Christian hegemony of 60–1, 92,
95, 116
future of the discipline 117–21, 146
history of 2–9, 39–47, 143–4, 146
as *Religionswissenschaft* (*see also*
science of religion) 41, 43
vs. theology xii–xiii, 47
Religion slot 30–1, 34, 37
religious experience xv–xvi, 2–4, 19–27,
39–42, 44–5, 70, 73, 77–82,
85–6, 87–96, 103, 123–31, 133,
145, 148–50
essentialization of 42
interiority of 19–27
as lived (*see* lived religion)
as objective 78, 138
as social process 20, 57
as subjective 25, 133, 136
as universal 40, 42
Renan, Ernest 64
Ricoeur, Paul 74
Rig Veda 12, 50
Roberts, Martha Smith xvi, 149

INDEX

Romanticism, European 74
Rudy, Kathryn 56

sacred, the 16, 40, 43, 46, 55, 86,
99, 101–2, 111, 115–16. 123–8,
131, 151
and "ontological thirst" 126
as set apart or distinct 96
Said, Edward 117
Sanskrit 11–12, 50, 56, 89, 145
savage (*see also* civilization;
primitivism) xv, 6, 29–35, 37,
49, 51, 69, 70–2, 80, 113–17,
120, 146
Savage slot 29
Schaefer, Donovan 94
scholarship xiii–xv, 3, 6, 9, 16 23, 30–
1, 34, 46–7, 61, 69–70, 91–6, 111,
118, 134, 138, 143, 148, 150
hierarchy of 137
scholarly reflexivity 150
science of religion 2, 11–15, 41, 71,
103, 145
Smart, Ninian 103
Smith, Christian 53
Smith, Huston 4
Smith, Jonathan Z. 4, 15, 31–2, 42–3,
86, 143–4
Smith, Wilfred Cantwell 59–68, 147
Social Darwinism 6, 147
sociology of religion xii, 75, 111–13,
115–18, 120, 133–4, 142 151
Stewart, Kathleen 94
Straus, David 82
Strenski, Ivan 88
structuralism 74, 78
subjectivity (*see also* experience;
objectivity) 23, 25, 72, 133, 136,
148, 151

Szanto, Edith xv, 147

taboo 50, 69, 70, 72, 75
tautology 72, 75, 115
telos 61
text 16, 50–8, 61, 71, 138, 145, 147
as sacred 16, 40–1, 46, 53
theology xii–xiii, 1–2, 19, 33, 40, 52,
61, 81, 89, 149
threshold 124, 126–7, 131
Tiele, Cornelis P. 12–13, 152
Tobolowsky, Andrew 151
translation 12, 14, 16, 35, 41, 50,
56, 143
Trouillot, Michael-Rolph 5, 29
Tylor, Edward B. xv, 7–9, 29–37, 53,
102, 145–6

United Nations (UN) 63, 65, 147
Ute 35

van der Leeuw, Gerardus 77–85
voudou 22

Waardenburg, Jacques xii–xiii, 2
Wach, Joachim 39–40
Waitz, Theodor 8
Walsh, Robyn Faith 148
Weber, Max 133–9
Wenger, Tisa 35
White, Hayden xiv, 5
whiteness 129–30
Williamson, George S. 71
Winters, Joseph 151
world making 130, 151
world religions 4, 13, 15, 32, 43, 44,
66, 70, 95, 101, 150
World War II 60, 63, 76
Wynter, Sylvia 131

Milton Keynes UK
Ingram Content Group UK Ltd.
UKHW020958021123
431797UK00003B/41